The Data Protection Act

WITHDRAWN AND SOLD BY WALSALL P.L.

PRICE 50p

Pg: 59 — 2nd principle
Pg: 110
Pg: 129

35 principles / 2nd principle
              4th   "

6. no longer than the purpose
7. without delay inform the individual
8. App. security measures

Three may keep a secret –
if two of them are dead.

Benjamin Franklin

The Data Protection Act

A practical guide

Richard Sizer and Philip Newman

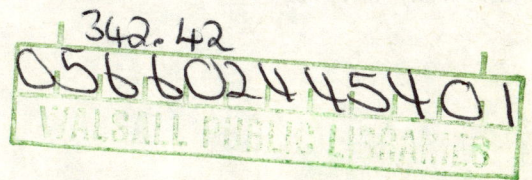

Gower

© Richard Sizer and Philip Newman 1984

All rights reserved. No part of this publication may be reproduced, stored in a retrieval system, or transmitted in any form or by any means, electronic, mechanical, photocopying, recording, or otherwise without the prior permission of Gower Publishing Company Limited.

Published by Gower Publishing Company Limited, Gower House, Croft Road, Aldershot, Hants GU11 3HR, England

Gower Publishing Company, Old Post Road, Brookfield, Vermont 05036, U.S.A.

British Library Cataloguing in Publication Data
Sizer, Richard
   The Data Protection Act.
   1. Data protection – Great Britain
   I. Title   II. Newman, Philip
344.102′858   KD4080
ISBN 0-566-02445-4

Library of Congress Cataloging in Publication Data
Sizer, Richard
   The Data Protection Act.
   Includes bibliographies and index.
   1. Data protection – Great Britain. 2. Records – Law and legislation – Great Britain. 3. Privacy, Right of – Great Britain. I. Newman, Philip. II. Title.
KD3756.S57 1984   342.41′0858   84-18702
ISBN 0-566-02445-4   344.102858

The authors and Gower Publishing Company Limited have used their best efforts in collecting and preparing material for inclusion in *The Data Protection Act*. They do not assume, and hereby disclaim, any liability to any party for any loss or damage caused by errors or omissions in *The Data Protection Act* whether such errors or omissions result from negligence, accident or any other cause.

Reprinted 1985

Typeset in Great Britain by Graphic Studios (Southern) Limited, Godalming, Surrey.
Printed and bound by Billing & Sons Limited, Worcester.

Contents

Acknowledgements ix

Preface xi

PART I THE CONTEXT

1   Historical Background to Data Protection 3
Data Subject 3
Data User 4
Privacy 4
Philosophical Components 5
Legal Components 14
Technical Components 17
General Components 22
Responsibility 22
Work in Europe 24
OECD Guidelines 26
Conclusion 30
References 31

PART II THE DATA PROTECTION ACT 1984

2   The Act in Summary 35
The Data Protection Principles 35

Delegation of Responsibility	37
Uncertainty	38
Security and Rights of Access	40
Registration	41
Rights of Data Subjects	42
Inaccurate Data	43
Exemptions	44
Summary	45
References	45

3	**The Act Examined**	**46**
Arrangement of Sections and Schedules		47
Part I	Preliminary	48
Part II	Registration and Supervision of Data Users and Computer Bureaux	68
Part III	Rights of Data Subjects	109
Part IV	Exemptions	122
Part V	General	143

PART III AFTER THE ACT

4	**The Implications of the Act for Managers and Professionals**	**155**
Accesss		156
Hierarchies		158
The Need for Inspection or Audits		161
Data Protection Audits – Who Might Do Them?		162
The Form a Data Protection Audit Could Take		164
Data Protection and Information Technology		165
Some Relevant Facts about Computers		167
Steps to be Taken by Computer Professionals		169
Conclusion		171
Checklists for Senior Management		172
References		179

5	**The Security Aspects**	**180**
Corporate Awareness		181
Data Protection and Security		183
Security		185
Data as an Asset, and Risk Assessment		188

Protecting the Asset	194
Physical Environment	194
The Computer	196
Access Control	197
Audit Procedures	202
Encryption	202
Contingency Planning	203
Summary	204
References	207
Appendix 1 – Some Legal Facts Associated with Computers	209
Appendix 2 – Some Relevant Technical Facts about Computers	219
Index	228

Acknowledgements

The authors gratefully acknowledge the following sources of material:

    Chapter 1. Allen and Unwin, *The Data Bank Society* by Warner and Stone (Reference 1)
AFIPS and Time Inc – Table 29 (Reference 2)
OECD Guidelines on the Protection of Privacy and Transborder Flows of Personal Data, OECD, Paris, 1981
International Chamber of Commerce, Endorsement of the OECD Guidelines and Council of Europe Convention
Butterworth Scientific, *Managing Information as a Corporate Resource*, by Richard Sizer
    Chapter 3. The Controller of Her Majesty's Stationery Office, *The Data Protection Act 1984*
    Chapter 5. *Journal of Accountancy*, USA – Tables on losses due to computer frauds by Brandt Allen, Copyright © 1977 by the American Institute of Certified Public Accountants, Inc. (Figures 5.2 to 5.4)
MIT Press, *Operating System Philosophy* by Organick, Copyright © 1972 by the Massachusetts Institute of Technology

Appendix 1. Alistair Kelman, in relation to hearsay evidence

The authors also record their grateful thanks to Sheena Currie and Valerie Sizer for their assistance and timely attention to details.

Preface

In this book we explain the UK Data Protection Act 1984 to people professionally concerned with data protection. However, as individuals they will each certainly have information held on them on one or more computers. The primary purpose of the Act is to afford protection for individuals. Particularly it enhances their rights by defining a legal framework to protect an individual from having his privacy invaded. At the same time, for the business community, the Act reflects a determination to do this without discouraging the increased application of computers.

Over the period in which we were writing the book, a point in time was reached when computers became a domestic commonplace rather than a specialist preserve. Knowledge of computing is now widespread, but some of the knowledge may be deceptively and unwittingly superficial – computing, privacy, security and data protection are complex issues.

A reader's knowledge may well be extensive in one area, sparse in another. We have, therefore, explained the law and practice of data protection from first principles to enable the book to be read by managers with no previous knowledge of data protection, as well as by computer professionals and by lawyers. But a reader will be able to by-pass any part that is going to add nothing to his or her knowledge.

We show the historical background of data protection to be full of paradoxes: what means one thing in one country often means something entirely different in another, or there may be no equivalent; one person will regard A as wholly good and acceptable whilst another will regard A as wholly bad and unacceptable; one person may regard A as wholly good in one context but wholly bad in another.

Philip Newman	Richard Sizer
Gray's Inn	Farnborough
London	Hampshire

PART I
THE CONTEXT

Chapter 1
Historical Background to Data Protection

The primary purpose of this book is to explain the working of the UK Data Protection Act 1984 (hereafter called the Act) and the effect it will have on people practising in areas covered by it. To help to understand the Act, which is complex, we devote this first chapter to a brief review of the historical background, showing how "data protection" evolved from the earlier issue of "privacy". For convenience we use from the outset the two relatively new terms from the Act – data subject and data user – so that by the time the descriptive material on the Act itself is reached the reader should be thoroughly familiar with their meaning. We start by defining the two terms.

Data Subject

"Data subject" is the name chosen to describe the individual for the purposes of the Act which gives a data subject rights of access to information about him stored in a computer. The definition in the Act is a simple one – the data subject is an individual who is the subject of personal data. Personal data are described in PART I, Section 1(3) (see Chapter 3), and in the definition of data user.

Data User

The definition of "data user" is complex and warrants careful study. Data user means a person who holds personal data. A person holds data if (a) the data form part of a collection processed or intended to be processed by equipment operating automatically, and (b) that person either alone or jointly or in common with other persons controls the contents and use of the data comprised in the collection. Thus the storage of data *per se* which are not processed or intended to be processed is not a matter dealt with by the Act.

Thus access by a person to certain personal data does not mean that that person is a data user. In order for that person to be a data user, he must, on his own or with others, control the contents and use of the data held in a collection of data processed or intended to be processed. The definition of data user is not limited to a person who holds personal data, but simply to a person who holds data. However, bearing in mind that the provisions of the Act are aimed at the occasions when a data user holds personal data, the fact that in PART I of the Act the definition of a data user is somewhat wider than it otherwise might be appears to be irrelevant.

Privacy

The subjects of privacy and computers have been studied for several years in the USA, UK, Canada and the European Community. Even a modest bibliography would fill a book of the present size. No attempt is made here to provide one but, apart from drawing on personal experience and responsibilities over several years, we used as source material a great many books, articles and papers published between 1962 and 1982 when drafting this chapter.

Treatments of the subject of privacy varied widely, depending on the field of specialisation of the author – legal, technical, scientific, social, political, professional or civil liberties. Disparate though the specialisations were, the authors of the time displayed a common syndrome – that of "we" and "they". George Orwell's *1984* had clearly had considerable psychological impact. Many authors wrote with the dramatic conviction possessed by the writers of Victorian melodrama: the villains "owned" computers and the data whilst the maidens in distress were the data subjects. Every author gave the impression of himself as a hero, dashing to the rescue and wielding his pen to capture the data user and hand him over to the authorities.

We draw the analogy only to provide a background for our own approach, which is based on the assumption that the Victorian melodrama mentality is no longer appropriate. In the 1980s we maintain there is no "we" and no "they" in computing because the technology explosion of the last two decades has resulted in a society which largely consists of "owners": computers now abound in every walk of life.

Take, for instance, the television advertisement based on the family of four – father, mother and two children, each with their own table-top computer. As is to be expected, Father has the one with the largest memory, the most flexible character set, a bigger and brighter screen, solid colour and a means of attaching larger capacity discs and a printer. Thus equipped he dominates the family unit and, for all we know, the neighbours and the street in which the family lives. With such an example fresh in our minds we move with the times and do not attempt to dramatise the privacy issue. We review instead only enough of the three components – philosophical, technical and legal – to establish a prerequisite understanding for Chapters 2 to 5. We look first at some of the philosophical components of the privacy issue.

Philosophical Components

The distinction between data and information is an important one to understand. In fact, as shown in Figure 1.1, data, information, the state of knowledge of the peruser of the information, and a consequential decision stage are all relevant.

An historical example clearly illustrates the relation

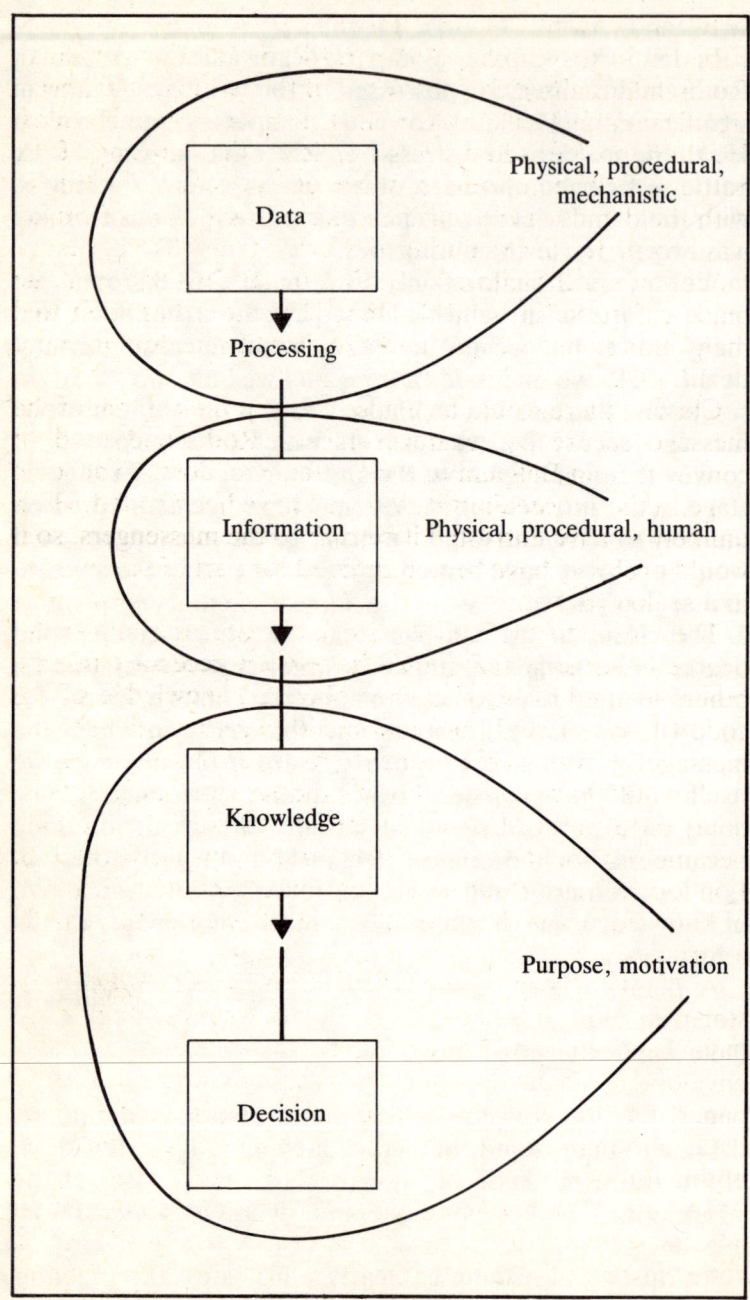

Figure 1.1

between the four.

In 1815, at the time of the Battle of Waterloo, Nathan Rothschild realised that the result of the battle would have a significant effect on the value of British Government bonds. He therefore devised a scheme to learn the outcome of the battle well ahead of others. We need not concern ourselves with the details of the scheme, except to say that the outlay was worth it, since, during the brief time that he had a monopoly on the information that the British had won, he made a fortune in bond dealings. The story has been told many times, but we can usefully examine it now in more detail.

Clearly, there would be a need to keep the content of the message secure by whatever means Rothschild used to convey it from Belgium to the United Kingdom, so at some stage in the proceedings it may well have been coded. He is unlikely to have entrusted it *en clair* to the messengers, so it would probably have been contained for part of the journey in a sealed packet.

The closer to the London stock market, the higher the degree of security that would have been necessary in case others learned of his plan, had obtained knowledge of the code (if one existed) and had made plans to intercept the message. A reasonable assumption also is that the message itself would have consisted of characters (for our purposes, data) on a piece of paper in the sealed packet. The data became information only when read by Rothschild in London, but as a result of the information content, his state of knowledge was changed, he made his decision, and made a fortune.

A point to bear in mind is that, had the message been stolen *en route*, it is not at all clear with what the thief might have been charged. Assuming the existence of a sealed envelope he could have been charged only with the theft of paper, of practically no value. Information conveyed by data, although of considerable potential value, counts for nothing in itself.

To return to privacy, in considering the philosophical aspects a number of paradoxes are revealed. The first concerns privacy itself. The word is used *per se* in Article 12 of the United Nations Declaration of Human Rights, but whilst this guarantees "privacy", it does not define it – just as well as the word means different things to different people as illustrated by our second paradox for which we choose "credit" as an example. One data subject may choose to live entirely on a credit basis and be largely insensitive to the requirement that as much of his personal financial data as is necessary to acquire a credit status be made available to a data user. Another data subject who regards credit as anathema finds offensive any process which makes his personal financial data and pattern of spending available to a data user. Thus, whilst the man who uses, say, credit cards would regard constraint on movement of his personal data as a restriction on (if not an invasion of) his privacy, the anti-credit man would take precisely the opposite view. This problem of individual opinion as to the relative importance or sensitivity of certain categories of personal data threads through data protection and is, we believe, a potential source of difficulty for data users. The difficulty should not arise so long as the data user complies with the statutory provisions without regard to his personal view of data sensitivity.

Apart from personal financial data for credit purposes there are other categories of data of a potentially sensitive nature – medical, habits, hobbies, family connections, social service record, career assessment, and, in certain circumstances, address and telephone numbers: the list is not exhaustive. Whilst the data subject who likes credit will be insensitive so far as availability of his personal financial data is concerned, he may take great exception to a computing process carried out by a data user which, by analysing his financial data in a certain way, detects that he spends numerous weekends at Brighton.

Clearly, there are also degrees of sensitivity. A data subject will expect different degrees of protection (security) to be applied by a data user who may be a legitimate custodian and processor of a data subject's personal data. The data subject will then instinctively feel that his "privacy" is protected.

A dilemma of the 1960s was that since privacy could not

be defined, was security the issue that should be considered? When faced with this question, some people took the view that the argument should, indeed, only be concerned with security, because it is tangible, factual, specific and the techniques used to obtain security are not matters of opinion. However, security and privacy (now data protection) are not synonymous terms; security is the core of data protection but another paradox, as we show in Chapter 5, is that it does not necessarily ensure freedom from invasion of privacy.

Apart from the personal interpretations already mentioned, what on an international basis a data subject would regard as an invasion of his privacy depends to a great extent on what constitutes invasion in different countries, as for example between Sweden and the UK; those in the UK concerned with the moral aspects of privacy and computers berated successive UK governments and the computing fraternity for not following the course of events in Sweden, where legislation controlling data and computer applications had been in force for some years. When finally various UK bodies charged with looking at such matters visited Sweden, they found a social system based on the existence of a mandatory, unique personal identifier for each Swedish citizen. The system had existed long before computers but had been made the cornerstone of Swedish data protection procedures. It is no exaggeration to write that anyone seriously proposing the use of a unique personal identifier for each UK citizen would, even now, let alone in the 1960s and 1970s, be treated as a renegade or social outcast. A recent demonstration of the truth of this statement was the uproar when the plastic identification cards were introduced by the DHSS in January 1984.

To return to the problem of different understandings of privacy and invasion thereof, a second example of a totally different viewpoint is the acceptance by citizens in a number of European countries of the use of a personal *fiche* (or file) as a means of monitoring personal movements. It has been a legal requirement in France, for example, since Napoleonic times for each citizen to deposit his or her personal *fiche* with the local police station on moving residence. In the UK such a proposal would be regarded as a prime act of privacy invasion.

In lighter vein, a third example is the European country where privacy, translated literally, means the freedom to enjoy solitude in a water-closet. Finally in the UK, with no written constitution, it is questionable whether anyone has any "right" to privacy although it should be said that there is a "right" of silence at Common Law whereby a person cannot in certain circumstances be obliged to answer questions. Also there is a substantial body of case law providing civil remedies for actionable nuisance, trespass to land or goods, trespass to the person, breach of confidence, passing off, infringement of copyright, trademarks and patents. Furthermore at common law there is a privilege against self-incrimination which has recently been upheld and reinforced by the House of Lords – Rank Film Distributors Ltd. *v* Video Information Centre (1981) ref: 2 AII E.R.

Considerations of which the above examples are typical led eventually to a shift in emphasis: whilst privacy was still the key word, 'invasion of privacy' was clearly the act to be worried about as the argument then no longer need be concerned with what different people regarded as private but with protecting "it" from invasion regardless of what "it" might be.

To return to generalities, a good example of early beliefs about computers is provided by Warner and Stone[1]. They describe a state of affairs that they saw as resulting from their uncontrolled use:

> The catastrophe we have in mind is the potential destruction of freedom in our society which the computer may cause: but only if nothing is done to avoid it. There is provision for a lesser degree of upset, because action can be taken to avoid the catastrophe. To determine the necessary action demands that an appraisal be made of the computer power which is available now, and still rapidly developing, together with a review of the consequential changes that this power may bring. The potential benefits must then be weighed against what would be destroyed, and society as a whole will be allowed to determine the relative values involved. What do we gain: what do we lose: are the changes greater than we can afford to allow?
>
> The choice is there: the values must be weighed. The serious danger is that changes will just happen. On the one hand there are the

computer men, dedicated to proving their own ingenuity and their machines' versatility: on the other are public and private managements, quite rightly desperate to improve efficiency and economy by using modern tools. Between the two, the side-effects of computer systems which will vastly modify the accepted customs of society could be overlooked. New projects, new ideas, new tools and new techniques, may imperceptibly remove the opportunity for choice. Individual liberties are at stake: a large part of our freedom will be seriously threatened if computers take over more and more tasks without serious questioning of the kind of society to which they may be leading us.

The quoted paragraphs are typical of many of the serious and responsible arguments developed by authors who were greatly concerned at the way in which society was being influenced by the computer.

We referred earlier to the existence of a number of paradoxes and have given some examples. Another lies in the apparent conflict between moral arguments mounted in the 1960s and 1970s, of which Warner and Cox's are typical, and the results of surveys conducted by other people endeavouring to establish a view of matters based on factual analysis. One such survey[2] conducted in America in 1971 was based on interviews with 1001 people of eighteen years and over, 15 per cent of whom had jobs which required some knowledge of computers. Whilst the survey undoubtedly revealed a concern about privacy, 54 per cent of those interviewed did not regard it as a real threat. The surprising result, however, was that in response to the question "In what areas did the interviewee consider the use of computers could be increased", 78 per cent voted for "keeping track of criminals"; 56 per cent for surveillance of activist or radical groups; 50 per cent for compiling information files on US citizens.

Table 29 from the survey, reproduced overleaf, was even worse from the moralists' point of view. Clearly a considerable majority were prepared to accept the use of computers in areas which others regarded as prime examples of misuse. It is interesting to speculate on what might be the trend in use now that the ability to store and process such information as is shown in the table lies within the grasp of anyone willing to spend a relatively small sum of money on a domestic micro: in 1971, when the survey was conducted, computers were centralised and formed a highly specialised preserve.

Beliefs about what types of information should be kept in a computer file	Should be Kept	Total (1,001) Don't know No answer	Should Not be Kept
Police records	83%	3%	14%
Medical records	81	2	17
School records	77	3	20
Tax records	76	2	22
Credit ratings	75	3	22
Employment records	74	2	24
Salary records	54	3	43
Political activity records	50	5	45
The brands of products people buy	46	7	47

Based on the question: "For each type of information about people that I mention, please tell me whether you believe this information should or should not be kept in a central computerized information file."

(Table 29, Schiller and Gilchrist: see reference (2))

It is interesting to speculate also on the reasons why the survey did not attract attention at the time of publication. It was certainly contentious but perhaps the lack of publicity was evidence of yet another paradox – suppression of information (we use the word deliberately here) by the moralists then campaigning for "freedom of information", always an element in the privacy debate.

An important part of the historical background lies in the attempts made to define the problem in analytical terms. We give two examples of which the first is Alan Gotlieb[3] who in 1970 had the following to say:

HISTORICAL BACKGROUND

> In the privacy domain there may be found the desire to be left alone, to be left in peace by the rest of the community, which means the availability of sufficient space to provide protection from the static of one's neighbours, to die alone if one so wished, to rest outside of society, to be non-productive, to be off-beat, to be alone if one so desired, to turn off the connection. It may also involve respect for one's anonymity in a public place, it may involve being able to establish intimate relationships with others in the understanding that whatever passes between those concerned will not be made public.

This point of view gave rise to argument, as the act of opting out is one-sided. For example, suppose a person subscribing to Gotlieb's view is knocked down in the street. Though he as an individual, up to the point of impact, may have been opting out, a humane society such as the Welfare State in the UK is not free to opt out, and will assume the responsibility for dealing with him as an injured human being. The fact that society may be able to do it all the better and more cheaply as a result of previously stored data concerning the man cannot seriously be disputed.

Willis Ware[4] had a different approach:

> Suppose a data bank exists and some of the information is used and I do not like it, I sue. If I win the case there is a precedent for what is in the individual's best interest and all other operators of data banks take notice. If I lose the case, then I as an individual have to conclude that that class of information has been decided collectively by society and by the legal processes of society to be necessary for the general welfare and benefit of society and I must yield.

Some people considered this to be a too matter of fact approach, but at least it could have been workable in legal terms under the right circumstances.

In spite of all the activity of the 1960s and early 1970s, there was a dearth of factual information on actual invasions of privacy taking place as a result of computing activity. Cynical observers (and there were many of those as well) were of the opinion that the whole problem was in the minds of the beholders. Most computer professionals were rather like agnostics in that they could not accept that there was a problem without factual evidence, yet knew enough of the weaknesses inherent in computer systems to be uneasy, certainly with regard to security of data.

It became clear that three basic issues were involved in privacy – "motive", "sensitivity" and "accessibility". The last two we deal with in Chapter 5 and here we need only consider motive in so far as to make clear that a data user will incur expense when processing a data subject's data by means of a computer, because searching even the simplest collection of data takes time and facilities, and costs money. A non-benevolent data user will therefore need to have a motive, possess or have access to computing resources, and have his own cost-effective criteria to be able to judge whether a given act of privacy invasion is to be worthwhile. With the Act now in force a data user will also need to assess the risk in terms of the Act's penalties, both civil and criminal.

As we have stated, the motives for invasion of privacy do not concern us beyond the comments above, but we note that the successful invasion of a data subject's privacy by a data user could result in the data subject's being compelled to do something he might not otherwise have done or, conversely, being compelled to stop doing something he might otherwise have done. This summarises the threat to the individual in the context of computers, data, information and privacy.

Legal Components

Prior to the 1984 Act there was no common law remedy available in England to a data subject for invasion of his privacy as such, though there was nothing to stop the courts from developing such a right. The main difficulty confronting the legislators was how to develop it; personal data is not a tangible property, although recently intangibles such as copyright have been protected. We have shown that privacy and invasion thereof are difficult concepts to define in precise terms, and particularly difficult to define in the case of a complaint to be laid before a court.

As the law stood prior to the Act, and in the absence of a definite right, a plaintiff had to show that the action he complained of was actionable under some other head of complaint recognised by the law; possibilities would have been defamation, negligent mis-statement, breach of confidence, breach of contract, breach of copyright, or trespass; or there may have been indirect protection of his alleged right by specific Act of Parliament. Each of these heads of complaint (with the exception of the statutory indirect protection) had disadvantages.

For example, in breach of contract, if there was a contractual relation between a data subject and a set of data (in whatever form), there would probably have had to be an express or implied term in the contract that the information supplied by the subject would be kept confidential. Similar arguments would have been applicable to trespass, defamation and copyright.

There might have been indirect protection of privacy by Acts of Parliament, but it is worth noting that these would have had to cover particular cases rather than privacy in general. For example, in 1967 an Act imposed on staff of the, then, Post Office Data Processing Service an obligation of secrecy. The Income Tax Management Act 1964 also requires the relevant staff to make a non-disclosure declaration so far as information received in the execution of their official duties is concerned.

Whilst the Theft Act 1968 covers by implication things in action and other intangible property, a prosecution where personal data is concerned could only succeed if the proof existed to show that the accused dishonestly intended permanently to deprive the other of his intangible property. The Theft Act 1968 deals not only with stealing pure and simple but also with deception. Clearly property, including intangible property such as "credit", may be obtained by deception. Personal data, perhaps forged, may be used in the course of the deception and prosecutions could take place in this area as well. Thus, the fact that the UK legal system required that a claim for invasion of privacy, to succeed, had to be associated with a claim for infringement of another right was highly unsatisfactory and contributed to the demand for Parliamentary action which has resulted in the Act.

Three Private Members' Bills, none of which became law,

are worth mentioning. The Bill of Mr Kenneth Baker provided for a register of "data banks" kept by Government, public corporations, and private operators, including credit and detective agencies and those offering information for sale. The Bill defined a data bank as a computer or computers which recorded and stored information. A clause provided that the operator must supply the following details to any person who is the subject of a file; a print-out of all data concerning him, together with a statement of the purposes for which the data was to be used; the purposes for which it had been used since the date of the last print-out; and the names and addresses of recipients of all or any of the data since the last print-out. These were to have been free in the first instance but obtainable on payment of a fee thereafter.

The Bill of Mr Brian Walden sought to establish a general right of privacy, which it defined as the right of any person to be protected from intrusion upon himself, his home, his family, his relationships and communications with others, his property and business affairs, by such means as spying, or unauthorised recordings, copying of documents or use of or disclosure of confidential information or of facts calculated to cause him distress, annoyance or embarrassment, or to place him in a false light.

The Bill of Mr Leslie Huckfield was designed to prevent the infringement of the right (explicitly created by the Bill) of the individual to control the collection, storage and use of information about him. The Bill sought to establish a data bank tribunal and an Inspectorate of Data Banks.

To summarise, the problems presented to the law by computers were first recognised some years ago in most Western countries. America and Australia were amongst the first to amend statute law (both Federal and State) to cope with computers. Member countries of the EEC also amended the law, whilst in the UK the Civil Evidence Act (1968) and the Criminal Evidence Act (1965) had clauses inserted dealing specifically with computers and output. Unfortunately in the UK statutes the distinction between hardware and software was either not drawn at all or drawn in a way that allowed of ambiguous interpretation with regard to the relations between hardware, software, errors and output.

Computer outputs can present courts with twin problems of accuracy and admissibility. Reliance is often placed on the use of expert witnesses, and the course of justice may be made more difficult by the combination of jargon (which abounds in computing) and the lack of sufficient technical know-how on the part of lawyers to mount an effective cross-examination. However it must be said that many lawyers (and here we refer primarily to barristers) have great experience in utilising the services of expert witnesses in order to mount effective cross-examination of other expert witnesses. To a large extent such cases will turn, as in any legal dispute concerning technical evidence, upon the court's view as to the quality of each side's respective expert evidence. We examine the issue in more detail in Appendix 1.

Technical Components

Nowadays because of the proliferation of computers one is apt to forget the nature of the computer itself, but in order to understand the problems in the context of data protection one has to delve below the popular "keyboard and visual display unit" face of computing. It was fashionable at one time to compare the computer with the human brain. Most comparisons then were unrewarding and often based on a misunderstanding of how the human brain was organised and operated. Recently the comparison has been made again[5] on the basis of a better understanding of both the brain's function and construction and computing processes, with the result that a complex relation between computers, human beings and society becomes apparent.

Thring[6] argues that people themselves can be categorised in a way we consider to be germane to discussion on the technical component. He maintains there are those who see only disorder in society, and groups them as "uneducated"; there are others who are happy to perceive and follow a set of rules, and these he classifies as the "half-educated";

finally there are those who appreciate the exceptions to the rules, and these he classifies as "educated". If a computer has to be compared usefully with a human being, then it probably best corresponds with the half-educated, as it needs to follow rules, which it can do both quickly and precisely, but in so doing its performance will be better than that of the half-educated human being. However, unlike the half-educated human being, who will be tolerant of exceptions, the computer will be quite unable to cope. One has here therefore an indication of an effect the computer can have on citizens in many walks of life – the imposition of regimentation and an elimination of the exceptions. This need for regimentation arises because a computer (whatever its size) is a machine which functions in terms of a very simple system – the difference between two states usually represented by the symbols 0 and 1. The reader who wishes to pursue this aspect is referred to Reference 3 on page 217. Here we merely remark on the fact that the computer's strength and weakness lie in its ability to distinguish between one of the two symbols – a strong tool but of moronic simplicity. In the context of data protection we need to describe some of the features of this tool.

We consider again data and information; the relationship between the two has been shown in Figure 1.1. Sufficient information to give a comprehensive profile on a typical data subject can be conveyed in a few thousand English words or, put another way, several thousand characters, including punctuation, spaces and new line. It is probable that much of this information on an individual will have been available for years in the manila file form, often referred to as his record – for example, personal or medical. Records of this kind and others need to be converted into alphabetic and numeric characters in digital form to become data in the computer sense.

The computer can do two things with such data: store them *en masse* to a far greater degree than was ever possible with manila files and filing cabinets, and process them (read, write, amend, sort etc.) extremely quickly and cheaply. A twelve inch reel of half-inch wide magnetic tape (used on many computers) is cheap and can contain 24 million characters of data in magnetically coded form. It can generally be read at a rate of many thousands of characters a second, though a magnetic disc allows reading of characters at an even higher rate. The sorting, correlation, editing and merging of sets of data to produce new sets can be carried out by most computers in a matter of minutes.

Some categories of data were protected before the advent of the current legislation. For example, some medical information has been statutorily classed as secret for a considerable time. Under the Act other data is now protected but in the early 1970s such was not the case. Even so, it was realised that some data is more sensitive than other data of more potential value, and therefore a potential "target". Thus the concepts of sensitivity rating and relative ease of data accessibility were made more apparent. Cost-effective criteria can apply, one for the protection aspect, the other for the invasion aspect. The latter can be typified by the data user performing as an information speculator who, once in possession of data from two or more sources, can by means of computer-based analysis carry out a correlation process. The results can be new information never voluntarily offered by a data subject, and the identification of data subjects either individually or as groups.

Consideration of the technical components came later than the philosophical and legal considerations, possibly because the technical specialists with the necessary understanding of computers, hardware and software did not themselves participate widely in the privacy debate for some considerable time. When eventually they did, the pace of transition from privacy to data protection was quickened.

The move towards a more technical approach first started in the European Community, although in the UK the British Computer Society (BCS) and other bodies such as the National Computing Centre (NCC) and the Computing Services Association (CSA) had also injected many arguments based on practicality into the debate. Two were concerned with the mundane process of the production of eye-readable output such as printed processed records. The moralists were arguing, idealistically as it transpired, for a "right to see print-out" to be exercised by any citizen who wished to know what was contained about him in a given computer file. The BCS in an attempt to put the matter into perspective pointed out that usually a given computer had only the number (and type) of printing devices attached to it for the amount of output generated by the applications for which the computer had been acquired in the first place. To have met an additional demand of quite indeterminable proportions resulting from a general right to print-out would have resulted in the need for an enormous additional investment in the printing devices themselves, which at that time cost a minimum of £15,000 each. It was argued, therefore, that whilst all accepted that such a print-out should be made available, the conditions under which it should be obtainable by a data subject would need careful definition if only to avoid mass bankruptcies on the part of data users. Further, it would be essential to call for a fee to be paid by the data subject, a point now embodied in PART III Section 21, subsection 2 of the Act.

A second vital point in the context of control of the distribution of sensitive data in eye-readable form is that, as a general rule, 10 per cent of all addresses held in a computer-based address file will be incorrect. People and organisations are notoriously lax in informing others of changes in address and similar items of data.

Computer professionals argued that no computer-based address file should be used, therefore, for the distribution of sensitive documents without thorough checks, for without these one data subject might unwittingly be the recipient of another data subject's sensitive personal record – an invasion of the privacy, by default, of the legitimate data subject. A third point concerns "proof of identity", which is particularly important in computing systems with remote terminals. We deal with this at a technical level in Chapter 5, but it is relevant here to explain to the non-technical reader that it cannot be assumed that a person at a remote terminal (who should be, say, a legitimate data subject accessing his own file) is, in fact, "legitimate". The data user (custodian of the file) has only limited means at his disposal to carry out legitimacy checks, and all of these cost money to implement; the performance of a computer is degraded when its time is spent on checking identities of terminal users rather than doing work – the more checks the less time spent on data processing. There are, therefore, commercial disincentives to the use of more checks than is absolutely necessary in a given set of circumstances – a good example of the need for the legislative framework provided by the Act, and independent data protection audits as we discuss in Chapter 4.

We have already remarked on the fact that the use of computers is widespread but not all uses are relevant to data protection. In order, therefore, to place the data protection issue in its technical context we indicate below some typical uses of computers which are of no concern to us. These are the controlling of factory production lines; helping pilots in flying aircraft; gun aiming; the firing of missiles; controlling motorway signals; scheduling buses and trains; controlling complex chemical processes, and so on. For the remainder, almost any type of computer can perform a role in areas covered by the Act and will, therefore, need to be registered when so doing.

In Appendix 2 we describe in more detail the different types of computer, the software and system components. It is sufficient here to point out that in terms of data protection even micro-computer systems can pose a threat, but so long as mass storage devices remain physically large and relatively expensive, the dangers from micro systems will be less than those from the larger machines described in Appendix 2. However, mass storage devices are constantly being reduced in size and cost, whilst increasing in capacity. In time, therefore, there will be no effective distinction between the different types of computer. It is a sobering thought that many of today's desk-top computers are more powerful than the computing leviathans of the 1960s and 1970s which caused the issue of privacy to be raised in the first place. The Act covers the use of "domestic" computers in PART IV, Section 33, where we comment on the hobbyist and personal data.

General Components

Above we have considered first the philosophical and legal components relevant to computers and data protection, then the computer itself. Here we consider the ways in which all three now tend to interact. It is essential to balance the protection of a data subject's privacy against the benefits which he himself or society can derive from the collection and use of personal data. It follows that data ought to be collected only where there is a clear requirement, within the law and where the data subject has given specific consent.

The Act now makes clear that the data subject should always be made aware of the use that is to be made of the data. This requires that all files should indicate their approved use and should be accessible to those authorised to have access, but not that unsolicited publication of the contents of files at periodic intervals is necessary. At the time of supplying data, therefore, a data subject would be expected to stipulate the following:

(*a*) that data are filed correctly,
(*b*) that data are intrinsically accurate,
(*c*) that the people to whom data are given are to use them for the purpose indicated and take steps to prevent others using them, and using them for correlation purposes,
(*d*) that other data are not added to them from sources other than that supplied by the individual,
(*e*) that records are maintained of all amendments to the data, and, finally,
(*f*) that data are not being passed between third parties.

Responsibility

This is possibly the most difficult and potentially contentious part of data protection. Problems arise because of the nature of computing activity and the manner in which it is practised. Sir Kenneth Younger[7] had drawn attention in the UK to the fact that in computing someone has to be responsible for the data processing activity as a whole. Some people argue that this had significance only at the time of Younger, when computers tended to be physically large and mostly owned, rented or leased by organisations. We believe that it is self-deluding to think that, in the era of the micro-computer (where considerable processing power is now available cheaply and on a wide scale), the concept of personal responsibility for the activity does not apply. In any environment where computing takes place there will, as Lindop also showed,[8] always be a need for well delineated responsibilities, and the Act supports this view.

The BCS drew a parallel[9] between the responsibilities of a data processing manager and a mine manager whose role had been defined by statute in the nineteenth century. It was more a debating point than a serious proposition in the context of privacy then, but it nevertheless drew attention to the crucial nature of the issue of responsibility which was developed further by others: for example, those responsible for holding personal information in computers, and the operator of the system.

The use of the term "operator" was, and is, confusing, as it has a meaning in the computing profession different from that implied in the Act. A better term (the one used in the Act) is "data user" – someone who is actually responsible for processing data for a given purpose. Again, however, the issue is not a simple one. For example is "responsibility" to be for a given application, a computer installation, or the contents of a file? An application can consist of several files and there can be several computer systems for a given application. A particular computer installation can be running a number of systems, particularly if it is a bureau. There could be a separate responsible person for each of these but each would be regarded as a "customer" of the bureau in question.

There is also a further complication; for a given system responsibility is frequently divided between two or more people: for example between a data processing manager and the head of a user department, or between an operations manager and systems analyst. Thus, here again, two or more people would frequently need to be regarded as responsible, each for a different aspect.

If, under the Act, responsibility is meant to be borne by a person in charge of an installation, then it would be difficult, to say the least, for such a person to assume responsibility for, say, the contents of all files, because to assume this he would need to be able to confirm the accuracy and relevance of the data that were being handled without necessarily being responsible for their initial acquisition and recording and without necessarily knowing how and for what purpose they were being processed. There is yet another paradox inherent in the proposition that one person should be aware of the contents of all files, because implementing this would increase those "needing to know" and hence reduce the level of protection. The argument returns to the use of security measures, operating procedures and operational standards dealt with more fully in Chapter 5.

Work in Europe

By 1974 the European nations were more advanced in studies connected with data protection than the UK, probably owing to the influence of the Organisation for Economic Co-operation and Development (OECD). For example, a seminar in 1974 dealt with many fundamental issues in data protection of direct relevance to the UK 1984 Act. At the seminar attention was drawn to the problems arising from the flow of data across national boundaries. Speakers regarded it as a necessary condition for free interaction among nations. Transnational flow was seen as consisting of three main elements – the origin of the data, the means of transmission, and the destination of the data. A number of examples were given, including money transfers, insurance transactions, airline reservations and so on.

Reference was made to the International Civil Aviation Authority (ICAA), which had already looked at an electronic passport, enabling "more effective control of people at airports" to be implemented. It was pointed out that the passports would need to be accepted by all member nations, be standardised in size and data format, and that unique personal identification would be essential.

Probably arising from the land-based frontiers common throughout Europe, there was recognition of the problem of movements of a data subject across a frontier and the consequent need for him to be able to identify himself unambiguously. It was recognised that with the increasing spread of data processing systems a data subject would need to identify himself with such systems in a way which was compatible with an electronic data processing interface. It was proposed that the electronic passport could be adopted for such general identification purposes. It was concluded that, whilst considerable advantages could accrue to data users from the electronic passport, there was a need for prior adoption of special principles and rules.

It followed from this that international regulations were required because national regulations provide not only restrictions on data flows but also define permitted uses. International harmonisation, certainly in a European context, was thus necessary to resolve the fundamental conflict between freedom of communicating information as against allowing the circumvention of national regulations.

Whilst accepting that data should be correct and up-to-date, it was recognised that it would be more difficult to validate data from a "foreign" source or indeed to recognise a source as foreign without the adoption of "foreign source identification" attached to data. To this end it was seen as essential that "transnational transmission and use of data" should be a stated purpose of a data user when registering.

It was recognised that geographical distances did, in fact, present problems. The data subject has a right to know what information is stored about him, but a large physical distance between a potential point of enquiry and the data bank was seen as presenting an insurmountable barrier in certain circumstances. Clearly there was a need for stricter rules.

OECD Guidelines

Out of such deliberations arose the OECD guidelines, which are set out in full below:

PART ONE – GENERAL

Definitions

1 For the purposes of these Guidelines:
   a) 'data controller' means a party who, according to domestic law, is competent to decide about the contents and use of personal data regardless of whether or not such data are collected, stored, processed or disseminated by that party or by an agent on its behalf;
   b) 'personal data' means any information relating to an identified or identifiable individual (data subject);
   c) 'transborder flows of personal data' means movements of personal data across national borders.

Scope of Guidelines

2 These Guidelines apply to personal data, whether in the public or private sectors, which, because of the manner in which they are processed, or because of their nature or the context in which they are used, pose a danger to privacy and individual liberties.

3 These Guidelines should not be interpreted as preventing:
   a) the application, to different categories of personal data, of different protective measures depending upon their nature and the context in which they are collected, stored, processed or disseminated;
   b) the exclusion from the application of the Guidelines of personal data which obviously do not contain any risk to privacy and individual liberties; or
   c) the application of the Guidelines only to automatic processing of personal data.

4 Exceptions to the Principles contained in Parts Two and Three of these Guidelines, including those relating to national sovereignty, national security and public policy (*ordre public*), should be:
   a) as few as possible, and
   b) made known to the public.

5 In the particular case of Federal countries the observance of these Guidelines may be affected by the division of powers in the Federation.

6 These Guidelines should be regarded as minimum standards which are capable of being supplemented by additional measures for the protection of privacy and individual liberties.

PART TWO – BASIC PRINCIPLES OF NATIONAL APPLICATION

Collection limitation principle
7 There should be limits to the collection of personal data and any such data should be obtained by lawful and fair means and, where appropriate, with the knowledge or consent of the data subject.

Data quality principle
8 Personal data should be relevant to the purposes for which they are to be used, and, to the extent necessary for those purposes, should be accurate, complete and kept up-to-date.

Purpose specification principle
9 The purposes for which personal data are collected should be specified not later than at the time of data collection and the subsequent use limited to the fulfilment of those purposes or such others as are not incompatible with those purposes and as are specified on each occasion of change of purpose.

Use limitation principle
10 Personal data should not be disclosed, made available or otherwise used for purposes other than those specified in accordance with Paragraph 9 except:
    a) with the consent of the data subject; or
    b) by the authority of law.

Security safeguards principle
11 Personal data should be protected by reasonable security safeguards against such risks as loss or unauthorized access, destruction, use, modification or disclosure of data.

Openness principle
12 There should be a general policy of openness about developments, practices and policies with respect to personal data. Means should be readily available of establishing the existence and nature of personal data, and the main purposes of their use, as well as the identity and usual residence of the data controller.

Individual participation principle
13 An individual should have the right:
    a) to obtain from a data controller, or otherwise, confirmation of whether or not the data controller has data relating to him;
    b) to have communicated to him, data relating to him
        i) within a reasonable time;
        ii) at a charge, if any, that is not excessive;
        iii) in a reasonable manner; and
        iv) in a form that is readily intelligible to him;
    c) to be given reasons if a request made under sub-paragraphs (a) and (b) is denied, and to be able to challenge such denial; and
    d) to challenge data relating to him and, if the challenge is

successful, to have the data erased, rectified, completed or amended.

Accountability principle
14 A data controller should be accountable for complying with measures which give effect to the principles stated above.

PART THREE – BASIC PRINCIPLES OF INTERNATIONAL APPLICATION:
FREE FLOW AND LEGITIMATE RESTRICTIONS

15 Member countries should take into consideration the implications for other member countries of domestic processing and re-export of personal data.

16 Member countries should take all reasonable and appropriate steps to ensure that transborder flows of personal data, including transit through a member country, are uninterrupted and secure.

17 A member country should refrain from restricting transborder flows of personal data between itself and another member country except where the latter does not yet substantially observe these Guidelines or where the re-export of such data would circumvent its domestic privacy legislation. A member country may also impose restrictions in respect of certain categories of personal data for which its domestic privacy legislation includes specific regulations in view of the nature of those data and for which the other member country provides no equivalent protection.

18 Member countries should avoid developing laws, policies and practices in the name of the protection of privacy and individual liberties, which would create obstacles to transborder flows of personal data that would exceed requirements for such protection.

PART FOUR – NATIONAL IMPLEMENTATION

19 In implementing domestically the principles set forth in Parts Two and Three, member countries should establish legal, administrative or other procedures or institutions for the protection of privacy and individual liberties in respect of personal data. Member countries should in particular endeavour to:
- a) adopt appropriate domestic legislation;
- b) encourage and support self-regulation, whether in the form of codes of conduct or otherwise;
- c) provide for reasonable means for individuals to exercise their rights;
- d) provide for adequate sanctions and remedies in case of failures to comply with measures which implement the principles set forth in Parts Two and Three; and
- e) ensure that there is no unfair discrimination against data subjects.

PART FIVE – INTERNATIONAL COOPERATION

20 Member countries should, where requested, make known to other member countries details of the observance of the principles set forth in these Guidelines. Member countries should also ensure that procedures for transborder flows of personal data and for the protection of privacy and individual liberties are simple and compatible with those of other member countries which comply with these Guidelines.

21 Member countries should establish procedures to facilitate:
   a) information exchange related to these Guidelines; and
   b) mutual assistance in the procedural and investigative matters involved.

22 Member countries should work towards the development of principles, domestic and international, to govern the applicable law in the case of transborder flows of personal data.

What we regard as the final stage in the European work was the endorsement, in 1980, by the International Chamber of Commerce (ICC), of the OECD and CoE Convention. We give, in full, the statement made by the Secretary-General of the ICC at the time.

ICC ENDORSEMENT OF OECD GUIDELINES AND COUNCIL OF EUROPE CONVENTION

In September 1980 the Council of the OECD and the Council of Ministers of the Council of Europe each adopted instruments designed to produce coherence of national data protection legislation. The ICC welcomes these developments. When equivalent legal protection is afforded to personal data in whatever country they are held, the need for regulations and controls on the transmission of those data between countries is reduced.

The OECD Guidelines and the Council of Europe Convention both specify general principles which should be adopted in national legislation to protect the interests of the individual. The business community has a legitimate interest in the protection of individual freedoms through limited access to and careful handling of personal information. The ICC therefore endorses those basic principles designed for this purpose and laid out in the two international instruments and recommends them to all governments as the basis for national legislation.

At the same time the ICC notes that the instruments themselves offer flexibility to governments in the way that the principles are implemented. The ICC wishes to express the sincere hope that this flexibility (e.g., to derogate from the undertaking to allow free flows of data, to extend the regulatory powers of national authorities to data which do not concern the rights of individuals) will not be misused, and that governments will respect the legitimate information needs of the business community operating at local national and international levels. Undue interference in the freedom to transmit and use legitimate business data could have serious impacts on the level of economic activity.

Conclusion

The late 1970s saw increasing attention to technical detail symptomatic of a wider understanding of computing matters. The shift from the moral and philosophical aspects of privacy to the legal and technical consideration of data protection was real and irreversible. It is to the credit of the draughtsmen of the current UK Act that, out of a mass of jargon, computing minutiae and complex legal considerations, a readable statute has been produced though we have serious reservations as to its workability in certain areas, as we have discussed already, and shall again in Chapter 2.

At the time of writing not only has computing technology itself changed out of all recognition in that computers are widespread, cheap and easily accommodated in ordinary domestic environments, but new complex technical structures such as national/international communication systems are in wide use. Satellite communications allow data to be transmitted quickly round the world, and even the most fervent moralists have to recognise that massive files of personal data can be transmitted virtually immediately out of one country and into another over a network, from one jurisdiction to a different one.

No High Street is now without a vending point for hardware and software, and yet there is evidence that many of these fall below an acceptable standard of reliability and accuracy. Thus the situation is compounded by a lowering of standards, which exacerbates an already difficult situation. We develop some of the arguments for improving professional standards in computing generally in Chapter 4. However, it is as well to realise that without precise legal processes and a professional approach to computing at all levels of society, the lowering (or lack) of professional standards as a result of commercial pressures will have a profound effect on computing as a whole. The situation may well get worse before it gets better. Increased professionalism is an essential component of effective data protection.

There is, however, a final paradox; though throughout two decades the moralists had called the tune and mounted an impressive argument based on the need to protect an individual from having his privacy invaded, it was the potential threat to UK business interests arising from non-ratification of the European Data Protection Convention which was finally recognised by the UK Government as being a prime motivator.[10]

References

1. Warner, M. and Stone, M., *The Data Bank Society: Organisation Computers and Social Freedom,* Allen and Unwin, UK, 1970
2. Schiller, C. and Gilchrist, B., "A National Survey of the Public's Attitude Towards Computers", AFIPS and TIME Inc, July 1971
3. Gotlieb, A., "Computers: Privacy and Freedom of Information", Conference Report, Queen's University, Kingston, Ontario, Canada, 1970
4. Ware, W., "Computers: Privacy and Freedom of Information", Conference Report, Queen's University, Kingston, Ontario, Canada, 1970
5. Campbell, J., *Grammatical Man – Information, Entropy, Language and Life,* Allen Lane, 1982
6. Thring, M., *Machines – Masters or Slaves of Man?* Peter Peregrinus, 1974
7. Younger, K. (Chairman), "Report of the Committee on Privacy", Cmnd 5012, HMSO, July 1972
8. Lindop, N. (Chairman), "Report of the Committee on Data Protection", Cmnd 6353, HMSO, December 1975
9. British Computer Society, *Privacy and the Computer: Steps to Practicality,* British Computer Society, July 1972
10. Leon Brittan, The Secretary of State for The Home Department, *Hansard,* Vol 53, 1 January 1984, p. 31

PART II
THE DATA PROTECTION ACT 1984

Chapter 2
The Act in Summary

In this chapter we give an overview of the Act which implements the proposals set out in the White Paper on Data Protection.[1] In so doing it enables the UK "to comply with and ratify the European Convention for the Protection of Individuals with regard to the Automatic Processing of Personal Data".

Forming the basis of the Act are eight data protection principles, a Data Protection Registrar, and an associated public register of data users. In essence the Act requires all data users to register and, in so doing, to give full details of their operations. The eight principles, then, form a set of standards against which the Registrar will ensure compliance.

The Data Protection Principles

1. The information to be contained in personal data shall be obtained, and personal data shall be processed, fairly and lawfully.
2. Personal data shall be held only for one or more specified and lawful purposes.
3. Personal data held for any purpose or purposes shall not be used or disclosed in any manner incompatible with

that purpose or those purposes.
4. Personal data held for any purpose or purposes shall be adequate, relevant, and not excessive in relation to that purpose or those purposes.
5. Personal data shall be accurate and, where necessary, kept up to date.
6. Personal data held for any purpose or purposes shall not be kept for longer than is necessary for that purpose or those purposes.
7. An individual shall be entitled –
(a) at reasonable intervals and without undue delay or expense –
   (i) to be informed by any data user whether he holds personal data of which that individual is the subject; and
   (ii) to access any such data held by a data user; and
(b) where appropriate, to have such data corrected or erased.
8. Appropriate security measures shall be taken against unauthorised access to, or alteration, disclosure, or destruction of, personal data and against accidental loss or destruction of personal data.

The Act itself incorporates the data protection principles in Section 2, and Section 2(3) provides that the Secretary of State may modify or supplement those data protection principles by order with the aim of providing additional safeguards in respect of personal data concerning:

(a) the racial origin of the data subject;
(b) his political opinions or religious or other beliefs;
(c) his physical or mental health or his sexual life;
(d) his criminal convictions.

Section 2(4) of the Act provides that an order under Section 2(3) may modify a principle either by modifying the principle *per se* or by modifying its interpretation thereof, and that where an order modifies a principle or provides for an additional principle of data protection, it may contain provisions for the interpretation of the modified or additional principle. The principles also form operational guidelines for data users – an equivalent of the Highway Code

THE ACT IN SUMMARY

but, unlike the Highway Code, which is advisory and often forgotten once a driver has a licence, the data user will diverge from the principles and the provisions of the Act at his peril.

Clearly, as is shown by Section 2(3), the government and Parliament have had well in mind much of the philosophical and moral argument we illustrate in Chapter 1 and which has attracted, and still does attract, media attention. It may be said, with justification, that while Bills laid before Parliament are "political" in their nature, Statutes emanating from Parliament should be "legal" in their nature. However, it is clear that, in allowing for modification or additions to the data protection principles and, moreover, specifying parameters for such modifications or additions, the Act is both a legal and political instrument.

Everyone should be worried if data on citizens are processed or stored in circumstances whereby the data subjects are categorised in respect, say, of their racial origins. The same comment applies to categorisation in respect of political opinions or religious or other beliefs, physical or mental health or sexual life, or criminal convictions. Indeed, categorisation may not be the only complaint; the use or storage or production of data based on such information may itself be questionable.

Delegation of Responsibility

The crucial and difficult issues to resolve are the occasions or circumstances which should by law be considered as improper in contravening a data protection principle. It seems that on these contentious issues Parliament has chosen to avoid reaching any conclusions and to delegate the responsibility for reaching those conclusions to the Secretary of State. On some of the more important issues, however, we note that Section 40 subsection 4 requires the approval of a draft Order of the Secretary of State by both Houses of Parliament in the form of a resolution. It would have been advantageous to both the data user and data subject if Parliament had been able properly to debate the issues, in the context of data protection, relating to race, politics, religion, physical or mental health, sexual life and criminal convictions – and, importantly, to reach some conclusions on those matters for the purpose of providing clear and reasonable legislation as a framework for future conduct by all concerned.

Uncertainty

Parliament has failed in fact to provide clear legislation. The resultant uncertainty is demonstrated by the following example. A firm of debt collectors, or, as they are sometimes called, credit controllers, may have information concerning a Mr A who owes money to one or more of their clients; Mr A may be, for instance, a Chinese Fascist atheist suffering from gout with a history of suicide attempts, who frequents the red light areas of London in the early hours of the morning and at weekends, and who has criminal convictions for dishonesty. The debt collectors hold the aforesaid information on Mr A primarily for the purpose of dealing with him as a debtor of their clients.

The question arises as to what relevance is his nationality to the primary purpose of the data user – the credit controllers. The answer may be given that, in itself, Mr A's nationality would not be relevant, but, taken in the context of the data user's legitimate business (as a debt collector) might well be relevant. For instance, bearing in mind the offences of dishonesty for which Mr A has been convicted in the past, it might be thought that any monies or assets which he had in the UK he would siphon abroad, perhaps to his country of origin or to a country with a Fascist regime in accordance with his political beliefs. Of course Mr A's connections with his country of origin would be relevant, but on the basis that a court considered in the light of evidence that there was a reasonable prospect of Mr A siphoning monies or assets out of the country to his country of origin or elsewhere in order to avoid an eventual judgment debt being executed against him effectively, then a Mareva Injunction* could be ordered restraining the removal from the jurisdiction of assets or money to a certain value and further restraining their dissipation within the UK.

The above example, whilst highlighting the sensitive nature of certain data and the difficulties of legislating against the use, storage or processing of such data, also illustrates the importance of data protection principles 1, 2, 3, 4, 5 and 6, which deal with, in essence, the purpose or purposes for which personal data are held by a data user, and seek to control the means by which the purpose or purposes are to be achieved. Thus the Act is intended to control the means to the end as far as the data user is concerned ("data purpose").

Mr A is, in fact, a personification of the elements dealt with in Section 2(3) (a), (b), (c) and (d), which gives the Secretary of State power to modify or supplement the eight data protection principles to provide extra safeguards in respect of personal data relating to racial origin, political opinions, religious or other beliefs, physical or mental health, sexual life or criminal convictions. Clearly Mr A will be of particular interest to any Secretary of State exercising the power under Section 2, subsection 3. The power in question is controlled to some extent by the requirement under Section 40 subsection 4 of prior approval by a resolution of both Houses of Parliament.

---

*Mareva Injunction: Mareva Compania Noviera S.A. v Int. Bulk Carriers Ltd, [1980] I AII ER.213 (C.A.). A Mareva Injunction is a method of halting the disposal of or dissipation of assets or monies by a person against whom legal proceedings have been commenced. Thus, it may be that a debtor against whom proceedings are commenced would wish to transfer all his monies to a Swiss bank numbered account; in the event that reasonable evidence could be advanced that this was on the balance of probabilities a likelihood, then to preserve the status quo the courts would generally grant a Mareva Injunction to stop him from doing so to the extent necessary to preserve the amount being claimed in the legal proceedings. If the debtor breached the injunction, he would be liable to contempt of court proceedings, with the result of unlimited fines or imprisonment or both.

Security and Rights of Access

Security is a sub-set of data protection. The Act in operation can be viewed as consisting of an upper and lower layer, where the upper contains the philosophical and moral principles of the original privacy debate. For example, the issues are "racial origin of the data subject", "political and religious beliefs", "mental health and sexual life". The lower layer (lower only in logical relationships) contains the techniques by which a candidate for protection shall be so protected; in other words, the security techniques.

Our Chinese Fascist, Mr A, is entitled by principle 8 of the Act to have his personal data held securely under "computerised lock and key", with suitable controls on the use of the key, the physical environment where the data are stored and processed, and the integrity of the staff there. We devote Chapter 5 to computer security.

Principle 7 concerns the entitlement of the individual data subject to full information in matters relevant to where a data user has personal data in respect of the subject and, if so, allows the subject access to such data. The issue also concerns the correction or erasure of data in certain circumstances ("data access") which is dealt with in Chapter 5.

The way in which the Act attempts to deal with the three issues specified above, namely data purpose, data security, and data access, is described in PART II of the Act with a system of registration, supervision, appeals, and what are referred to as matters of a "miscellaneous and supplementary" nature. As is usual in recent statutes, the teeth of the legislation are embodied under the heading, "Miscellaneous and Supplementary", or some other equally innocuous title. This heading comprises Sections 15–20 of the Act and deals with the following matters: unauthorised disclosure by computer bureaux; powers of entry and inspection; disclosure of information; service of notices; prosecutions and penalties; and the liability of directors, managers, secretaries or similar officers of a body corporate, or any person purporting to act in such a capacity.

As to prosecutions and penalties, it is clear that breaches may give rise to either civil or criminal liability or both. The penalties as far as criminal breaches are concerned are set out in Section 19. We are unable to comment on the likely extent of the penalties since this will be an entirely new matter for courts to determine in terms of sentencing policy. As to civil proceedings, the amount involved must clearly be closely related to the loss and damage sustained by the plaintiff in the litigation.

Registration

It may fairly be stated that the basis of PART II of the Act is the system of registration of data users and computer bureaux. Quite simply, those who do not have the benefit of being entered on the register cannot hold personal data, save by breaching the Act. It is therefore important to note the basis upon which the Registrar is entitled to refuse registration of a data user or computer bureau. This aspect is dealt with in Section 7, subsection 2; the Registrar may refuse an application for registration when, but only when:

(a) he considers that the particulars provided for registration are insufficient;
(b) he is satisfied that the applicant for registration is likely to contravene any of the data protection principles; or
(c) he considers that the information available to him is insufficient to satisfy him that the applicant is unlikely to contravene any of the data protection principles.

Clearly very wide discretionary powers are invested in the Registrar by Section 7, subsection 2(b) for him to conclude that he is satisfied that an applicant is "likely to contravene any of the data protection principles". Obviously the applicant may with his application make representation in support to the Registrar, although this is not statutorily provided for, somewhat surprisingly. In addition any data user refused registration has the right of appeal, and of course may tender evidence to the appeal tribunal in support of his case to show that the Registrar's decision was unfounded in the circumstances. However, even wider discretionary powers are invested in the Registrar at Section 7, subsection 2(c), enabling him to refuse registration to an applicant whom he considers has provided insufficient information to satisfy him that the applicant is "unlikely to contravene any of the data protection principles". This is a sweeping provision, in our view, but it must be recalled that again a right of appeal is embodied in the Act in Section 13.

Rights of Data Subjects

PART III specifically deals with the rights of data subjects, whereby an individual shall be entitled, (a) to be informed by any data user whether the data held by him includes personal data of which that individual is the data subject, and (b) to be supplied by any data user with a copy in writing of the information based on any such personal data held by him (together with any necessary explanation of such information, if it would otherwise be unintelligible). This part of the Act in Section 22 also deals with providing a remedy for damage sustained by a data subject by reason of the inaccuracy of the data held; proceedings may be brought for compensation in such circumstances. There are here the important riders that, in proceedings brought by virtue of this section, it will be a defence to prove that the data user had taken such care as in all the circumstances was reasonably required to ensure the accuracy of the data at the material time (Section 22(3)). Section 22(2) covers situations where data are held which accurately records information received or obtained by the data user from the data subject or a third party and (a) the data indicate that the information was received or obtained from the data subject or a third party or (b) the information is not extracted from the data except in a form which includes an indication to that effect. In all these data shall not be regarded as inaccurate because the information is itself incorrect or misleading.[2]

There is provision in Section 23(1) for compensation to be payable to a data subject for the loss, destruction or unauthorised disclosure of personal data. Again, there is the important rider that it will be a defence for the data user to prove that he has taken such care as in all the circumstances is reasonably required to prevent the loss, destruction or disclosure of the personal data in question. In Chapter 4 we show how important a previously prepared 7-stage deposition or Statutory Declaration could be in this respect.

Inaccurate Data

Under Section 24 of the Act an application may be made to the High Court or a County Court for the rectification or erasure of personal data held by a data user if:

(a) the personal data are inaccurate (that is, that they are incorrect or misleading as to any matter of fact), or
(b) the data subject has suffered damage by reason of the disclosure of personal data in circumstances entitling him to compensation under Section 23, and that there is a substantial risk of the data being further disclosed without such authority as is mentioned in that section.

Of course, once the High Court or a County Court has made an order under Section 24, breach of such an order would constitute a contempt of court, placing the person in breach at risk as to a fine or imprisonment or both. Indeed, Section 24 gives the court wide powers, whereby the court, in addition to ordering rectification or erasure of data, may, in a case where personal data are inaccurate (subsection 1 thereof) make such further order, if any, as it thinks just, in respect of any *other* data appearing to the court to be based on inaccurate data. In a serious case this could, it is envisaged, lead to an injunction closing down a complete computer installation or a given registered system or ordering the complete destruction of certain data.

With regard to which court to use for the purpose of obtaining an order for compensation, rectification, or erasure, the basis of choice between the County Court and the High Court would appear to be no more than the upper limit of the County Court jurisdiction, which at present is £5,000 payable as damages, subject to any agreement between the parties being reached under the provisions of the County Courts Act 1959, whereby the monetary jurisdiction of the County Court is by consent increased to a higher level. There is no limit to the High Court jurisdiction.

Exemptions

By PART IV of the Act certain important exemptions are dealt with. Section 27 exempts personal data from the provisions of PART II (including the provisions as to registration), and of PART III insofar as it relates to the rights of data subjects, and insofar as the exemption is required for the purposes of safeguarding national security. Section 27(2) further provides that any question of an exemption being required for the purpose of safeguarding national security will be determined by a minister of the crown and that a certificate signed by a minister of the crown certifying that the exemption is, or at the time was, so required, will be *conclusive evidence* of that fact. Furthermore, personal data not exempt by reason of the foregoing provision will be exempt from the non-disclosure provisions of the Act in any case in which the disclosure in question is for the purpose of safeguarding national security. Once again, on this point, certification by a minister of the crown that the disclosure was for the purpose of safeguarding national security will be conclusive evidence of that fact.

It is provided by Section 27, subsection 6, that the powers of certification conferred on a minister of the crown shall not be exercisable except by a minister who is a member of the Cabinet or by the Attorney General or the Lord Advocate. Section 28 is important in that personal data held for any of the following purposes,

(a) the prevention or detection of crime,
(b) the apprehension or prosecution of offenders,
(c) the assessment or collection of any tax or duty,

are to be exempt from the data subject access provisions in any case in which the application of those provisions to the data would be likely to prejudice any of the matters mentioned in (a), (b) or (c) above.

The Act in Section 31 also provides for the exemption

from data subject access provisions in respect of data received from a third party and held by a government department which are held as information relevant to the making of judicial appointments. Further, personal data are exempt from data subject access provisions if the data consist of information in respect of which a claim to legal professional privilege could be maintained in legal proceedings.

Summary

The Act is designed to regulate and control the use, storage and processing of personal data on automatic equipment, in particular where there is some measure of risk to individual privacy. In Chapter 3 we deal in an annotated manner on a Section-by-Section basis, with the interpretation and likely operation of the Act's provisions.

References

1. HMSO, "Data Protection: the Government's Proposals for Legislation", Cmnd 8539, April 1982
2. See pages 114-16 which analyse Section 22 including the further provisions of 22 (2)(b) as to the rights of data subjects to notify data users of information being regarded as incorrect and misleading, and for an indication to that effect to be included in the data or information extracted therefrom.

Chapter 3
The Act Examined

This chapter sets out each section of the Act, followed, where necessary, by a comment or interpretation of that section and stating our views as to its likely operation. We give a strict interpretation of the Act but it may be that the Courts will interpret the Act in a more liberal manner to avoid the normal consequences of defective drafting of a Statute. There is no doubt in our minds that the Statute as a whole will provide almost endless possibilities for litigation as to its interpretation and effect, unfortunate for data subject and data user alike, although no doubt lawyers will not be complaining at this new source of business.

We start with the Arrangement of Sections found in the Act but we have inserted the Schedules at suitable places in the text for ease of reading.

THE ACT EXAMINED

ARRANGEMENT OF SECTIONS AND SCHEDULES

PART I
PRELIMINARY

Section	1.	Definition of "data" and related expressions.
Section 2. and Schedule I.		The data protection principles.
Section	3.	The Registrar and the Tribunal.
Schedule	2.	The Data Protection Registrar and the Data Protection Tribunal.

PART II
REGISTRATION AND SUPERVISION OF DATA USERS AND COMPUTER BUREAUX

Registration

Section	4.	Registration of data users and computer bureaux.
Section	5.	Prohibition of unregistered holding etc. of personal data.
Section	6.	Applications for registration and for amendment of registered particulars.
Section	7.	Acceptance and refusal of applications.
Section	8.	Duration and renewal of registration.
Section	9.	Inspection etc. of registered particulars.

Supervision

Section	10.	Enforcement notices.
Section	11.	De-registration notices.
Section	12.	Transfer prohibition notices.

Appeals

Section	13.	Rights of appeal.
Schedule	3.	Appeal Proceedings.
Section	14.	Determination of appeals.

Miscellaneous and supplementary

Section	15.	Unauthorised disclosure by computer bureaux.
Section 16. and Schedule 4.		Powers of entry and inspection.
Section	17.	Disclosure of information.
Section	18.	Service of notices.
Section	19.	Prosecutions and penalties.
Section	20.	Liability of directors etc.

THE DATA PROTECTION ACT 1984

PART III
RIGHTS OF DATA SUBJECTS

Section 21. Right of access to personal data.
Section 22. Compensation for inaccuracy.
Section 23. Compensation for loss or unauthorised disclosure.
Section 24. Rectification and erasure.
Section 25. Jurisdiction and procedure.

PART IV
EXEMPTIONS

Section 26. Preliminary.
Section 27. National security.
Section 28. Crime and taxation.
Section 29. Health and social work.
Section 30. Regulation of financial services etc.
Section 31. Judicial appointments and legal professional privilege.
Section 32. Payrolls and accounts.
Section 33. Domestic or other limited purposes.
Section 34. Other exemptions.
Section 35. Examination marks.

PART V
GENERAL

Section 36. General duties of the Registrar.
Section 37. Co-operation between parties to the Convention.
Section 38. Application to government departments and police.
Section 39. Data held, and services provided, outside the United Kingdom.
Section 40. Regulations, rules and orders.
Section 41. General interpretation.
Section 42. Commencement and transitional provisions.
Section 43. Short title and extent.

PART I PRELIMINARY
Section 1 Definition of "data" and related expressions

1.–(1) The following provisions shall have effect for the interpretation of this Act.
(2) "Data" means information recorded in a form in which it

THE ACT EXAMINED

can be processed by equipment operating automatically in response to instructions given for that purpose.

(3) "Personal data" means data consisting of information which relates to a living individual who can be identified from that information (or from that and other information in the possession of the data user), including any expression of opinion about the individual but not any indication of the intentions of the data user in respect of that individual.

(4) "Data subject" means an individual who is the subject of personal data.

(5) "Data user" means a person who holds data, and a person "holds" data if–
  (a) the data form part of a collection of data processed or intended to be processed by or on behalf of that person as mentioned in subsection (2) above; and
  (b) that person (either alone or jointly or in common with other persons) controls the contents and use of the data comprised in the collection; and
  (c) the data are in the form in which they have been or are intended to be processed as mentioned in paragraph (a) above or (though not for the time being in that form) in a form into which they have been converted after being so processed and with a view to being further so processed on a subsequent occasion.

(6) A person carries on a "computer bureau" if he provides other persons with services in respect of data, and a person provides such services if–
  (a) as agent for other persons he causes data held by them to be processed as mentioned in subsection (2) above; or
  (b) he allows other persons the use of equipment in his possession for the processing as mentioned in that subsection of data held by them.

(7) "Processing", in relation to data, means amending, augmenting, deleting or re-arranging the data or extracting the information constituting the data and, in the case of personal data, means performing any of those operations by reference to the data subject.

(8) Subsection (7) above shall not be construed as applying to any operation performed only for the purpose of preparing the text of documents.

(9) "Disclosing", in relation to data, includes disclosing information extracted from the data; and where the identification of the individual who is the subject of personal data depends partly on the information constituting the data and partly on other information in the possession of the data user, the data shall not be regarded as disclosed or transferred unless the other information is also disclosed or transferred.

Subsection 1 introduces the definitions, interpretations and meanings to have effect in respect of the Act's interpretation. It is essential for a proper understanding of the Act that the definitions are read together and, in any event, in context. In addition, it is important in our view that the definitions are read in conjunction with the definitions of certain other terms in the general interpretation section, being Section 41.

Subsection 2 states that "data" means information recorded in a form in which it can be "processed". It is important to note here that the term "processed" should be construed in relation to the definition of processing in subsection 7. Subsection 2 limits the operation of the term "processed" to equipment operating automatically in response to instructions given for that purpose. Hence the key to the interpretation of the term "data" is the automatic operation of equipment in response to instructions given for that purpose. It would appear that instructions for processing must have been given in advance of the processing actually taking place, whereby, once started, the process is carried out "automatically" without the assistance of any person prior to the process being completed.

The effect of subsection 2 is further limited by the definition in subsection 5 of "data user" as meaning a person who "holds" data, but disclosing that the circumstances in which a person holds data are restricted to where the data is processed or intended to be processed (and here again see subsection 7). In our view the manner in which the definition of "data" has been limited in scope, together with its operation, means that written material of all types is prevented from falling within the definition, unless automatically processed or intended to be processed, or is in a form into which it has been converted after being so processed and with a view to being further processed later.

Subsection 3 defines the term "personal data" as consisting of information relating to a living individual who can be identified from such information. (The term "consisting", however, is vague, as "information" is represented by data. It must be emphasised that "information" comes first and data come second. "Data" is the means of communication of information, and therefore to say that data "consist" of information is likely to lead to confusion.) In terms of operation of subsection 3, one must therefore consider the methods by which a living individual can be so identified: the most common method is by name and, for further clarity, by address combined with the name. Other methods would include the following: a National Insurance number, a membership number, a bank account number, a building society roll number; and further we consider that photographs produced automatically from digital data or otherwise would constitute personal data in that they are a means of identifying a living individual. We consider that the combination of data representing information with "other information in the possession of the data user" gives considerable breadth to the definition in that it may be that the data themselves represent information which *per se* could not probably identify an individual but that combined with other information identification could be made. The data may refer to "Mr X" whereas Mr X is actually identified in a paper file of documents marked "confidential". We take the view that the data would then be personal data.

"Personal data" is held to include expressions of opinion about the individual, but not an indication of the intentions of the data user in respect of that individual. The use of the term "opinion" must be taken in contradistinction to factual "information". In the event that the expressions of intention of one data user in respect of a particular individual are transferred to another data user, it is likely that, to the extent that those expressions of intention did not constitute personal data as far as the first data user was concerned, they would constitute personal data insofar as they are held by the second transferee data user.

Subsection 4 defines the "data subject" as meaning an individual who is the subject of personal data. It is extremely important to be aware as to the operation of the Act that it relates as a whole to data relating to living persons, as opposed to legal persons, and in particular here one is talking about companies or corporate bodies of any kind, with which the Act is not concerned. It is therefore the case that, as far as the operation of the Act is concerned, it is not intended to deal with corporate industrial espionage. It may be that certain corporations, for instance insurance companies and credit reference agencies, hold individuals' personal data as part of their "business". Such data could be of immense value to a competitor corporation. In the event of such data being held, compliance with the Act would be required. However, in the event of the information data, for instance, being that a large oil company was in one month's time going to commence drilling for oil in the English Channel, that would not, *per se*, be within the scope of the Act.

Subsection 5 defines the term "data user" as meaning a person who "holds data". It is stated that a person "holds" data in the event that two separate matters are complied with – first, the data form part of a collection of data processed or intended to be processed (as dealt with in subsection 2) *and*, secondly, that the person in question either alone or jointly or in common with other persons controls the contents and use of the data comprised in the collection and, thirdly, the data are in the form in which they have been or are intended to be processed *or* in a form in which they have been converted after having processed *and* with a view to being further processed later. Thus, the data form part of a collection of data which has been processed or is intended to be processed by automatic equipment operating in response to instructions given for that purpose, and the user, either by himself or together with others, has control over the contents and use of the data. It is clear, therefore, that within the companies, or organisations, or bodies, in which the data user is playing a part in relation to personal data, the Act is aimed at management levels and above. A person who is solely responsible, for instance, for the storage of data but has no control over its contents and use will not be a data user. Further, computer terminal or computer keyboard operators who may "access" data via printers or visual display units will not, simply by that fact, be data users, for they will not have control over the contents and use of the data comprised in the collection. However, the data user may well be liable in the event of security being breached by computer terminal or keyboard operators in the event of appropriate security measures not having been taken as provided for in data protection principle 8.

We note here that the term used in subsection 5(b) is "controls the contents *and* use" (the italicisation is our own) as opposed to the term "controls the contents or use". In our view, therefore, the use of the term "and" in this particular context means that both control of contents and use must be present for subsection 5(b) to be fulfilled. Subsection 5 provides for the possibility of more than one person having control over the contents and use of the data, and to this extent it is possible that, jointly or in common with other persons, the control of the contents and use of the data may be split or categorised, whereby one person or one group of persons has control of the contents and another person or another group of persons has control of the use, but that acting jointly or in common (that is to say, in combination) they together have control of the contents *and* use of the data comprising the collection. In our view this is a practical provision, bearing in mind the manner in which certain organisations, corporations and other bodies actually work, and is an example of the statute being practically applied to real situations.

The importance of subsection (c) is that in the event of data being *converted* after having been processed but with no view to there being any further processing as a subsequent decision, data would not be *held* and any person possessing such converted material would not be a data user. Whether this was the intention of the draftsmen of the Statute is open to doubt. On the face of it the use of the word "converted" provides a simple method of avoidance to anyone not wishing to be a data user under the Act.

The term "converted" has both technical and general meanings. The most common technical meanings may be summarised as follows:–

Converted from one computer system to another; from one computer language to another; from one character code such as ASCII to EBCDIC – all methods of effecting compatibility.

The general meaning of "converted" to the layman would

appear to be for instance the printing in eye-readable form of the contents of a disc file and the subsequent destruction of the data on the disc-file. We feel it is important that the Act does not provide a definition of "converted" at Section 41.

Subsection 6 defines a person carrying on a "computer bureau". A person carries on a computer bureau if he provides other persons with services in respect of data, and provides such services in two *alternative* situations: first, as an agent for other persons where he causes data held by them to be processed, as defined in subsection 2, *or*, secondly, he allows other persons holding data the use of equipment in his possession for the processing of that data as defined in subsection 2. It will be noted that persons carrying on computer bureaux are not data users unless they additionally have control over the contents and use made of the data being processed on their equipment, and are in a situation where they can provide individual access to the data. Without the additional circumstances, such persons are only liable in respect of data protection principle 8 in Schedule 1 that appropriate security measures shall be taken against unauthorised access to, or alteration, disclosure, or destruction of, personal data, and against accidental loss or destruction of personal data. It is apparent also that by reason of the wording of subsection 6, and in particular at subsection 6(b), whereby the equipment shall be in the possession of the person carrying on the computer bureau, the situation of a person selling, leasing or hiring equipment to others for the purposes of processing data will not fall within the provisions of subsection 6.

Subsection 7 defines the term "processing" in relation to data as meaning the amending, augmenting, deleting or rearranging of the data or the extracting of the information constituting the data, and further, in the case of personal data, as meaning the performing of any of those operations by reference to the data subject. It is our view that this particular definition is of importance in that it restricts the Act's operation to activities which might result in an invasion of individual privacy, in that in relation to personal data as covered by the Act, amending, augmenting, deleting, rearranging and extracting are operations which are taken to be performed under subsection 7, by reference to the data subject. Under subsection 5, a necessary constituent element of a "data user" is that the person in question holds data forming part of a collection of data processed or intended to be processed.

Subsection 2 is relevant as referring to information recorded in the form in which it can be processed by equipment operating automatically in response to instructions *given for that purpose*. "Purpose" appears to be a key word; this means that even though there may be information recorded in a form in which it can be processed by equipment operating automatically, it will not constitute "data" under the Act unless the equipment itself is capable of operating in response to instructions given for the specific purpose of processing the information. This point is made purely because the phrase "in response to instructions given for that purpose" as used in the subsection is itself taken to be included for some purpose. It would appear at this point that there is a possibility that certain data users will take positive measures in order to avoid or evade the provisions of the Act by deliberately "hiding" personal data within a large body of other data, and it will clearly be difficult to prove the intentions of such data users in relation to the personal data held within that body of other data. We see a need for highly sophisticated audit techniques to discover personal data embedded with a body of other data. The responsible data user will in our view wish to demonstrate to data subjects and to the Registrar that he is not indulging in these practices. However, for those unscrupulous data users who do so indulge, the problem is as to who will track them down. In theory the answer is either (i) a data subject or a group of data subjects or (ii) the Registrar. We envisage perhaps insurmountable problems for effective policing. Other European legislation provides of data inspectors with more on-the-ground powers than the Registrar, and we would commend this.

Subsection 8 is an explanatory provision whereby it is stated that subsection 7 (processing) shall not be construed as applying to any operation performed only for the purpose of preparing the text of documents.

Subsection 9 defines the term "disclosing" in relation to data as *including* disclosing information extracted from that data. One example which has formed the subject of considerable press comment is client lists or potential client lists which are sold for, generally, large sums of money, to provide certain companies and organisations with "mailshot" material. In addition, this subsection is important in that the manner in which the information is extracted is immaterial; it can, for instance, be in the form of eye-readable computer print-out. However, there is no reason why it could not be in the form of a handwritten document copied from a computer print-out or from a visual display unit, or in the form of a photograph of such information obtained from a visual display unit or computer print-out, or even in the form of a tape recording, where information extracted from the data in question has been dictated on to tape. It is arguable that the disclosing is a "once and for all" provision and that it will not apply to second and subsequent disclosures of the information in question; however, we do not consider that such an argument would succeed. The definition of disclosing properly incorporates the provision relating to the definition of "personal data" as including not only the data themselves but also other information which in combination can identify the data subject. It is provided that disclosure will not occur unless both the data and the other information are disclosed. Additionally the question of data being transferred is dealt with on the same basis and we would consider that this is relevant to a proper interpretation of Section 12 relating to transfer prohibition notices.

Section 2 and Schedule 1   The data protection principles

2.–(1) Subject to subsection (3) below, references in this Act to the data protection principles are to the principles set out in Part I of Schedule 1 to this Act; and those principles shall be interpreted in accordance with Part II of that Schedule.
(2) The first seven principles apply to personal data held by data users and the eighth applies both to such data and to personal data in respect of which services are provided by persons carrying on computer bureaux.
(3) The Secretary of State may by order modify or supplement

those principles for the purpose of providing additional safeguards in relation to personal data consisting of information as to—
  (a) the racial origin of the data subject;
  (b) his political opinions or religious or other beliefs;
  (c) his physical or mental health or his sexual life; or
  (d) his criminal convictions;
and references in this Act to the data protection principles include, except where the context otherwise requires, references to any modified or additional principle having effect by virtue of an order under this subsection.
(4) An order under subsection (3) above may modify a principle either by modifying the principle itself or by modifying its interpretation; and where an order under that subsection modifies a principle or provides for an additional principle it may contain provisions for the interpretation of the modified or additional principle.
(5) An order under subsection (3) above modifying the third data protection principle may, to such extent as the Secretary of State thinks appropriate, exclude or modify in relation to that principle any exemption from the non-disclosure provisions which is contained in Part IV of this Act; and the exemptions from those provisions contained in that Part shall accordingly have effect subject to any order made by virtue of this subsection.
(6) An order under subsection (3) above may make different provision in relation to data consisting of information of different descriptions.

The key to the Act is the group of eight principles governing the collection and use of personal data specified in Schedule 1 of the Act. The provisions of Section 2 and the likely operation of those provisions can only be understood if they are read in the context of the data protection principles, which are set out below in the form in which they appear in the Act (as regards principle 8, see also Chapter 5).

THE DATA PROTECTION PRINCIPLES (SCHEDULE 1)

Personal data held by data users

1. The information to be contained in personal data shall be obtained, and personal data shall be processed, fairly and lawfully.
2. Personal data shall be held only for one or more specified and lawful purposes.

3. Personal data held for any purpose or purposes shall not be used or disclosed in any manner incompatible with that purpose or those purposes.

4. Personal data held for any purpose or purposes shall be adequate, relevant and not excessive in relation to that purpose or those purposes.

5. Personal data shall be accurate and, where necessary, kept up to date.

6. Personal data held for any purpose or purposes shall not be kept for longer than is necessary for that purpose or those purposes.

7. An individual shall be entitled—
  (a) at reasonable intervals and without undue delay or expense—
    (i) to be informed by any data user whether he holds personal data of which that individual is the subject; and
    (ii) to have access to any such data held by a data user; and
  (b) where appropriate, to have such data corrected or erased.

Personal data held by data users or in respect of which services are provided by persons carrying on computer bureaux

8. Appropriate security measures shall be taken against unauthorised access to, or alteration, disclosure or destruction of, personal data and against accidental loss or destruction of personal data.

The principles relate to the collection and use of personal data, the quality of the data in question, the purposes for which that data is used, the rights of data subjects to have access to personal data relating to them, and the requirement for appropriate security measures to protect personal data against accidental or deliberate access, or its loss or corruption.

Subsection 1 introduces the principles set out above and states that those principles are to be interpreted in accordance with PART II of Schedule 1 as follows:

The first principle

1.—(1) Subject to sub-paragraph (2) below, in determining whether information was obtained fairly regard shall be had to the method by which it was obtained, including in particular whether any person from whom it was obtained was deceived

THE ACT EXAMINED

or misled as to the purpose or purposes for which it is to be held, used or disclosed.

(2) Information shall in any event be treated as obtained fairly if it is obtained from a person who—
- (a) is authorised by or under any enactment to supply it; or
- (b) is required to supply it by or under any enactment or by any convention or other instrument imposing an international obligation on the United Kingdom;

and in determining whether information was obtained fairly there shall be disregarded any disclosure of the information which is authorised or required by or under any enactment or required by any such convention or other instrument as aforesaid.

The second principle

2. Personal data shall not be treated as held for a specified purpose unless that purpose is described in particulars registered under this Act in relation to the data.

The third principle

3. Personal data shall not be treated as used or disclosed in contravention of this principle unless—
- (a) used otherwise than for a purpose of a description registered under this Act in relation to the data; or
- (b) disclosed otherwise than to a person of a description so registered.

The fifth principle

4. Any question whether or not personal data are accurate shall be determined as for the purposes of section 22 of this Act but, in the case of such data as are mentioned in subsection (2) of that section, this principle shall not be regarded as having been contravened by reason of any inaccuracy in the information there mentioned if the requirements specified in that subsection have been complied with.

The seventh principle

5.—(1) Paragraph (a) of this principle shall not be construed as conferring any rights inconsistent with section 21 of this Act.

(2) In determining whether access to personal data is sought at reasonable intervals regard shall be had to the nature of the data, the purpose for which the data are held and the frequency with which the data are altered.

(3) The correction or erasure of personal data is appropriate only where necessary for ensuring compliance with the other data protection principles.

The eighth principle

6. Regard shall be had—
   (a) to the nature of the personal data and the harm that would result from such access, alteration, disclosure, loss or destruction as are mentioned in this principle; and
   (b) to the place where the personal data are stored, to security measures programmed into the relevant equipment and to measures taken for ensuring the reliability of staff having access to the data.

Use for historical, statistical or research purposes

7. Where personal data are held for historical, statistical or research purposes and not used in such a way that damage or distress is, or is likely to be, caused to any data subject—
   (a) the information contained in the data shall not be regarded for the purposes of the first principle as obtained unfairly by reason only that its use for any such purpose was not disclosed when it was obtained; and
   (b) the data may, notwithstanding the sixth principle, be kept indefinitely.

Subsection 2 provides that the first seven principles apply to personal data held by data users and that the eighth principle applies both to such data and to personal data in respect of which services are provided by persons carrying on a business based on the computer bureaux principle (as defined in Section 1, subsection 6).

In respect of principle 8, we consider that security measures are not limited simply to the technical measures which can be incorporated into computer systems but extend to the totality, as discussed in Chapter 5.

Subsection 3 empowers the Secretary of State to modify or supplement the eight principles for the purpose of providing additional safeguards in relation to personal data relating to racial origin, political opinions or religious or other beliefs, physical or mental health or sexual life, or criminal convictions. Article 6 of the Council of Europe Convention provides that these particular categories are sensitive data, which should not be processed automatically unless member state law provides appropriate safeguards. The Convention does not require that different provisions be made, and it may be the case that the Act provides sufficient safeguards in its present form.

It is known that consultation between government and various interest and pressure groups is taking place with regard to additional protection. It may be, therefore, that the Secretary of State will, when acceptable specific proposals have been formulated, use his power under subsection 3 to modify or supplement principles embodied in Schedule 1. It is, as previously stated, an important power, bearing in mind the sensitive nature of the data in question. It may be considered also that the Act is defective in failing effectively to deal with these important aspects even in broad terms, and in leaving such sensitive matters effectively to the discretion of the Secretary of State and both Houses of Parliament at a later date by an enabling power. In this respect we criticise the drafting of the Act in that it is extremely difficult to comment on the likely operation of the Act in these circumstances. It is provided in Section 38, subsection 4, that the Secretary of State will not make an order under Section 2, subsection 3, unless a draft of the Order has been laid before both Houses of Parliament and approved by a resolution of each House.

Subsection 4 is an explanatory provision in respect of subsection 3, whereby it is stated that in modifying any data protection principle the modification can either take the form of modifying the principle itself, or modifying its interpretation, and to that extent subsection 3 will apply to both the principles set out at PART I of Schedule 1 and to the interpretation to be accorded to those principles set out in PART II of Schedule 1.

Subsection 5 attempts to make it clear that the modification of the third principle may make specific provision for any exemption from the non-disclosure provision contained in PART IV of the Act.

Subsection 6 provides that any order made under subsection 3 by the Secretary of State may make different provisions in respect of data consisting of information of different descriptions. In practical terms data concerning the political opinions of a data subject may be dealt with differently by the Secretary of State modifying or supplementing the data protection principles from, for instance, data concerning the racial origin of the data subject. In effect, the Secretary of State may make different provisions modifying or supplementing the data protection principles in relation to any one of the matters raised in subsection 3 (a), (b), (c) and (d). Consequently, in our opinion, although, for instance, (b) deals with political opinions or religious or other beliefs, the Secretary of State is entitled by the Act to deal with political opinions in a different way from religious or other beliefs. Again in subsection 3(c) the Secretary of State may modify or supplement the data protection principles differently in respect of physical health, mental health, and sexual life of the data subject.

Section 3   The Registrar and the Tribunal

3.–(1) For the purposes of this Act there shall be–
  (a) an officer known as the Data Protection Registrar (in this Act referred to as "the Registrar"); and
  (b) a tribunal known as the Data Protection Tribunal (in this Act referred to as "the Tribunal").
(2) The Registrar shall be appointed by Her Majesty by Letters Patent.
(3) The Tribunal shall consist of–
  (a) a chairman appointed by the Lord Chancellor after consultation with the Lord Advocate;
  (b) such number of deputy chairmen appointed as aforesaid as the Lord Chancellor may determine; and
  (c) such number of other members appointed by the Secretary of State as he may determine.
(4) The members of the Tribunal appointed under subsection (3) *(a)* and *(b)* above shall be barristers, advocates or solicitors, in each case of not less than seven years' standing.
(5) The members of the Tribunal appointed under subsection (3)*(c)* above shall be:
  (a) persons to represent the interests of the data users
  (b) persons to represent the interests of data subjects.
(6) Schedule 2 to this Act shall have effect in relation to the Registrar and the Tribunal.

This section introduces the officer known as the Data Protection Registrar ("the Registrar") and the tribunal known as the Data Protection Tribunal ("the Tribunal"). The Registrar plays an important part, being responsible for the maintenance of a register of data users and bureaux in accordance with the provisions of Section 4.

The Registrar will have certain powers in order to obtain compliance with the Act. The provisions whereby the Registrar will be appointed provide for such appointments to be by Her Majesty by Letters Patent. The Registrar will thereby be invested with the same sort of independence as a High Court Judge and can only be removed in the same fashion. In this respect, we feel that the Registrar is provided, by statute, with a high degree of judicial independence in that his office is not within the control of a government minister and to this extent his notices and decisions can be made entirely impartially, without fear of removal from office. It may also be noted that he has the same independence as the Parliamentary Commissioner for Administration (the Ombudsman).

Subsection 3 specifies that the Tribunal is to consist of a chairman, appointed by the Lord Chancellor after consultation with the Lord Advocate; such number of deputy chairmen, appointed in the same way, as the Lord Chancellor may determine; and such number of other members appointed by the Secretary of State as he may determine.

Subsection 4 provides that the Tribunal chairman and deputy chairmen shall be drawn from barristers, advocates, or solicitors, in each case of not less than seven years' standing. By this means it is ensured that the office of chairman or deputy chairman shall be occupied by persons trained in the law and of reasonable seniority within their profession. This, of course, is extremely important, if the public (and we envisage that virtually the entire population will be data subjects in one form or another) are to have an appropriate degree of confidence in the Tribunal, which is, after all, an appeal body. It is likely that the members of the public choosing to use the Tribunal will already have been dissatisfied with a decision or notice of the Registrar, and it will thus be all the more important that they are satisfied that, win or lose, they have had a fair hearing.

Subsection 5 provides for other membership of the Tribunal, appointed by the Secretary of State in accordance with subsection 3(c), to be persons to represent the interests of data users and persons to represent the interests of data subjects. The Act has allowed the Secretary of State a wide discretion as to whom to appoint as members. Such persons will no doubt to some extent be put forward by the various interest and pressure groups, such as the Consumers Association and the National Council for Civil Liberties for the data subject, and the British Institute of Management, the Institute of Directors, the British Computer Society and the Institute of Personnel Management for the data users. No doubt the professional bodies of the Bar, Solicitors and Accountants would also propose potential members to represent the interests of data users and data subjects. We note that there is no provision for the interests of third parties to be represented. No doubt it has been considered that the tribunal should be akin to an industrial tribunal where there is a legally qualified (neutral) chairman, an "employee" member and an "employer" member (in this case read "data subject" for employee and "data user" for employer).

Subsection 6 relates Schedule 2 to the Registrar and the Tribunal. Schedule 2 describes the status, tenure of office, salary, etc., officers and servants, receipts and expenses, and accounts of the Registrar, and, for the Tribunal, tenure of office of members, salary and allowances to be paid to members, services of officers and servants for the purpose of the Tribunal discharging its functions and the expenses of the Tribunal. Schedule 2 reads as follows:

PART I

THE REGISTRAR

Status

1.–(1) The Registrar shall be a corporation sole by the name of "The Data Protection Registrar".
(2) Except as provided in section 17(2) of this Act, the Registrar and his officers and servants shall not be regarded as servants or agents of the Crown.

Tenure of office

2.–(1) Subject to the provisions of this paragraph, the Registrar shall hold office for five years.

THE ACT EXAMINED 65

(2) The Registrar may be relieved of his office by Her Majesty at his own request.
(3) The Registrar may be removed from office by Her Majesty in pursuance of an Address from both Houses of Parliament.
(4) The Registrar shall in any case vacate his office on completing the year of service in which he attains the age of sixty-five years.
(5) Subject to sub-paragraph (4) above, a person who ceases to be Registrar on the expiration of his term of office shall be eligible for re-appointment.

Salary etc.

3.–(1) There shall be paid–
　(a) to the Registrar such salary, and
　(b) to or in respect of the Registrar such pension,
as may be specified by a resolution of the House of Commons.
(2) A resolution for the purposes of this paragraph may either specify the salary or pension or provide that it shall be the same as that payable to, or to or in respect of, a person employed in a specified office under, or in a specified capacity in the service of, the Crown.
(3) A resolution for the purposes of this paragraph may take effect from the date on which it is passed or from any earlier or later date specified in the resolution.
(4) Any salary or pension payable under this paragraph shall be charged on and issued out of the Consolidated Fund.
(5) In this paragraph "pension" includes an allowance or gratuity and any reference to the payment of a pension includes a reference to the making of payments towards the provision of a pension.

Officers and servants

4.–(1) The Registrar–
　(a) shall appoint a deputy registrar; and
　(b) may appoint such number of other officers and servants as he may determine.
(2) The remuneration and other conditions of service of the persons appointed under this paragraph shall be determined by the Registrar.
(3) The Registrar may pay such pensions, allowances or gratuities to or in respect of the persons appointed under this paragraph, or make such payments towards the provision of such pensions, allowances or gratuities, as he may determine.
(4) The references in sub-paragraph (3) above to pensions, allowances or gratuities to or in respect of the persons appointed under this paragraph include references to pensions, allowances or gratuities by way of compensation to or in respect of any of those persons who suffer loss of office

or employment.

(5) Any determination under sub-paragraph (1)*(b)*, (2) or (3) above shall require the approval of the Secretary of State given with the consent of the Treasury.

5.—(1) The deputy registrar shall perform the functions conferred by this Act on the Registrar during any vacancy in that office or at any time when the Registrar is for any reason unable to act.

(2) Without prejudice to sub-paragraph (1) above, any functions of the Registrar under this Act may, to the extent authorised by him, be performed by any of his officers.

Receipts and expenses

6.—(1) All fees and other sums received by the Registrar in the exercise of his functions under this Act shall be paid by him into the Consolidated Fund.

(2) The Secretary of State shall out of moneys provided by Parliament pay to the Registrar such sums towards his expenses as the Secretary of State may with the approval of the Treasury determine.

Accounts

7.—(1) It shall be the duty of the Registrar—
- *(a)* to keep proper accounts and other records in relation to the accounts;
- *(b)* to prepare in respect of each financial year a statement of account in such form as the Secretary of State may direct with the approval of the Treasury; and
- *(c)* to send copies of that statement to the Comptroller and Auditor General on or before 31st August next following the end of the year to which the statement relates or on or before such earlier date after the end of that year as the Treasury may direct.

(2) The Comptroller and Auditor General shall examine and certify any statement sent to him under this paragraph and lay copies of it together with his report thereon before each House of Parliament.

(3) In this paragraph "financial year" means a period of twelve months beginning with 1st April.

PART II

THE TRIBUNAL

Tenure of office

8.—(1) A member of the Tribunal shall hold and vacate his office in accordance with the terms of his appointment and

shall, on ceasing to hold office, be eligible for re-appointment.
(2) Any member of the Tribunal may at any time resign his office by notice in writing to the Lord Chancellor (in the case of the chairman or a deputy chairman) or to the Secretary of State (in the case of any other member).

Salary etc.

9. The Secretary of State shall pay to the members of the Tribunal out of moneys provided by Parliament such remuneration and allowances as he may with the approval of the Treasury determine.

Officers and servants

10. The Secretary of State may provide the Tribunal with such officers and servants as he thinks necessary for the proper discharge of its functions.

Expenses

11. Such expenses of the Tribunal as the Secretary of State may with the approval of the Treasury determine shall be defrayed by the Secretary of State out of moneys provided by Parliament.

PART III

GENERAL

Parliamentary disqualification

12.—(1) In Part II of Schedule 1 to the House of Commons Disqualification Act 1975 (bodies whose members are disqualified) there shall be inserted at the appropriate place "The Data Protection Tribunal".
(2) In Part III of that Schedule (disqualifying offices) there shall be inserted at the appropriate place "The Data Protection Registrar".
(3) Corresponding amendments shall be made in Parts II and III of Schedule 1 to the Northern Ireland Assembly Disqualification Act 1975.

Supervision by Council on Tribunals

13. The Tribunals and Inquiries Act 1971 shall be amended as follows—
- (a) in section 8(2) after "paragraph" there shall be inserted "5A";
- (b) in section 19(4) after "46" there shall be inserted the words "or the Data Protection Registrar referred to in paragraph 5A";

(c) in Schedule 1, after paragraph 5 there shall be inserted—
"Data protection. 5A. *(a)* The Data Protection Registrar;
(b) The Data Protection Tribunal."

Public records

14. In Part II of the Table in paragraph 3 of Schedule 1 to the Public Records Act 1958 there shall be inserted at the appropriate place "the Data Protection Registrar"; and after paragraph 4(1)*(n)* of that Schedule there shall be inserted—
"*(nn)* records of the Data Protection Tribunal;".

PART II REGISTRATION AND SUPERVISION OF DATA USERS AND COMPUTER BUREAUX
Section 4 Registration of data users and computer bureaux

4.—(1) The Registrar shall maintain a register of data users who hold, and of persons carrying on computer bureaux who provide services in respect of, personal data and shall make an entry in the register in pursuance of each application for registration accepted by him under this Part of this Act.

(2) Each entry shall state whether it is in respect of a data user, of a person carrying on a computer bureau or of a data user who also carries on such a bureau.

(3) Subject to the provisions of this section, an entry in respect of a data user shall consist of the following particulars—
   (a) the name and address of the data user;
   (b) a description of the personal data to be held by him and of the purpose or purposes for which the data are to be held or used;
   (c) a description of the source or sources from which he intends or may wish to obtain the data or the information to be contained in the data;
   (d) a description of any person or persons to whom he intends or may wish to disclose the data;
   (e) the names or a description of any countries or territories outside the United Kingdom to which he intends or may wish directly or indirectly to transfer the data; and
   (f) one or more addresses for the receipt of requests from data subjects for access to the data.

(4) Subject to the provisions of this section, an entry in respect of a person carrying on a computer bureau shall consist of that person's name and address.

(5) Subject to the provisions of this section, an entry in respect of a data user who also carries on a computer bureau shall

consist of his name and address and, as respects the personal data to be held by him, the particulars specified in subsection (3)*(b)* to *(f)* above.

(6) In the case of a registered company the address referred to in subsections (3)*(a)*, (4) and (5) above is that of its registered office, and the particulars to be included in the entry shall include the company's number in the register of companies.

(7) In the case of a person (other than a registered company) carrying on a business the address referred to in subsections (3)*(a)*, (4) and (5) above is that of his principal place of business.

(8) The Secretary of State may by order vary the particulars to be included in entries made in the register.

Section 4 deals with the registration of data users and computer bureaux, and specifies the particulars required of a data user or of a data user who carries on a computer bureau (see Section 4(3)). Article 8(a) of the Council of Europe Convention requires that provision be made to enable a person to discover the existence of an automatically processed personal data file together with its primary purpose and the identity and whereabouts of the data user in control of the file. Of particular importance is the provision at Section 4, subsection 3(d), that the register entry shall include a description of any person or persons to whom the data user intends or may wish to disclose the data. A major factor behind this legislation is the practice of personal data being passed from one person to another (not necessarily a data user) without the knowledge of the data subject. Media coverage, in particular, has highlighted the problem of "mail-shot lists".

Subsection 1 needs no comment. Subsection 2 requires each entry to state whether it is in respect of a data user or a person carrying on a computer bureau, or of a data user who also carries on a computer bureau. The distinctions are necessary, bearing in mind that, of the eight data protection principles, only the eighth principle applies to computer bureaux which are not also data users.

Subsection 3 provides for the particulars which must be supplied in respect of every entry in the register, namely: the name and address of the data user; a description of the personal data held by the data user and the purpose or purposes for which the data are being held or used; a description of the source or sources from which the data user intends or may wish to obtain the data, or the information to be contained in the data; a description of any person or persons to whom he intends, or may wish to disclose the data; the name or a description of any country or territories outside the UK to which the data user is in the practice of or intends, directly or indirectly, to transfer the data; and one or more addresses for the receipt of requests from a data subject for access to his data. It may be difficult if not impossible in certain cases to link the data user to each and every data system within his power and control. To avoid the difficulties of proving the data users' power and control in each case over a particular data system, we feel that a provision requiring each data system to be specified would have been virtually essential for effective enforcement.

Subsection 3 is a particularly important provision. The Registrar will be able to assess the expressly stated purpose or purposes for which the data are being held or used under subsection 3(b). He will also know the person or persons to whom the data user intends or may wish to disclose the data under subsection 3(d). It is envisaged that the Registrar will generally make such assessments upon some complaint or request being made, since to police independently the activities of every data user would be an impossible and, in any case, an unrewarding task. The register entry will provide data subjects with the necessary address in respect of which they may enforce their rights of access to data under Section 21. Importantly, in the event of a data user holding, obtaining, transferring or providing disclosure of personal data in contravention of or not in accordance with the registered particulars under Section 4, subsection 3, the data user would, pursuant to Section 5, subsection 5, be guilty of an offence, in the event of such conduct being carried out knowingly or recklessly.

The terms used in subsection 3, "name", "address", "description", are all key words within the subsection and should be interpreted in contradistinction with one another. It is unlikely that in subsection 3(c) a description of the source or sources requires that the name of the person or organisation involved has in all cases to be provided. The question of how specific or how general the description may be is, of course, one of degree, and the Registrar has discretion in this respect pursuant to Section 7 of the Act to refuse the applications for entry upon the register which, *inter alia*, are insufficient in terms of particulars given.

Subsection 4 makes provision in respect of a person carrying on a computer bureau whereby the entry is to consist of that person's name and address. Subsection 5 also deals with a person carrying on a computer bureau whereby that person is to provide the particulars required by subsection 3(b) to (f), i.e. all the other particulars required of any other data user. We would point out the distinction, made in comparing subsection 4 with subsection 5, between a "person" carrying on a computer bureau and a "data user" who also carries on a computer bureau. Reference must be made to Section 1, subsections 5 and 6, where the terms "data user" and "a person who carries on a computer bureau" are defined. The basic reason for the distinction is that a person who carries on a computer bureau does not necessarily control the contents and use of the data held in the bureau, in which case he would *not* be a data user, and hence would only be obliged to provide his name and address as required by Section 4, subsection 4.

Subsection 6 states that in the case of a registered company in the capacity of a data user or a computer bureau the address required to be given is its registered office and the particulars will include the company's number in the Register of Companies, allowing other public material, such as the company's memorandum and articles of association, and submitted accounts, to be obtained and inspected.

Subsection 7 provides that, in the case of a person other than the registered company, the address required under subsection 3(a) and subsection 4 will be that of his principal place of business.

Subsection 8 provides that the Secretary of State may vary the particulars to be included in entries made in the register. The Secretary of State may thereby amend, delete or add to the particulars specified in subsection 3(a) to (f) and Section 3, subsections 4, 5 and 6.

Section 5 Prohibition of unregistered holding etc. of personal data

5.–(1) A person shall not hold personal data unless an entry in respect of that person as a data user, or as a data user who also carries on a computer bureau, is for the time being contained in the register.

(2) A person in respect of whom such an entry is contained in the register shall not—

    (a) hold personal data of any description other than that specified in the entry;

    (b) hold any such data, or use any such data held by him, for any purpose other than the purpose or purposes described in the entry;

    (c) obtain such data, or information to be contained in such data, to be held by him from any source which is not described in the entry;

    (d) disclose such data held by him to any person who is not described in the entry; or

    (e) directly or indirectly transfer such data held by him to any country or territory outside the United Kingdom other than one named or described in the entry.

(3) A servant or agent of a person to whom subsection (2) above applies shall, as respects personal data held by that person, be subject to the same restrictions on the use, disclosure or transfer of the data as those to which that person is subject under paragraphs *(b)*, *(d)* and *(e)* of that subsection and, as respects personal data to be held by that person, to the same restrictions as those to which he is subject under paragraph *(c)* of that subsection.

(4) A person shall not, in carrying on a computer bureau, provide services in respect of personal data unless an entry in respect of that person as a person carrying on such a bureau, or as a data user who also carries on such a bureau, is for the time being contained in the register.

(5) Any person who contravenes subsection (1) above or knowingly or recklessly contravenes any of the other provisions of this section shall be guilty of an offence.

Section 5 provides that a person will not hold, use, obtain, disclose or directly or indirectly transfer data in specified circumstances, unless an entry in respect of that person as a data user, or as a data user who carries on a computer bureau, is for the time being contained in the register. Further, Section 5 provides the "teeth" of a criminal offence in respect of contravention by unregistered data users and by registered data users acting outside the ambit of the particulars specified under their register entry.

It is important to cross-refer to the definitions provided in Section 1, subsection 5, in respect of, in this instance, "holding". This subsection is clearly aimed at those who are not registered at all as data users. It is an offence without the requirement of *mens rea* in that it is not provided that there should be any element of knowledge, or recklessness. Subsection 1, therefore, provides for an offence of absolute liability, to which there can be no defence but only mitigation. The offence pursuant to Section 19, subsection 2, may be tried either summarily (in a Magistrates Court) or upon indictment (in a Crown Court). The chief distinction between an offence triable summarily on the one hand, or upon indictment on the other, in the context of Section 19, subsection 2, is that, upon conviction on indictment, the person found guilty is liable to an unlimited fine, whereas upon summary conviction he would be liable to a fine not exceeding the statutory maximum as defined in Section 74 of the Criminal Justice Act 1982, or, in respect of Northern Ireland, to a maximum fine of £1,000.

Subsection 2 provides for certain prohibitions in relation to conduct by a data user in respect of whom an entry is contained in the register. It is thereby provided that the data user will not hold personal data of any description other than that specified in the entry, will not hold or use any such data for any purpose other than the purpose or purposes described, will not obtain such data or information to be contained in such data from any source which is not described, will not pass such data or disclose such information to any person who is not described, and will not directly or indirectly transfer any such data to any country or territory outside the UK other than one named or described. A criminal offence is committed in respect of a contravention of the provisions of subsection 2 in the event of any person in respect of whom an entry is contained in the register knowingly or recklessly breaching the provisions laid down. It will be extremely important, therefore, for those who are required to register and provide particulars under Section 4, subsection 3, to ensure that full and sufficiently expansive particulars are provided for the register to ensure that an offence will not be committed by reason of Section 5, subsection 2, combined with Section 5, subsection 5.

Subsection 3 relates to subsections 2(b), (c), (d) and (e). The prohibitions set out apply in addition to any servant or agent of the person to whom the entry relates.

Subsection 4 is a similar provision to subsection 1, whereby a person who carries on a computer bureau shall not provide services in respect of personal data unless an entry in respect of that person as a person carrying on such a bureau, or as a data user who also carries on such a bureau, is, at the time, contained in the register. However, it should be noted that subsection 4 does not create an offence of absolute liability, and that, for an offence to be committed, the person in question must have contravened subsection 4 knowingly or recklessly. It is thereby envisaged that a person or body using the services provided by a computer bureau may "hoodwink" the person carrying on the bureau as to the nature of the data being dealt with (that is, by deliberately stating the said data are not personal data). Again, it is important to note that the register only has application pursuant to Section 4, subsection 1, in respect of data users who hold, and persons carrying on computer bureaux who provide services in respect of, *personal data*. Here the reader might wish to refer to the definition of "personal data" provided in Section 1, subsection 3.

Subsection 5 provides that an offence will be committed by any person who contravenes subsection 1 (i.e. an offence of absolute liability, as described above) and by any person who knowingly or recklessly contravenes any of the other provisions of Section 5. The criminal offences in respect of Section 5 generally may be dealt with either by summary trial or trial upon indictment, as previously described, and the penalties as stated, in either case, are in the form of fines (see Section 19, subsection 2).

Section 6 Applications for registration and for amendment of registered particulars

6.–(1) A person applying for registration shall state whether he wishes to be registered as a data user, as a person carrying

on a computer bureau or as a data user who also carries on such a bureau, and shall furnish the Registrar, in such form as he may require, with the particulars required to be included in the entry to be made in pursuance of the application.
(2) Where a person intends to hold personal data for two or more purposes he may make separate applications for registration in respect of any of those purposes.
(3) A registered person may at any time apply to the Registrar for the alteration of any particulars included in the entry or entries relating to that person.
(4) Where the alteration would consist of the addition of a purpose for which personal data are to be held, the person may, instead of making an application under subsection (3) above, make a fresh application for registration in respect of the additional purpose.
(5) A registered person shall make an application under subsection (3) above whenever necessary for ensuring that the entry or entries relating to that person contain his current address; and any person who fails to comply with this subsection shall be guilty of an offence.
(6) Any person who, in connection with an application for registration or for the alteration of registered particulars, knowingly or recklessly furnishes the Registrar with information which is false or misleading in a material respect shall be guilty of an offence.
(7) Every application for registration shall be accompanied by the prescribed fee, and every application for the alteration of registered particulars shall be accompanied by such fee, if any, as may be prescribed.
(8) Any application for registration or for the alteration of registered particulars may be withdrawn by notice in writing to the Registrar at any time before the applicant receives a notification in respect of the application under section 7(1) below.

Section 6 deals with applications for registration and for the amendment of registered particulars. This section is of importance, bearing in mind the interrelation between the particulars provided for registration under Section 4 and the prohibitions set out in Section 5, whereby criminal liability may be incurred for a contravention carried out knowingly or recklessly by a person in respect of whom such an entry is contained. The section is also of importance in that it is provided that any person in connection with an application for registration or the alteration of registered particulars who knowingly or recklessly furnishes the Registrar with information that is false or misleading in any material respect will be guilty of an offence.

Subsection 6 should be read in the context of Section 19, subsection 2.

With regard to subsection 8 it would appear that, in the event of the application for registration or for the alteration of registered particulars containing information which is false or misleading and which was knowingly or recklessly furnished to the Registrar, even in the event of a withdrawal by notice in writing as provided for by Section 8, an offence would have been committed.

Section 7   Acceptance and refusal of applications

7.–(1) Subject to the provisions of this section, the Registrar shall as soon as practicable and in any case within the period of six months after receiving an application for registration or for the alteration of registered particulars notify the applicant in writing whether his application has been accepted or refused; and where the Registrar notifies an applicant that his application has been accepted the notification shall contain a statement of—

(a) the particulars entered in the register, or the alteration made, in pursuance of the application; and

(b) the date on which the particulars were entered or the alteration was made.

(2) The Registrar shall not refuse an application made in accordance with section 6 above unless—

(a) he considers that the particulars proposed for registration or, as the case may be, the particulars that would result from the proposed alteration, will not give sufficient information as to the matters to which they relate; or

(b) he is satisfied that the applicant is likely to contravene any of the data protection principles; or

(c) he considers that the information available to him is insufficient to satisfy him that the applicant is unlikely to contravene any of those principles.

(3) Subsection (2)(a) above shall not be construed as precluding the acceptance by the Registrar of particulars expressed in general terms in cases where that is appropriate, and the Registrar shall accept particulars expressed in such terms in any case in which he is satisfied that more specific particulars would be likely to prejudice the purpose or purposes for which the data are to be held.

(4) Where the Registrar refuses an application under this section he shall give his reasons and inform the applicant of the rights of appeal conferred by section 13 below.
(5) If in any case it appears to the Registrar that an application needs more consideration than can be given to it in the period mentioned in subsection (1) above he shall as soon as practicable and in any case before the end of that period notify the applicant in writing to that effect; and in that event no notification need be given under that subsection until after the end of that period.
(6) Subject to subsection (8) below, a person who has made an application in accordance with section 6 above shall—
- (a) until he receives a notification in respect of it under subsection (1) above or the application is withdrawn; and
- (b) if he receives a notification under that subsection of the refusal of his application, until the end of the period within which an appeal can be brought against the refusal and, if an appeal is brought, until the determination or withdrawal of the appeal,

be treated for the purposes of section 5 above as if his application had been accepted and the particulars contained in it had been entered in the register or, as the case may be, the alteration requested in the application had been made on the date on which the application was made.
(7) If by reason of special circumstances the Registrar considers that a refusal notified by him to an applicant under subsection (1) above should take effect as a matter of urgency he may include a statement to that effect in the notification of the refusal; and in that event subsection (6)(b) above shall have effect as if for the words from "the period" onwards there were substituted the words "the period of seven days beginning with the date on which that notification is received".
(8) Subsection (6) above shall not apply to an application made by any person if in the previous two years—
- (a) an application by that person has been refused under this section; or
- (b) all or any of the particulars constituting an entry contained in the register in respect of that person have been removed in pursuance of a de-registration notice;

but in the case of any such application subsection (1) above shall apply as if for the reference to six months there were substituted a reference to two months and, where the Registrar gives a notification under subsection (5) above in respect of any such application, subsection (6) above shall apply to it as if for the reference to the date on which the application was made there were substituted a reference to the date on which that notification is received.

(9) For the purposes of subsection (6) above an application shall be treated as made or withdrawn—
   (a) if the application or notice of withdrawal is sent by registered post or the recorded delivery service, on the date on which it is received for dispatch by the Post Office;
   (b) in any other case, on the date on which it is received by the Registrar;
and for the purposes of subsection (8)(a) above an application shall not be treated as having been refused so long as an appeal against the refusal can be brought, while such an appeal is pending or if such an appeal has been allowed.

Section 7 makes provision in respect of the acceptance and refusal of applications for entries to be made upon the register. Here, the Registrar may use his discretion in refusing applications for registration if he considers that the particulars are materially insufficient, if he is satisfied that the applicant is likely to contravene any of the data protection principles, or if he considers that the information available to him is insufficient to satisfy him that the applicant is unlikely to contravene any of the data protection principles.

Subsection 1 provides for the Registrar, as soon as is practicable and in any event within a period of six months after receipt of an application, to give the applicant written notice as to whether his application has been accepted or refused. In the event of the written notification stating that the application had been accepted, the notification shall contain a statement of, first, the particulars entered in the register or the alteration made to the particulars entered in the register in pursuance of the application, and, secondly, the date on which the particulars were entered or the alteration was made. In our view, in the event of the Registrar failing to comply with Section 7, legal proceedings could be commenced by an applicant to enforce compliance, most probably by an application to the Divisional Court of the Queen's Bench Division, requiring judicial review, by means of an order of *Mandamus* obliging the Registrar to comply with his statutory duty. (An order of *Mandamus* is an order of the Court obliging an authority such as the Registrar to perform his duties and functions.)

Subsection 2 provides that the Registrar will not refuse an application for a number of reasons. Subsection 2(c) appears to be broadly worded. In any event, subsection 2(b) is subsumed within (c), since any person whom the Registrar is satisfied is likely to contravene any of the data protection principles must necessarily be a person in respect of whom the information available to the Registrar is insufficient to satisfy him that that person is unlikely to contravene any of the data protection principles. Clearly, subsection 2(c) is a broad provision giving the Registrar a wide discretion to refuse applications.

Subsection 3 deals with the balance which needs to be struck by the Registrar, in the case of every particular application, between sufficient particularity on the one hand and the undesirability of prolix or over-detailed particulars on the other.

Subsection 4 requires that the Registrar, in refusing an application, must give his reasons (although it is not provided that the Registrar shall notify the applicant of any evidence in support of those reasons), and inform the applicant of the rights of appeal conferred by Section 13. It seems likely that in the case of there being any doubt on the part of the Registrar as to whether he should refuse under subsection 2(b) or (c), he would be likely to refuse on the basis of (c).

Subsection 5 provides that, in the event of it appearing to the Registrar that an application requires more consideration than can be given to it in the six-month period set out in subsection 1, he shall be under a duty as soon as practicable and in any case before the end of that period to notify the applicant in writing to that effect. In that event, no notification need be given under subsection 1 until after the end of that period.

Subsection 6 requires no comment.

Subsection 7 deals with the special circumstances in which the Registrar considers that a refusal notified by him to an applicant under subsection 1 should take effect as a matter of urgency, whereby he may include a statement to that effect in the notification of refusal. In that event, the provision of subsection 6(b) will have effect on the basis that it *should* in that event read:

> Section 7, subsection 6. ... A person who has made an application in accordance with section 6 above shall—
> (a) until he receives a notification in respect of it under subsection (1) above, or the application is withdrawn; and
> (b) if he receives a notification under that subsection of the refusal of his application, until the end of the period of seven days beginning with the date on which the notification is received,
>
> be treated for the purposes of section 5 above as if his application had been accepted and the particulars contained in it had been entered in the register or, as the case may be, the alteration requested in the application had been made on the date on which the application was made.

Effectively, therefore, subsection 7 provides a power for use by the Registrar, whereby a person who has made an application in accordance with Sections 4 and 6 for an entry on the register, to halt operations within seven days beginning with the date on which notification of refusal is received by him.

The continuance provisions of subsection 6 are subject to the provisions of subsection 8, which provide that those continuance provisions will not apply to an application made by any person if, in the previous two years, an application by that person had been refused under Section 7 or all or any of the particulars constituting an entry contained in the register in respect of that person had been removed in pursuance of a de-registration notice. However, it is further provided that, in the case of any such application as just described, subsection 1 (which places a duty on the Registrar to give written notification as soon as is practicable and in any case within a period of six months after receipt of an application for registration or alteration) will read as if the reference to six months was substituted by a reference to two months. In the event of the Registrar giving a notification under subsection 5 (that is, where it appears to the Registrar that an application needs more consideration than can be given to it in the period of two months, in this case), the provisions of subsection 6 will apply, and a person who has made an application will be treated as if his application had been accepted and the particulars contained in it had been entered in the register. Alternatively the alteration requested in the application having been made, it shall apply as from the date on which notification is received, rather than the date upon which application is made. Thus in these circumstances cleared "acceptance" of an application for registration cannot be claimed. "Acceptance" can only be claimed from the date of receipt of the Registrar's notification requiring more time to consider the application, and not from the date of the application itself.

Subsection 9 requires no comment.

Section 8   Duration and renewal of registration

8.–(1) No entry shall be retained in the register after the expiration of the initial period of registration except in pursuance of a renewal application made to the Registrar in accordance with this section.
(2) Subject to subsection (3) below, the initial period of registration and the period for which an entry is to be retained in pursuance of a renewal application ("the renewal period") shall be such period (not being less than three years) as may be prescribed beginning with the date on which the entry in question was made or, as the case may be, the date on which that entry would fall to be removed if the renewal application had not been made.
(3) The person making an application for registration or a renewal application may in his application specify as the initial period of registration or, as the case may be, as the renewal period, a period shorter than that prescribed, being a period consisting of one or more complete years.
(4) Where the Registrar notifies an applicant for registration that his application has been accepted the notification shall include a statement of the date when the initial period of registration will expire.
(5) Every renewal application shall be accompanied by the prescribed fee, and no such application shall be made except in the period of six months ending with the expiration of–
   (a) the initial period of registration; or
   (b) if there have been one or more previous renewal applications, the current renewal period.
(6) Any renewal application may be sent by post, and the Registrar shall acknowledge its receipt and notify the applicant in writing of the date until which the entry in question will be

retained in the register in pursuance of the application.
(7) Without prejudice to the foregoing provisions of this section, the Registrar may at any time remove an entry from the register at the request of the person to whom the entry relates.

Section 8 requires no comment.

Section 9 Inspection etc. of registered particulars

9.–(1) The Registrar shall provide facilities for making the information contained in the entries in the register available for inspection (in visible and legible form) by members of the public at all reasonable hours and free of charge.
(2) The Registrar shall, on payment of such fee (if any) as may be prescribed, supply any member of the public with a duly certified copy in writing of the particulars contained in the entry made in the register in pursuance of any application for registration.

Section 9 requires no comment.

Section 10 Enforcement notices

.10.–(1) If the Registrar is satisfied that a registered person has contravened or is contravening any of the data protection principles he may serve him with a notice ("an enforcement notice") requiring him to take, within such time as is specified in the notice, such steps as are so specified for complying with the principle or principles in question.
(2) In deciding whether to serve an enforcement notice the Registrar shall consider whether the contravention has caused or is likely to cause any person damage or distress.
(3) An enforcement notice in respect of a contravention of the fifth data protection principle may require the data user—
   (a) to rectify or erase the data and any other data held by him and containing an expression of opinion which appears to the Registrar to be based on the inaccurate data; or
   (b) in the case of such data as are mentioned in subsection (2) of section 22 below, either to take the steps mentioned in paragraph (a) above or to take such steps as are specified in the notice for securing compliance with the requirements specified in that subsection and, if the Registrar thinks fit, for supplementing the data with such statement of the true facts relating to the

matters dealt with by the data as the Registrar may approve.

(4) The Registrar shall not serve an enforcement notice requiring the person served with the notice to take steps for complying with paragraph *(a)* of the seventh data protection principle in respect of any data subject unless satisfied that the person has contravened section 21 below by failing to supply information to which the data subject is entitled and which has been duly requested in accordance with that section.

(5) An enforcement notice shall contain—
> *(a)* a statement of the principle or principles which the Registrar is satisfied have been or are being contravened and his reasons for reaching that conclusion; and
> *(b)* particulars of the rights of appeal conferred by section 13 below.

(6) Subject to subsection (7) below, the time specified in an enforcement notice for taking the steps which it requires shall not expire before the end of the period within which an appeal can be brought against the notice and, if such an appeal is brought, those steps need not be taken pending the determination or withdrawal of the appeal.

(7) If by reason of special circumstances the Registrar considers that the steps required by an enforcement notice should be taken as a matter of urgency he may include a statement to that effect in the notice; and in that event subsection (6) above shall not apply but the notice shall not require the steps to be taken before the end of the period of seven days beginning with the date on which the notice is served.

(8) The Registrar may cancel an enforcement notice by written notification to the person on whom it was served.

(9) Any person who fails to comply with an enforcement notice shall be guilty of an offence; but it shall be a defence for a person charged with an offence under this subsection to prove that he exercised all due diligence to comply with the notice in question.

It is clear that the Registrar has discretion as to whether to serve an enforcement notice or not (not unlike the discretion of a local planning authority as to whether to serve an enforcement notice in respect of a breach of planning control). The Registrar will consider whether contravention has caused, or is likely to cause, any person damage or distress in deciding whether to serve an enforcement notice or not.

Subsection 1 provides that the Registrar may serve an

enforcement notice in the circumstances already described above, and subsection 2 deals with the matter of the Registrar considering whether the contravention has caused or is likely to cause any person damage or distress, upon deciding whether to serve an enforcement notice.

Subsection 3 provides that an enforcement notice in respect of a breach of data protection principle 5 (that is, that "personal data shall be accurate and where necessary kept up to date") may require the data user (by subsection 3(a)) to rectify or erase *the data* and any other data held by him and containing an expression of opinion appearing to the Registrar to be based on inaccurate data. We consider that Section 10, subsection 3(a) is particularly badly worded. The words "the data" are used but not defined. We assume that this means data specified which is inaccurate or not kept up to date *and* which is specified in the enforcement notice, in contradistinction to "any other data held by him and containing an expression of opinion . . ." The clumsy use of words by the Statutory draftsman makes interpretation all the more difficult.

By subsection 3(b) it is provided that in the case of data as referred to in Section 22 subsection 2 (that is, data which accurately record information received or obtained by the data user from the data subject or a third party) the enforcement notice may alternatively require *either* rectification or erasure *or* the data user to take steps to ensure (a) the data indicate that the information was received as obtained by the data user from the data subject or a third party or that the information has not been extracted from the data except in a form which includes an indication to that effect and (b) in the event of the data subject having informed the data user that he regards the information as incorrect or misleading, that an indication to that effect has been included in the data and that information has not been extracted from the data except in a form which includes an indication to that effect (see Section 22 and the commentary thereon). It is further provided that in the case of such data, the Registrar may require in the enforcement notice that the data user supplements the data with a statement of the true facts relating to the matters dealt with by the data, as approved by the Registrar. We consider that the Act here is of special importance to the data subject. The data subject is given, in effect, something approaching a "right of reply".

During the final stages of the Data Protection Bill becoming the Act there was considerable political debate as to the "right of reply" in the sphere of the ethics of journalism. Certain politicians have sought a statutory right of reply in respect of articles appearing in the newspaper columns or magazines. With the introduction of automated data processing into the newspaper industry and in respect of magazines, the data subject will be able to ensure an indication that he regards certain information as incorrect is included in the data and information extracted from the data. Obviously, and initially, there must be "data" from which information is "extracted" for such an indication to appear in a printed article. We would point out, however, (as we do later in relation to Section 22 subsection 2) that the size and extent and prominence of the "indication" provided for is not dealt with in the Act and constitutes a source of potential abuse by data users.

The Registrar has a broad power in that he may require data to be supplemented by a statement of the true facts approved by him. This would be included as part of the requirements of the enforcement notice. We note that no provision is made for representations to be made to the Registrar by the data subject, data user or relevant third party. It is of great importance that non-compliance with this aspect of an enforcement notice as with any other would by subsection 9 constitute a criminal offence unless the data user could prove as a defence that he had used all due diligence to comply with the enforcement notice. We find it unsatisfactory that a data user should be subjected to the prospect of criminal proceedings in the event of his non-compliance with the enforcement notice as to the aspect of the inclusion of a supplemental statement of the "true facts" as approved by the Registrar when rights of representation before the Registrar are not provided for by the Act. The Registrar could simply choose to act on the information of a data subject with no obligation whatsoever to seek the views of the data user – we consider this could lead to injustice and discontent among the data user community.

Subsection 4 states that the Registrar will *not* serve an enforcement notice requiring the persons served with the notice to comply with paragraph (a) of data protection principle 7 (being that an individual shall be entitled, at reasonable intervals and without undue delay or expense, (i) to be informed by any data user whether he holds personal data of which that individual is the subject; and (ii) access to any such data held by the data user) unless the Registrar is satisfied that the person has contravened Section 21, which sets out the rights of data subjects in respect of access to personal data.

Subsection 5 specifies that the enforcement notice is to contain a statement of the principle or principles of data protection which the Registrar is satisfied have been or are being contravened. The Registrar must specify reasons for reaching his conclusion, and it is our view that, to that extent, the Registrar will be bound by those reasons from an evidential and legal viewpoint.

Subsection 6 provides that the time for compliance under the enforcement notice cannot expire before the end of the period within which an appeal may be brought against the notice, and that, if such an appeal is brought, those steps need not be taken pending the determination or withdrawal of the appeal (this is analogous to the position in respect of an enforcement notice issued by a local planning authority).

Subsection 7 is a provision similarly drafted to that of Section 7, subsection 7.

Subsection 8 requires no comment.

In subsection 9 it should be noted that it is for the defendant to prove that he exercised all due diligence, rather than for the prosecution to prove that he did not do so. The standard of proof is not specifically dealt with at subsection 9 or elsewhere in the Act, and it is open to considerable question whether or not it would be for the defendant in a criminal prosecution to prove beyond reasonable doubt that he exercised all due diligence. This would need to be to the satisfaction of the presiding magistrates or stipendiary magistrate in the case of summary trial, or to the satisfaction of a jury in the case of trial upon indictment in a Crown

Court. Our view is that this is unlikely, and that the standard of proof required of the defendant under subsection 9 would be held to be proof "on the balance of probabilities", i.e. that it was more likely than not that he had exercised all due diligence to comply with the notice in question.

Section 11   De-registration notices

11.–(1) If the Registrar is satisfied that a registered person has contravened or is contravening any of the data protection principles he may–
    (a) serve him with a notice ("a de-registration notice") stating that he proposes, at the expiration of such period as is specified in the notice, to remove from the register all or any of the particulars constituting the entry or any of the entries contained in the register in respect of that person; and
    (b) subject to the provisions of this section, remove those particulars from the register at the expiration of that period.

(2) In deciding whether to serve a de-registration notice the Registrar shall consider whether the contravention has caused or is likely to cause any person damage or distress, and the Registrar shall not serve such a notice unless he is satisfied that compliance with the principle or principles in question cannot be adequately secured by the service of an enforcement notice.

(3) A de-registration notice shall contain–
    (a) a statement of the principle or principles which the Registrar is satisfied have been or are being contravened and his reasons for reaching that conclusion and deciding that compliance cannot be adequately secured by the service of an enforcement notice; and
    (b) particulars of the rights of appeal conferred by section 13 below.

(4) Subject to subsection (5) below, the period specified in a de-registration notice pursuant to subsection (1)(a) above shall not expire before the end of the period within which an appeal can be brought against the notice and, if such an appeal is brought, the particulars shall not be removed pending the determination or withdrawal of the appeal.

(5) If by reason of special circumstances the Registrar considers that any particulars should be removed from the register as a matter of urgency he may include a statement to that effect in the de-registration notice; and in that event

subsection (4) above shall not apply but the particulars shall not be removed before the end of the period of seven days beginning with the date on which the notice is served.
(6) The Registrar may cancel a de-registration notice by written notification to the person on whom it was served.
(7) References in this section to removing any particulars include references to restricting any description which forms part of any particulars.

Subsection 1 requires no comment.

There is no doubt that a de-registration notice is more serious in its nature than an enforcement notice, and it is specifically provided (subsection 2) that the Registrar will not serve a de-registration notice unless he is satisfied that compliance with the principle or principles of data protection in question cannot be adequately secured by service of an enforcement notice. It is envisaged, therefore, that the contravention or contraventions in question are of a fundamental or serious nature in themselves, or are so numerous as to pervade the entire system or a large part of the system operated by the registered person. Further, it may be that the registered person has failed to comply in the past with enforcement notices, whereby the Registrar is satisfied that compliance could not adequately be secured by service of yet another enforcement notice.

Subsections 3 to 6 require no comment.

Subsection 7 provides that references to the removing of any particulars by the Registrar include reference to restricting any description which forms part of such particulars. For example, it may be that a data user has stated in the entry on the register pursuant to Section 4, subsection 3(e), that he intends or may wish directly or indirectly to transfer data to the USA, the USSR, Canada, the EEC countries or states and Argentina. The Registrar might choose to issue a de-registration notice in respect of the transfer of data to certain of these countries, and the data user would then no longer be legally able to transfer data to those countries. He would thereby be liable to prosecution in the event of contravention of the provision of Section 5, subsection 2(e). Such contravention would need to have been carried out knowingly or recklessly by the data user.

Section 12 Transfer prohibition notices

12.–(1) If it appears to the Registrar that–
- (a) a person registered as a data user or as a data user who also carries on a computer bureau; or
- (b) a person treated as so registered by virtue of section 7(6) above,

proposes to transfer personal data held by him to a place outside the United Kingdom, the Registrar may, if satisfied as to the matters mentioned in subsection (2) or (3) below, serve that person with a notice ("a transfer prohibition notice") prohibiting him from transferring the data either absolutely or until he has taken such steps as are specified in the notice for protecting the interests of the data subjects in question.

(2) Where the place to which the data are to be transferred is not in a State bound by the European Convention the Registrar must be satisfied that the transfer is likely to contravene, or lead to a contravention of, any of the data protection principles.

(3) Where the place to which the data are to be transferred is in a State bound by the European Convention the Registrar must be satisfied either–
- (a) that–
  - (i) the person in question intends to give instructions for the further transfer of the data to a place which is not in such a State; and
  - (ii) that the further transfer is likely to contravene, or lead to a contravention of, any of the data protection principles; or
- (b) in the case of data to which an order under section 2(3) above applies, that the transfer is likely to contravene, or lead to a contravention of, any of the data protection principles as they have effect in relation to such data.

(4) In deciding whether to serve a transfer prohibition notice the Registrar shall consider whether the notice is required for preventing damage or distress to any person and shall have regard to the general desirability of facilitating the free transfer of data between the United Kingdom and other states and territories.

(5) A transfer prohibition notice shall specify the time when it is to take effect and contain–
- (a) a statement of the principle or principles which the Registrar is satisfied are likely to be contravened and his reasons for reaching that conclusion; and
- (b) particulars of the rights of appeal conferred by section 13 below.

(6) Subject to subsection (7) below, the time specified in a transfer prohibition notice pursuant to subsection (5) above

shall not be before the end of the period within which an appeal can be brought against the notice and, if such an appeal is brought, the notice shall not take effect pending the determination or withdrawal of the appeal.

(7) If by reason of special circumstances the Registrar considers that the prohibition should take effect as a matter of urgency he may include a statement to that effect in the transfer prohibition notice; and in that event subsection (6) above shall not apply but the notice shall not take effect before the end of the period of seven days beginning with the date on which the notice is served.

(8) The Registrar may cancel a transfer prohibition notice by written notification to the person on whom it was served.

(9) No transfer prohibition notice shall prohibit the transfer of any data where the transfer of the information constituting the data is required or authorised by or under any enactment or required by any convention or other instrument imposing an international obligation on the United Kingdom.

(10) Any person who contravenes a transfer prohibition notice shall be guilty of an offence; but it shall be a defence for a person charged with an offence under this subsection to prove that he exercised all due diligence to avoid a contravention of the notice in question.

(11) For the purposes of this section a place shall be treated as in a State bound by the European Convention if it is in any territory in respect of which the State is bound.

Section 12 provides for the Registrar to serve a transfer prohibition notice. This notice is confined to circumstances relating to the transfer of personal data outside the UK, whereby the Registrar is empowered to prevent the flow of data overseas where he considers that the data protection principles would be breached as a result of the transfer. The Registrar, however, is bound not to interfere with international agreements which provide for, or are reliant upon, the transfer of data. Further he is prevented from prohibiting the flow of personal data to countries which have ratified the Council of Europe Convention, except if otherwise provided for by the Convention itself.

Subsection 1 states that, if it appears to the Registrar that a person registered as a data user or as a data user who also carries on a computer bureau, or a person treated as so registered by reason of Section 7, subsection 6, proposes to transfer personal data held by him to a place outside the

UK, in certain circumstances, specified at subsections 2 and 3, the Registrar may serve a transfer prohibition notice upon the data user. Such a notice will prohibit the data user from transferring the data either absolutely or until he has taken such steps as specified in the notice for protecting the interests of the data subjects in question. It may be that there is a difference in meaning between the phrase used at the commencement of Section 12, "if it appears to the Registrar that", and the phrase used in the statute at, for instance, Section 19, subsection 1, and Section 11, subsection 1, "if the Registrar is satisfied that". We consider "if it appears to the Registrar that" has a somewhat wider ambit and gives the Registrar a certain degree of flexibility in his approach. This may be good as far as the data subject is concerned but bad as far as the data user is concerned.

In the case of subsection 2 the Registrar will clearly have in mind any statutory provisions or regulatory provisions in the country or state in question, and the probable or possible use which may be made of the data by the person or body to whom it is to be transferred.

Subsection 3 requires no comment.

Subsection 4 discloses the "general desirability of facilitating the free transfer of data" and, together with the question of whether the notice is required for preventing damage or distress to any person, presents the Registrar with a number of hurdles to surmount before he may issue and serve such a notice.

It is not clear whether a de-registration notice could apply via the provision of Section 11, subsection 7, in respect of particulars relating to the transfer, either directly or indirectly, of personal data. It is certainly the case that there is no exclusion with regard to the operation and use of a de-registration notice and it will be recalled that the example given in respect of Section 11, subsection 7, specifically deals with the prospect of, for instance, the USSR and Argentina being removed from the description of countries and territories required to be specified on the register by reason of Section 4, subsection 3(e). The Act could have been drafted differently in this respect. The matters covered by Section 11, subsection 2, which the Registrar will need to consider in deciding whether to serve a de-registration notice, do not include the general desirability of facilitating the transfer of data between the UK and other states and territories. This needs to be considered by the Registrar in deciding whether to serve a transfer prohibition notice (Section 12, subsection 4). In our view, on balance, we consider that a de-registration notice may apply in respect of the particulars relating to the transfer of data, as it applies to all other particulars.

We consider subsection 5 to be unsatisfactory in that the initial opening of Section 12, at subsection 1, is, "If it appears to the Registrar that – (a) a person registered as a data user or as a data user who also carries on a computer bureau; or (b) a person treated as so registered by virtue of Section 7 (6) above, proposes to transfer personal data held by him to a place outside the United Kingdom. . . ." In our view, the Registrar should have to justify his act by giving reasons why it appears to him that such a person proposes to transfer personal data held by him to a place outside the United Kingdom. As presently drafted, Section 5 makes no provision for the specifying of reasons.

Subsection 6 is a similar provision to Section 10, subsection 5, and Section 11, subsection 4.

Subsection 7 is a similar provision to that of Section 10, subsection 6, and Section 11, subsection 5.

Section 13   Rights of appeal

13.–(1) A person may appeal to the Tribunal against–
   (a) any refusal by the Registrar of an application by that person for registration or for the alteration of registered particulars;
   (b) any enforcement notice, de-registration notice or transfer prohibition notice with which that person has been served.

(2) Where a notification that an application has been refused contains a statement by the Registrar in accordance with section 7(7) above, then, whether or not the applicant appeals under paragraph (a) of subsection (1) above, he may appeal against the Registrar's decision to include that statement in the notification.

(3) Where any such notice as is mentioned in paragraph (b) of subsection (1) above contains a statement by the Registrar in

accordance with section 10(7), 11(5) or 12(7) above, then, whether or not the person served with the notice appeals under that paragraph, he may appeal against the Registrar's decision to include that statement in the notice or against the effect of the inclusion of the statement as respects any part of the notice.
(4) Schedule 3 to this Act shall have effect in relation to appeals under this section and to the proceedings of the Tribunal in respect of any such appeal.

Section 13 deals with the rights of appeal to the data protection Tribunal in respect of any refusal by the Registrar of an application for registration or for alteration of registered particulars, and against any enforcement notice, de-registration notice, or transfer prohibition notice, with which a person has been served.

Subsection 1 requires no comment.

Subsection 2 relates to those applicants for registration or alteration of particulars who have received notification from the Registrar in accordance with Section 7, subsection 7, and in respect of whom the Registrar determines that their applications are to be refused and that the refusal should take effect as a matter of urgency, whereby the continuance provisions will not apply, save in respect of a period of seven days beginning with the date on which the notification of refusal is received. This subsection provides that, in any event, the person may appeal against the Registrar's inclusion of the statement that the notification of refusal should take effect as a matter of urgency, whether or not that person should decide to appeal against the refusal of registration itself. Clearly, the operation of this particular subsection will require that an appeal on this particular point is heard with great speed. It is to be noted that Schedule 3, paragraph 3, provides, with regard to an appeal under Section 13, subsections 2 and 3, that such an appeal shall be exercised without the necessity of notice being given to the Registrar, by the chairman or a deputy chairman of the Tribunal sitting alone. The Act has therefore provided a means whereby a speedy remedy is available.

Again, in subsection 3 it will be noted that the procedure for a speedy appeal is given in Schedule 3, paragraph 3, and accordingly Section 13, subsection 4, provides that Schedule 3 will have effect in relation to appeals under the section and to the proceedings of the Tribunal in respect of any such appeal.

Section 13, subsection 4 specifically refers to Schedule 3 which reads as follows:

SCHEDULE 3
APPEAL PROCEEDINGS
Hearing of appeals

1. For the purpose of hearing and determining appeals or any matter preliminary or incidental to an appeal the Tribunal shall sit at such times and in such places as the chairman or a deputy chairman may direct and may sit in two or more divisions.

2.–(1) Subject to any rules made under paragraph 4 below, the Tribunal shall be duly constituted for an appeal under section 13(1) of this Act if it consists of
   (a) the chairman or a deputy chairman (who shall preside); and
   (b) an equal number of the members appointed respectively in accordance with paragraphs (a) and (b) of section 3(5) of this Act.

(2) The members who are to constitute the Tribunal in accordance with sub-paragraph (1) above shall be nominated by the chairman or, if he is for any reason unable to act, by a deputy chairman.

(3) The determination of any question before the Tribunal when constituted in accordance with this paragraph shall be according to the opinion of the majority of the members hearing the appeal.

3. Subject to any rules made under paragraph 4 below, the jurisdiction of the Tribunal in respect of an appeal under section 13(2) or (3) of this Act shall be exercised ex parte by the chairman or a deputy chairman sitting alone.

Rules of procedure

4.–(1) The Secretary of State may make rules for regulating the exercise of the rights of appeal conferred by section 13 of this Act and the practice and procedure of the Tribunal.

(2) Without prejudice to the generality of sub-paragraph (1) above, rules under this paragraph may in particular make provision—
   (a) with respect to the period within which an appeal can be brought and the burden of proof on an appeal;

(b) for the summoning of witnesses and the administration of oaths;
(c) for securing the production of documents and data material;
(d) for the inspection, examination, operation and testing of data equipment and the testing of data material;
(e) for the hearing of an appeal wholly or partly in camera;
(f) for hearing an appeal in the absence of the appellant or for determining an appeal without a hearing;
(g) for enabling any matter preliminary or incidental to an appeal to be dealt with by the chairman or a deputy chairman;
(h) for the awarding of costs;
(i) for the publication of reports of the Tribunal's decisions; and
(j) for conferring on the Tribunal such ancillary powers as the Secretary of State thinks necessary for the proper discharge of its functions.

Obstruction etc.

5.–(1) If any person is guilty of any act or omission in relation to proceedings before the Tribunal which, if those proceedings were proceedings before a court having power to commit for contempt, would constitute contempt of court, the Tribunal may certify the offence to the High Court or, in Scotland, the Court of Session.

(2) Where an offence is so certified, the court may inquire into the matter and, after hearing any witness who may be produced against or on behalf of the person charged with the offence, and after hearing any statement that may be offered in defence, deal with him in any manner in which it could deal with him if he had committed the like offence in relation to the court.

Section 14   Determination of appeals

14.–(1) If on an appeal under section 13(1) above the Tribunal considers–
 (a) that the refusal or notice against which the appeal is brought is not in accordance with the law; or
 (b) to the extent that the refusal or notice involved an exercise of discretion by the Registrar, that he ought to have exercised his discretion differently,
the Tribunal shall allow the appeal or substitute such other decision or notice as could have been made or served by the Registrar; and in any other case the Tribunal shall dismiss the appeal.

(2) The Tribunal may review any determination of fact on which the refusal or notice in question was based.

(3) On an appeal under subsection (2) of section 13 above the Tribunal may direct that the notification of the refusal shall be treated as if it did not contain any such statement as is mentioned in that subsection.

(4) On an appeal under subsection (3) of section 13 above the Tribunal may direct that the notice in question shall have effect as if it did not contain any such statement as is mentioned in that subsection or that the inclusion of the statement shall not have effect in relation to any part of the notice and may make such modifications in the notice as may be required for giving effect to the direction.

(5) Any party to an appeal to the Tribunal may appeal from the decision of the Tribunal on a point of law to the appropriate court; and that court shall be—
- *(a)* the High Court of Justice in England if the address of the person who was the appellant before the Tribunal is in England or Wales;
- *(b)* the Court of Session if that address is in Scotland; and
- *(c)* the High Court of Justice in Northern Ireland if that address is in Northern Ireland.

(6) In subsection (5) above references to the address of the appellant before the Tribunal are to his address as included or proposed for inclusion in the register.

This section provides that, in the event of a refusal or notice against which the appeal is brought being not in accordance with the law, or to the extent that the refusal or notice involved an exercise of discretion by the Registrar that he ought to have exercised differently, the Tribunal shall allow the appeal or substitute such other decision or notice as could have been made or served by the Registrar, and that in any other case, the Tribunal shall dismiss the appeal. Furthermore, the Tribunal may review any determination of fact upon which the refusal or notice in question was based. This is of particular importance in that the Tribunal will not be bound by the Registrar's findings of fact and, in this regard, the rules of procedure in respect of appeal proceedings under Schedule 3, paragraph 4, sub-paragraphs (1) and (2), deal specifically with rules which may be made by the Secretary of State in respect of the regulation of the exercise of the rights of appeal conferred by Section 13.

In Section 14, subsection 1 it is possible that the Tribunal could decide that the Registrar should have exercised his discretion more severely against the appellant: for instance, by serving a de-registration notice instead of an enforcement notice.

Subsection 2 is important in that the Tribunal may review any determination of fact upon which the refusal or notice in question was based, and this would include the calling of fresh evidence.

Subsection 3 provides that, in respect of an appeal against the Registrar's decision to include a statement in the notification of refusal, being a statement of urgency, the Tribunal may direct the notification of the refusal to be treated as if it did not contain any such statement, as is mentioned in Section 13, subsection 2.

Subsection 4 is similar to subsection 2, whereby, in respect of an appeal under Section 13, subsection 3, the Tribunal may direct that the notice in question (that is, an enforcement notice, a de-registration notice, or a transfer prohibition notice) will have effect as if it did not contain any such statement of urgency, as is mentioned in that subsection, or that the inclusion of such a statement shall not have effect in relation to any part of the notice, and may make such modifications in the notice as may be required.

Subsections 5 and 6 require no comment.

Section 15 Unauthorised disclosure by computer bureaux

15.–(1) Personal data in respect of which services are provided by a person carrying on a computer bureau shall not be disclosed by him without the prior authority of the person for whom those services are provided.
(2) Subsection (1) above applies also to any servant or agent of a person carrying on a computer bureau.
(3) Any person who knowingly or recklessly contravenes this section shall be guilty of an offence.

Section 15 deals with the question of unauthorised disclosure by a computer bureau of personal data and provides that personal data in respect of which services are provided by a person carrying on a computer bureau shall not be disclosed without the prior authority of the person for whom those services are provided. The person for whom such services are provided may well be a limited company, despite the fact that the personal data as defined at Section 1, subsection 3, means data representing information which relates to a living individual, who can be identified from the information, including any expression of opinion about the individual, but not any indication of the intentions of the data user in respect of that individual. Subsection 2 provides that subsection 1 applies also to any servant or agent of the person carrying on a computer bureau. Subsection 3 provides that any person who knowingly or recklessly contravenes the section will be guilty of an offence, the offence being dealt with in accordance with Section 19.

Section 16 Powers of entry and inspection

16. Schedule 4 to this Act shall have effect for the detection of offences under this Act and contraventions of the data protection principles.

Section 16 provides for powers of entry and inspection in accordance with Schedule 4, which, for convenience, we set out below.

Issue of warrants

1. If a circuit judge is satisfied by information on oath supplied by the Registrar that there are reasonable grounds for suspecting—
    (a) that an offence under this Act has been or is being committed; or
    (b) that any of the data protection principles have been or are being contravened by a registered person,
and that evidence of the commission of the offence or of the contravention is to be found on any premises specified in the information, he may, subject to paragraph 2 below, grant a warrant authorising the Registrar or any of his officers or servants at any time within seven days of the date of the warrant to enter those premises, to search them, to inspect, examine, operate and test any data equipment found there and to inspect and seize any documents or other material found there which may be such evidence as aforesaid.
2. A judge shall not issue a warrant under this Schedule

unless he is satisfied—
- (a) that the Registrar has given seven days' notice in writing to the occupier of the premises in question demanding access to the premises;
- (b) that access was demanded at a reasonable hour and was unreasonably refused; and
- (c) that the occupier has, after the refusal, been notified by the Registrar of the application for the warrant and has had an opportunity of being heard by the judge on the question whether or not it should be issued;

but the foregoing provisions of this paragraph shall not apply if the judge is satisfied that the case is one of urgency or that compliance with those provisions would defeat the object of the entry.

3. A judge who issues a warrant under this Schedule shall also issue two copies of it and certify them clearly as copies.

Execution of warrants

4. A person executing a warrant issued under this Schedule may use such reasonable force as may be necessary.

5. A warrant issued under this Schedule shall be executed at a reasonable hour unless it appears to the person executing it that there are grounds for suspecting that the evidence in question would not be found if it were so executed.

6. If the person who occupies the premises in respect of which a warrant is issued under this Schedule is present when the warrant is executed, he shall be shown the warrant and supplied with a copy of it; and if that person is not present a copy of the warrant shall be left in a prominent place on the premises.

7.—(1) A person seizing anything in pursuance of a warrant under this Schedule shall give a receipt for it if asked to do so.
(2) Anything so seized may be retained for so long as is necessary in all the circumstances but the person in occupation of the premises in question shall be given a copy of anything that is seized if he so requests and the person executing the warrant considers that it can be done without undue delay.

Matters exempt from inspection and seizure

8. The powers of inspection and seizure conferred by a warrant issued under this Schedule shall not be exercisable in respect of personal data which are exempt from Part II of this Act.

9.—(1) Subject to the provisions of this paragraph, the powers of inspection and seizure conferred by a warrant issued under this Schedule shall not be exercisable in respect of—
- (a) any communication between a professional legal

adviser and his client in connection with the giving of legal advice to the client with respect to his obligations, liabilities or rights under this Act; or

(b) any communication between a professional legal adviser and his client, or between such an adviser or his client and any other person, made in connection with or in contemplation of proceedings under or arising out of this Act (including proceedings before the Tribunal) and for the purposes of such proceedings.

(2) Sub-paragraph (1) above applies also to—
 (a) any copy or other record of any such communication as is there mentioned; and
 (b) any document or article enclosed with or referred to in any such communication if made in connection with the giving of any advice or, as the case may be, in connection with or in contemplation of and for the purposes of such proceedings as are there mentioned.

(3) This paragraph does not apply to anything in the possession of any person other than the professional legal adviser or his client or to anything held with the intention of furthering a criminal purpose.

(4) In this paragraph references to the client of a professional legal adviser include references to any person representing such a client.

10. If the person in occupation of any premises in respect of which a warrant is issued under this Schedule objects to the inspection or seizure under the warrant of any material on the grounds that it consists partly of matters in respect of which those powers are not exercisable, he shall, if the person executing the warrant so requests, furnish that person with a copy of so much of the material as is not exempt from those powers.

Return of warrants

11. A warrant issued under this Schedule shall be returned to the court from which it was issued—
 (a) after being executed; or
 (b) if not executed within the time authorised for its execution;

and the person by whom any such warrant is executed shall make an endorsement on it stating what powers have been exercised by him under the warrant.

Offences

12. Any person who—
 (a) intentionally obstructs a person in the execution of a warrant issued under this Schedule; or
 (b) fails without reasonable excuse to give any person

executing such a warrant such assistance as he may reasonably require for the execution of the warrant, shall be guilty of an offence.

Vessels, vehicles etc.

13. In this Schedule "premises" includes any vessel, vehicle, aircraft or hovercraft, and references to the occupier of any premises include references to the person in charge of any vessel, vehicle, aircraft or hovercraft.

Scotland and Northern Ireland

14. In the application of this Schedule to Scotland, for any reference to a circuit judge there shall be substituted a reference to the sheriff, for any reference to information on oath there shall be substituted a reference to evidence on oath and for the reference to the court from which the warrant was issued there shall be substituted a reference to the sheriff clerk.

15. In the application of this Schedule to Northern Ireland, for any reference to a circuit judge there shall be substituted a reference to a county court judge and for any reference to information on oath there shall be substituted a reference to a complaint on oath.

In paragraph 1 of Schedule 4 provision is made for the issue of warrants by a circuit judge if he is satisfied by information on oath supplied by the Registrar that there are reasonable grounds for suspecting (a) that an offence under the Act has been or is being committed, or (b) that any one of the data protection principles has been or is being contravened by a registered person. Evidence of the commission of the offence or of the contravention would need to be found on any premises specified in the information. The warrant will authorise the Registrar or any of his officers or servants at any time within seven days of the date of the warrant to enter the premises in question and to search them to inspect, examine, operate, and test any data-processing equipment found there and to inspect and seize any documents or other material found there which may constitute the evidence. Note that there is no power to seize or render inoperative any data-processing equipment found at the premises.

Paragraph 2 provides that a judge cannot issue a warrant under the schedule unless he is satisfied, first, that the Registrar has given seven days' notice in writing to the occupant of the premises in question demanding access to those premises; secondly, that access was demanded at a reasonable hour and was unreasonably refused; and, thirdly, that the occupier has, after the refusal, been notified by the Registrar of the application for the warrant and has had an opportunity of being heard by the judge on the question of whether or not it was to be issued. However, subsection 2 also stipulates that the provisions will not apply if the judge is satisfied that the case is one of urgency, or that compliance with those provisions would defeat the object of the entry. Paragraphs 4 to 7 of Schedule 4 deal with the execution of warrants. Paragraph 4 states that a person executing a warrant issued under the Schedule may use such reasonable force as may be necessary.

Paragraph 5 is a widely drafted provision, whereby it would seem that simple evidence (that the person executing the warrant honestly believed that there were grounds for suspecting that the evidence in question would not be found if it were executed at a reasonable hour) is good enough.

Paragraph 6 provides for the occupant, if he is present at the time when the warrant is executed, to be shown the warrant and supplied with a copy, and that if the person is not present, a copy of the warrant can be left in a prominent place on the premises. In practice, "a prominent place on the premises" would normally be by means of fixing the copy of the warrant to the front door of the premises.

In paragraph 7 it is important to note that a request must be made in order for there to be a duty to give a receipt. It is our view that the Act should, in any event, have provided for a receipt to be given, whether or not it was requested. Paragraph 7, sub-paragraph 2, further allows for anything seized under a warrant to be retained for so long as is necessary in all the circumstances, but that the person occupying the premises must be given a copy of anything that is seized, if he requests it, and the person executing the warrant considers that it can be done, without undue delay.

Clearly a "copy" of anything that is seized would generally mean a photostat copy of documents seized, but other material found may be seized and could be in the form of photographs, microfilm, microfiche, microdots, computer tape, audio tape, video tape, and so on. In such cases it might well be that undue delay would be incurred in providing such copies. Sub-paragraph 2, in our view, is poorly drafted because, on the one hand, it envisages that a copy of anything seized will be given to the occupant of the premises upon request being made, which would appear to include a request after the seizure and during the period of retention of the documentation or other material so seized, yet it is further provided that the person executing the warrant must consider that provision of a copy can be done without undue delay for the duty to operate. In our view there should be a distinction between the provision of a copy at the time of seizure and the provision of a copy after seizure but during the period of retention.

Paragraph 8 requires no comment (but see Sections 22–33 inclusive).

Paragraph 9 provides that the powers of inspection and seizure conferred by a warrant shall not be exercisable within the meaning of the Act, first in respect of any communication between a professional legal adviser and his client and, secondly, in respect of any communication between a professional legal adviser and his client or between such an adviser and his client or any other person made in connection with the Act. This is clearly a necessary provision to preserve the confidentiality and privilege of such communications between a lawyer and his client. A professional legal adviser would not necessarily be limited to being a solicitor, but could include a barrister, a firm of business consultants providing legal advice, or a legal executive.

In the case of sub-paragraph 3 we consider that there is an element of poor drafting, in that paragraph 9(1)(b) allows that there could be communications between not only a professional legal adviser and his client, but between such an adviser or his client and any other person in connection with or in contemplation of proceedings under or arising out of the Act and for the purposes of such proceedings. Thus, for instance, the lawyer may be in correspondence with a firm of data protection consultants, with an accountant, with an auditor, or with a firm of private investigators. It would appear that in such cases communications in the hands of, for instance, the data protection consultants, the accountants and auditors, or the private investigators, would be liable to inspection and seizure. In our view this is a defect not simply because it impinges in an unjustifiable way upon the relation of a client and his lawyer, but also because it is plainly inconsistent with the provision of paragraph 9(1)(b).

Sub-paragraph 4 states that references to the client of a professional legal adviser include references to any person representing such a client. It may be that the problem just mentioned may be protected on the basis that such bodies or persons represent the client of the professional legal adviser, but, in our view, to provide exemption on this basis would be unnecessarily circuitous and involve an over-technical and unreal reading of the statute.

The meaning of paragraph 10 is unclear. Is it really thought that if the person executing the warrant is met with the objection that the material in question is exempt from inspection or seizure, that the person so executing will request a copy of all material that is not exempt from the powers under the warrant? Or is it really more likely that the person executing the warrant will use such reasonable force as may be necessary, as provided by paragraph 4 of the schedule, disregard the objections made by the occupant of the premises that the material in question consists partly of matters in respect of which the powers under the warrant are not exercisable, and inspect all the material, and/or seize all the material? In our view the latter situation is more likely in practice, and those who had seized the material in question would take the risk of proceedings being brought in respect of unlawful seizure and/or contempt of court.

Paragraphs 11 and 12 require no comment.

Paragraph 13 provides that the term "premises" are to include any vessel, vehicle, aircraft, or hovercraft, and the references to the "occupier" of any premises include references to the person in charge of any such vessel, etc.

It is likely that the warrants will be obtained by an application to a circuit judge sitting in a Crown Court, although this is not expressly provided, and it would be possible for a warrant to be obtained from a circuit judge sitting in a County Court, or a circuit judge at his home or elsewhere.

Section 17   Disclosure of information

> 17.–(1) No enactment or rule of law prohibiting or restricting the disclosure of information shall preclude a person from furnishing the Registrar or the Tribunal with any information necessary for the discharge of their functions under this Act.
> (2) For the purposes of section 2 of the Official Secrets Act 1911 (wrongful communication of information)–
> (a) the Registrar and his officers and servants;
> (b) the members of the Tribunal; and
> (c) any officers or servants of the Tribunal who are not in the service of the Crown,
> shall be deemed to hold office under Her Majesty.
> (3) The said section 2 shall not be construed as precluding the disclosure of information by any person mentioned in subsection (2)(a) or(b) above or by any officer or servant of the Tribunal where the disclosure is made for the purpose of discharging his duties under this Act or for the purpose of proceedings under or arising out of this Act, including proceedings before the Tribunal.

Section 17 deals with disclosure of information and is aimed at providing the Registrar with such information as may be necessary for him to discharge his duties.

Subsections 1 and 2 require no comment.

Subsection 3 provides that the application of the provisions of the Official Secrets Act 1911, as to the wrongful communication of information, will not preclude disclosure of information by the Registrar and his officers or servants or by members of the Tribunal where the disclosure is made in order that their respective duties may be carried out under the Act, or for the purpose of proceedings arising out of the Act (and we take this to mean civil or criminal proceedings as well as proceedings before the Tribunal). Whether proceedings would include applications to the Registrar for registration or alteration of registered particulars, or actions by the Registrar such as the issuing of notices (e.g. an enforcement notice) is unclear; we take the view that these matters would probably not constitute "proceedings", but this is certainly open to argument.

Section 18 Service of notices

18.—(1) Any notice or notification authorised or required by this Act to be served on or given to any person by the Registrar may—
- (a) if that person is an individual, be served on him—
  - (i) by delivering it to him; or
  - (ii) by sending it to him by post addressed to him at his usual or last-known place of residence or business; or
  - (iii) by leaving it for him at that place;
- (b) if that person is a body corporate or unincorporate, be served on that body—
  - (i) by sending it by post to the proper officer of the body at its principal office; or
  - (ii) by addressing it to the proper officer of the body and leaving it at that office.

(2) In subsection (1)(b) above "principal office", in relation to a registered company, means its registered office and "proper officer", in relation to any body, means the secretary or other executive officer charged with the conduct of its general affairs.

(3) This section is without prejudice to any other lawful method of serving or giving a notice or notification.

Section 18 requires no comment.

Section 19 Prosecutions and penalties

19.—(1) No proceedings for an offence under this Act shall be instituted—
- (a) in England or Wales except by the Registrar or by or with the consent of the Director of Public Prosecutions;
- (b) in Northern Ireland except by the Registrar or by or with the consent of the Director of Public Prosecutions for Northern Ireland.

(2) A person guilty of an offence under any provision of this Act other than section 6 or paragraph 12 of Schedule 4 shall be liable—
- (a) on conviction on indictment, to a fine; or
- (b) on summary conviction, to a fine not exceeding the statutory maximum (as defined in section 74 of the Criminal Justice Act 1982).

(3) A person guilty of an offence under section 6 above or the said paragraph 12 shall be liable on summary conviction to a fine not exceeding the fifth level on the standard scale (as defined in section 75 of the said Act of 1982).

THE ACT EXAMINED

(4) Subject to subsection (5) below, the court by or before which a person is convicted of an offence under section 5, 10, 12 or 15 above may order any data material appearing to the court to be connected with the commission of the offence to be forfeited, destroyed or erased.

(5) The court shall not make an order under subsection (4) above in relation to any material where a person (other than the offender) claiming to be the owner or otherwise interested in it applies to be heard by the court unless an opportunity is given to him to show cause why the order should not be made.

Section 19 deals with prosecutions and penalties and states who will be able to commence prosecutions. It also deals with the mode of trial (summary or trial upon indictment) and provides for penalties and judicial powers in respect of commissions of offences under the Act.

Subsection 1 provides that proceedings for an offence under the Act in England and Wales will be commenced by the Registrar or by or with the consent of the Director of Public Prosecutions. In Northern Ireland it will again be by the Registrar or by or with the consent of the Director of Public Prosecutions for Northern Ireland. Clearly, the main body of enforcement is the Registrar, who may act on his own initiative. It is probable, however, that he will also act by investigating complaints made to him by third parties, and will thereby act as a sieve in respect of sought-after prosecutions. We consider it likely that the Registrar will have insufficient manpower as presently conceived to act effectively as a policing authority on a broad scale. One matter of interest is that it would appear to be unlikely that in respect of an offence committed under Section 17, the Registrar would prosecute either himself, his officers or servants, members of the Tribunal, or officers or servants of the Tribunal, but that the Director of Public Prosecutions would bring such a prosecution or give his consent for such a prosecution.

Subsection 2 provides for the mode of trial as either being trial upon indictment or summary trial. In either case the convicted person would be liable to a fine. The difference between the modes of trial is described in Appendix 1 but, briefly, trial upon indictment is before a judge and jury, the judge being the arbiter of law and the jury the arbiter of fact.

In this event there is no limit to the fine that may be imposed by the judge. Summary trial, however, would be before a bench of lay magistrates or, alternatively, before a stipendiary magistrate (being a legally qualified and experienced person appointed by the Lord Chancellor), in which case the convicted person is liable to a fine not exceeding the statutory maximum as defined by Section 74 of the Criminal Justice Act 1982, which at present stands at £1,000. In practice, the prosecution will seek summary trial in relatively minor cases, and trial upon indictment in more serious cases. In any event the person charged will have the right to trial upon indictment before a judge and jury even if the prosecution is content with summary trial.

In the context of subsection 3 it will be recalled that Section 6, subsection 6, deals with a person tendering, knowingly or recklessly, information which is false or misleading in any material respect with regard to an application for registration or for alteration of registered particulars. Paragraph 12 of Schedule 4 deals with the person who intentionally obstructs someone seeking to execute a warrant or who fails without reasonable excuse to give any person executing such a warrant such assistance as that person might reasonably require. The effect of this subsection is not to provide for trial upon indictment in respect of those offences and thereby to limit the respective scale of punishment.

Subsection 4 should be read in the context of subsection 5. The first provides that where a person is convicted of an offence under Sections 5, 10, 12 or 15, the court may order any data appearing to the court to be connected with the commission of the offence to be forfeited, destroyed or erased. It is essential, however, that whoever carries out the destruction should be aware of the common (essential) practice of providing data "back-up" in the form of archived copies of the data. Several sets are often archived and known colloquially as grandfather, father and son (if three sets are retained), son being the most recent. All "generations" would need to be destroyed. Subsection 5 is not particularly clearly drafted, but it would appear to us that in the event of cause being shown why the order should

THE ACT EXAMINED

not be made by the person other than the offender claiming to be the owner or otherwise interested in the data material, the court should not make an order for the forfeiture, destruction or erasure of such material.

Section 20 Liability of directors, etc.

> 20.–(1) Where an offence under this Act has been committed by a body corporate and is proved to have been committed with the consent or connivance of or to be attributable to any neglect on the part of any director, manager, secretary or similar officer of the body corporate or any person who was purporting to act in any such capacity, he as well as the body corporate shall be guilty of that offence and be liable to be proceeded against and punished accordingly.
>
> (2) Where the affairs of a body corporate are managed by its members subsection (1) above shall apply in relation to the acts and defaults of a member in connection with his functions of management as if he were a director of the body corporate.

Section 20 deals with the liability of directors, managers, secretaries or similar officers of a corporation, or any person who was purporting to act in any such capacity. Further, in the event of the affairs of a corporation being managed by its members, the provisions will apply in relation to the acts and defaults of a member in connection with his functions of management as if he were a director.

PART III RIGHTS OF DATA SUBJECTS

PART III of the Act deals with the rights of data subjects and comprises Sections 21 to 25. We believe confusion may arise because of the way the Act uses the terms "data" and "information" (see Section 1). In commenting on Section 21 we use the words as they appear in the following extract from the statute:

Section 21 Right of access to personal data

> 21.–(1) Subject to the provisions of this section, an individual shall be entitled–
>
>   (a) to be informed by any data user whether the data held

by him include personal data of which that individual is the data subject; and

(b) to be supplied by any data user with a copy of the information constituting any such personal data held by him;

and where any of the information referred to in paragraph (b) above is expressed in terms which are not intelligible without explanation the information shall be accompanied by an explanation of those terms.

(2) A data user shall not be obliged to supply any information under subsection (1) above except in response to a request in writing and on payment of such fee (not exceeding the prescribed maximum) as he may require; but a request for information under both paragraphs of that subsection shall be treated as a single request and a request for information under paragraph (a) shall, in the absence of any indication to the contrary, be treated as extending also to information under paragraph (b).

(3) In the case of a data user having separate entries in the register in respect of data held for different purposes a separate request must be made and a separate fee paid under this section in respect of the data to which each entry relates.

(4) A data user shall not be obliged to comply with a request under this section—

(a) unless he is supplied with such information as he may reasonably require in order to satisfy himself as to the identity of the person making the request and to locate the information which he seeks; and

(b) if he cannot comply with the request without disclosing information relating to another individual who can be identified from that information, unless he is satisfied that the other individual has consented to the disclosure of the information to the person making the request.

(5) In paragraph (b) of subsection (4) above the reference to information relating to another individual includes a reference to information identifying that individual as the source of the information sought by the request; and that paragraph shall not be construed as excusing a data user from supplying so much of the information sought by the request as can be supplied without disclosing the identity of the other individual concerned, whether by the omission of names or other identifying particulars or otherwise.

(6) A data user shall comply with a request under this section within forty days of receiving the request or, if later, receiving the information referred to in paragraph (a) of subsection (4) above and, in a case where it is required, the consent referred to in paragraph (b) of that subsection.

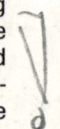

(7) The information to be supplied pursuant to a request under this section shall be supplied by reference to the data in question at the time when the request is received except that it may take account of any amendment or deletion made between that time and the time when the information is supplied, being an amendment or deletion that would have been made regardless of the receipt of the request.

(8) If a court is satisfied on the application of any person who has made a request under the foregoing provisions of this section that the data user in question has failed to comply with the request in contravention of those provisions, the court may order him to comply with the request; but a court shall not make an order under this subsection if it considers that it would in all the circumstances be unreasonable to do so, whether because of the frequency with which the applicant has made requests to the data user under those provisions or for any other reason.

(9) The Secretary of State may by order provide for enabling a request under this section to be made on behalf of any individual who is incapable by reason of mental disorder of managing his own affairs.

It is an essential characteristic of the Act and the *raison d'être* of the legislation that data subjects shall have rights of access to personal data. The section provides data subjects with a legally enforceable means of access. Once access is achieved, the data subject will be in a position to consider whether the data protection principles set out in Schedule 1 have been complied with by the data user. In particular, the data subject may be in a position to consider whether the information, for instance, was obtained and, as data, processed fairly and lawfully (see data protection principle 1) and particularly whether the said data are accurate and have been kept up to date (see data protection principle 5). Further, the data subject will be able to consider whether the personal data held and disclosed by reason of his rights under PART III are adequate, relevant and not excessive in relation to the purpose or purposes registered by the data user under Section 4, subsection 3(b). We envisage that the consequence of rights of access being exercised may be, in certain cases, complaints being raised by data subjects directly with the Registrar. The Registrar will then investigate those complaints. It would appear likely that in the event of the Registrar being satisfied that offences have been committed under the Act, statements would be taken from the complainants in a similar fashion to the manner in which police authorities take statements from complainants in other spheres of criminal activity. The complainants would then be called to give evidence in any proceedings in the Magistrates or Crown Courts. The reader's attention is drawn to Chapter 5, where rights of access are dealt with at length in the contexts of security and a corporate security policy.

The content of subsection 1 is self-evident but note that the right is conferred upon "an individual" – a living individual, as opposed to a corporate person.

Subsection 2 restricts the obligations of data users with regard to the supply of information under subsection 1, whereby the duty to supply such information will not arise other than in response to a request in writing and on payment of such fee (not exceeding a prescribed maximum) as the data user may require.

Subsection 3 provides that in the case of a data user having separate entries in the register in respect of data held for different purposes, a separate request (in writing) must be made and a separate fee paid in respect of the data to which each entry relates. It may be that a data user has a data retrieval system based primarily upon the purposes for which specific groups of personal data are used. In that event, it is likely that the data user will make separate entries in the register in respect of those different categories of purpose. Subsection 3 will therefore obviate the necessity of a data user making a retrieval search of his entire data system in respect of personal data relating to an individual.

Subsection 4 provides additional protection to the data user in that he will not be obliged to comply with a request under subsection 1, first, unless he is supplied with such information as he may reasonably require in order to satisfy himself as to the identity of the person making the request, and to locate the information which he requires; and, secondly, if he cannot comply with the request without disclosing information relating to another individual who is thereby identified, unless he is satisfied that that other individual has consented to the disclosure of the information to the person making the request. Clearly, it is essential that the data user is satisfied within reasonable limits that the data subject is genuine. Again we draw attention to Chapter 5, which discusses the present technical difficulties of achieving this degree of access control with many computer systems.

It is difficult to determine the correct interpretation of the provision whereby the data user is not obliged to comply with the data subject's request in circumstances where he could not do so without disclosing data about another individual who can be identified from information conveyed by the data. It is likely that the correct interpretation is that such information must of itself provide the capability of identifying the third party in question without the use of further knowledge on the part of the data subject or through further enquiries made by the data subject. However, it is possible that a wider interpretation could be placed upon subsection 4: for instance, it might be that in certain circumstances the supply of information in accordance with a request under Section 21 would disclose information relating to one of a number of other individuals. Thus it could be seen from the information disclosed, for instance, that certain information related either to Mr A, or Mr B. It might be, in those circumstances, that the damage would have been done in that the choice of third parties to whom such information related would be extremely limited.

Subsection 6 provides a time limit for compliance with a request under Section 21, whereby the data user must comply with such a request within forty days of receiving the request, or within forty days of receiving such data as he may reasonably require in order to satisfy himself as to the identity of the person making the request and to locate the data which he seeks (subsection 4(a)), and, in the event that it is so required, within forty days of receiving the consent referred to in subsection 4(b).

Subsection 7 makes provision for the specific parameters of the information to be supplied. This subsection states that such information should be supplied by reference to the data in question at the time the request is received *but* that such information *may* take account of any amendment or deletion made between the time of the request being received and the time of the information being supplied on the basis that such an amendment or deletion would have been made regardless of the receipt of the request.

This is a wide provision which could be the subject of serious abuse. We consider the burden of proof to be upon the data user but from a purely practical evidential viewpoint it seems improbable that a data subject could contradict the assertion of the data user that the amendment or deletion "would have been made regardless of" the request for information being received. We note that this is a wider provision than was expressed in the Bill brought from the House of Lords on November 3 1983 and is an amendment which was included by Standing Committee H in the revision of the Bill printed on April 26, 1984.

In subsection 8 the Act specifically brings to the court's attention the possibility of a data subject becoming "a pest" as far as the data user is concerned, and seeking data on numerous occasions. However, it should be noted that the slant of the legislation, in particular at subsection 8, is generally in favour of the data subject in that it is not stated, for instance, that the court should not make an order under the subsection unless it was reasonable to do so, but it is worded in favour of the data subject, so that the court will not make an order under the subsection in circumstances where it would be unreasonable to do so.

Subsection 9 requires no comment.

Section 22   Compensation for inaccuracy

22.–(1) An individual who is the subject of personal data held by a data user and who suffers damage by reason of the inaccuracy of the data shall be entitled to compensation from the data user for that damage and for any distress which the individual has suffered by reason of the inaccuracy.
(2) In the case of data which accurately record information received or obtained by the data user from the data subject or a third party, subsection (1) above does not apply if the following requirements have been complied with–
   (a) the data indicate that the information was received or obtained as aforesaid or the information has not been

extracted from the data except in a form which includes an indication to that effect; and
(b) if the data subject has notified the data user that he regards the information as incorrect or misleading, an indication to that effect has been included in the data or the information has not been extracted from the data except in a form which includes an indication to that effect.

(3) In proceedings brought against any person by virtue of this section it shall be a defence to prove that he had taken such care as in all the circumstances was reasonably required to ensure the accuracy of the data at the material time.

(4) Data are inaccurate for the purposes of this section if incorrect or misleading as to any matter of fact.

Subsection 1 provides that a data subject who suffers damage through the inaccuracy of personal data held by a data user will be entitled to compensation for that damage from the data user.

Subsection 2 limits the effect of Subsection 1 in providing that when data accurately represent information received and obtained by the data user from the data subject or a third party, subsection 1 shall not apply if, and only if, the two following conditions have been complied with:

First, that the data "indicate" the information was received and obtained by the data user from the data subject or a third party or that the information has not been extracted from the data other than in a form which contains such an "indication".

Second, in the event of the data subject having notified the data user that he considers the information to be incorrect or misleading, an "indication" to that effect has been included in the data, or information has not been extracted except in a form which includes such an indication.

We consider that the use of the words "indication" and "indicate" is open to potential abuse. The Act does not go so far as to say that there should be an express statement at the same or a similar level of prominence as the rest of the surrounding data or information. We consider that at present a footnote "indicator" would suffice as far as the data user is concerned.

In addition subsection 2 only deals with a data user having

received or obtained information rather than the data user, and servants or agents of the data user. This extension may be implied, but the matter itself is open to argument. We consider that it should be implied, since a body corporate could *only* act through its servants or agents and, of course, a data user may be a body corporate (a company), which is a legal "person" for the purposes of the definition of "data user" in Section 1, subsection 5.

There is no provision for the payment of compensation by a third party who has provided inaccurate or misleading information. We consider therefore that Section 22 is open to considerable abuse by third parties against data subjects. This will be of great importance in the fields of journalism and personnel matters, where information received or obtained from third parties will commonly be held.

Importantly, there is no express provision in Section 22 for the data subject to be initially informed of the intention of the data user to hold data supplied or obtained from that data subject or from a third party concerning that data subject. Therefore we see great difficulties in the effective operation of subsection 2(b) in that it is an "after the event" provision, whereas we consider that the Act should go further to provide an effective method of advance notice to the data subject prior to such data being held in the first place. Indeed it may be purely fortuitous that a data subject learns that incorrect or misleading data is held about him, when he will only at that stage make a notification to the data user under subsection 2(b).

Subsection 3 gives conditions under which the data user has a defence against proceedings brought by a data subject. Clearly, from a technical viewpoint, evidence of the system and *modus operandi* adopted by the data user will be highly relevant to the defence under this subsection.

Subsection 4 defines the term "inaccurate" for the purposes of Section 22 as data being "incorrect or misleading as to any matter of fact". In this respect it should be noted that the term "matter of fact" is not the same as "matter of opinion". An opinion or a view cannot be inaccurate in itself.

Section 23 Compensation for loss or unauthorised disclosure

23.–(1) An individual who is the subject of personal data held by a data user or in respect of which services are provided by a person carrying on a computer bureau and who suffers damage by reason of–
   (a) the loss of the data;
   (b) the destruction of the data without the authority of the data user or, as the case may be, of the person carrying on the bureau; or
   (c) subject to subsection (2) below, the disclosure of the data, or access having been obtained to the data, without such authority as aforesaid,
shall be entitled to compensation from the data user or, as the case may be, the person carrying on the bureau for that damage and for any distress which the individual has suffered by reason of the loss, destruction, disclosure or access.
(2) In the case of a registered data user, subsection (1)(c) above does not apply to disclosure to, or access by, any person falling within a description specified pursuant to section 4(3)(d) above in an entry in the register relating to that data.
(3) In proceedings brought against any person by virtue of this section it shall be a defence to prove that he had taken such care as in all the circumstances was reasonably required to prevent the loss, destruction or disclosure in question.

Subsection 1 ensures that the data subject will be entitled to compensation for such damage and distress from the data user, or the person carrying on the computer bureau, as the case may be. The last mentioned head in respect of which compensation for damage may be obtained, by reason of subsection 2, does not apply to disclosure by any person falling within the description specified in an entry in the register relating to the data user. Thus, if the recipient of the information was a *potential* recipient of the personal data by reason of an entry in the register relating to the data user, subsection 2 would apply, so that the data subject would not be entitled to compensation. If part of the business of a data user, therefore, is supplying "mail-shot lists" to commercial organisations, and that is a registered purpose for which the data is held, it would seem that disclosure can take place without any right to compensation for the data subject.

One can take the example also of a private detective agency or credit reference agency, both of which would register as data users. One purpose of their data gathering could include subsequent disclosure to clients who sought the services of either agency in the first place. Obviously, to obtain registration at all, such agencies must at the very least provide information to the Registrar sufficient to satisfy him that they would be unlikely to contravene any of the data protection principles – including the first principle that the information contained in the data must be obtained "fairly and lawfully". Furthermore, if the Registrar is satisfied that any of the data protection principles are being breached he may take appropriate action by serving, for instance, an enforcement notice or a de-registration notice. However, from a strict reading of the Act it would appear to be a major defect in the Act that in the example of a registered data user unfairly or illegally obtaining information which is represented by the personal data held, a data subject will not be entitled to compensation for disclosure of that information to a third party, if such disclosure falls within a description specified pursuant to Section 4(3)d. Nonetheless it may be that the data subject could maintain a claim for compensation under Section 23 (1)(a) in a case where a claim under Section 23 (1)(c) could not be brought. It should be noted that the authority required for destruction, disclosure of, or access to data is not that of the data subject but that of the data user.

So far as subsection 3 is concerned it is particularly important for a data user to be able to claim that his data protection system and *modus operandi* in handling personal data are effective. Clearly, evidence supporting such claims will be highly relevant as far as the statutory defence is concerned (see Chapter 4).

Section 24   Rectification and erasure

24.–(1) If a court is satisfied on the application of a data subject that personal data held by a data user of which the applicant is the subject are inaccurate within the meaning of section 22 above, the court may order the rectification or erasure of the data and of any data held by the data user and containing an expression of opinion which appears to the court to be based on the inaccurate data.

(2) Subsection (1) above applies whether or not the data accurately record information received or obtained by the data user from the data subject or a third party but where the data accurately record such information, then–
   (a) if the requirements mentioned in section 22(2) above have been complied with, the court may, instead of making an order under subsection (1) above, make an order requiring the data to be supplemented by such statement of the true facts relating to the matters dealt with by the data as the court may approve; and
   (b) if all or any of those requirements have not been complied with, the court may, instead of making an order under that subsection, make such order as it thinks fit for securing compliance with those requirements with or without a further order requiring the data to be supplemented by such a statement as is mentioned in paragraph (a) above.
(3) If a court is satisfied on the application of a data subject–
   (a) that he has suffered damage by reason of the disclosure of personal data, or of access having been obtained to personal data, in circumstances entitling him to compensation under section 23 above; and
   (b) that there is a substantial risk of further disclosure of or access to the data without such authority as is mentioned in that section,
the court may order the erasure of the data; but, in the case of data in respect of which services were being provided by a person carrying on a computer bureau, the court shall not make such an order unless such steps as are reasonably practicable have been taken for notifying the person for whom those services were provided and giving him an opportunity to be heard.

Section 24 should be read in the light of data protection principle 7(b), whereby an individual is to be entitled where appropriate to have "data corrected or erased". Subsection 1 provides that if the court is satisfied on the application of a data subject that data held are inaccurate, the court may order the destruction or erasure of the data and of any data held by the data user. Included are data containing an expression of opinion based on inaccurate data. It is provided by subsection 2 that subsection 1 applies *whether or not* the data accurately record information received or obtained from the data subject or a third party. This provision and the remainder of subsection 2 is in line with the corresponding provisions of Section 10 subsection 3 as to enforcement notices. The Court may by subsection 2(a) order a supplemental statement of the "true facts" as it may approve to be included in the data in the event that the requirements of Section 22 subsection 2 have been complied with. In the event of those requirements not having been complied with the Court may by subsection 2(b) order compliance with those requirements with or without a further order for the inclusion of a supplemental statement of the "true facts" as it may approve.

It is conceivable that a data subject could bring proceedings under Section 24 for rectification or erasure even if the data user had *complied* with an enforcement notice under Section 10 which had required compliance with the requirements of Section 22 subsection 2 and which had required the inclusion of a statement of the "true facts" as approved by the Registrar. Thus the Court's view of the "true facts" might materially differ from the view of the Registrar. The Court would be at liberty upon hearing evidence to find that the Registrar's approved supplemental statement of the "true facts" was wrong. The foregoing is open to argument however, in that it may be said that the statement of "true facts" included by reason of an enforcement notice is a case of a data user accurately recording information received from a third party, namely the Registrar; in which case, the same could not be said to be "inaccurate" within the meaning of Section 22! We take the view that the accuracy of the Registrar's approved statement of facts may be challenged in the Courts, but we acknowledge the arguments against this view. A difficulty which arises is that the words "inaccurate" or "inaccuracy" are not specifically defined in the Act. Section 24 subsection 1 refers to "personal data . . . inaccurate within the meaning of Section 22 . . ." However upon analysing Section 22 no particular meaning is actually attributed to the word "inaccurate" or indeed to the word "inaccuracy". At one stage during the passage of the Data Protection Bill it was thought by us that Section 22 was to convey the meaning that data were not "inaccurate" if Section 22 subsection 2 was complied with. This cannot be the case bearing in mind the provisions of

Section 24 subsection 2 which states that the Court may order rectification or erasure of "inaccurate" data whether or not the data accurately record information received or obtained from the data subject or a third party and whether or not the requirements of Section 22 subsection 2 have been complied with.

It is in these circumstances that we take the stance that it should properly be open to the Courts finally to determine what data are inaccurate and what are not and what are the "true facts" relating to the matters dealt with by the data.

The arguments advanced above that the Courts may in an appropriate case override the view of the "true facts" taken by the Registrar applies equally to any review of the "true facts" made the Data Protection Tribunal under Section 14 of the Act.

Subsection 3 provides that if the court is satisfied that the data subject has sustained damage by reason of the disclosure of personal data or of access having been obtained to personal data in circumstances entitling him to compensation under Section 23 and there is a substantial risk of further disclosure or access without the requisite authority, it may order erasure of the data. Thus a possible penalty for disclosure of or access to personal data unauthorised by the data user is the complete erasure of the data. The subsection seeks to safeguard the interests of those persons who engage the services of a computer bureau, so that they receive notification of the proceedings and have an opportunity to be heard by the Court prior to any order being made. We note that it is stated that "the Court *may* order" erasure, and thus the court have regard to the interests of the person who has engaged the services of a computer bureau in deciding *not* to order erasure in any specific case.

Section 25   Jurisdiction and procedure

25.–(1) The jurisdiction conferred by sections 21 and 24 above shall be exercisable by the High Court or a county court or, in Scotland, by the Court of Session or the sheriff.
(2) For the purpose of determining any question whether an applicant under subsection (8) of section 21 above is entitled to the information which he seeks (including any question

whether any relevant data are exempt from that section by virtue of Part IV of this Act) a court may require the information constituting any data held by the data user to be made available for its own inspection but shall not, pending the determination of that question in the applicant's favour, require the information sought by the applicant to be disclosed to him or his representatives whether by discovery (or, in Scotland, recovery) or otherwise.

It is provided that the High Court or County Court will have jurisdiction in respect of Sections 21 to 24. No particular division of the High Court is specified, and it would appear to us that a case could equally well be brought in the Chancery Division or in the Queen's Bench Division, Commercial Court, of the High Court of Justice. In our view, it will be largely a matter of personal preference as far as solicitors and barristers are concerned as to which High Court division is used. The powers of compensation in terms of awarding damages for loss sustained are unlimited in the High Court in either of the divisions mentioned, but are currently limited to the sum of £5,000 in the County Court, except in the case of an agreement between the parties in County Court proceedings whereby the £5,000 limit is raised.

In subsection 2 it should be noted that "discovery" is the legal procedural method whereby opposing parties find out what documents are or have been in the possession, power or control of their respective opponents, their servants or agents. It also enables inspection of such documents as remain in the possession, power or control of the opponent in question by himself, his servants or agents.

PART IV   EXEMPTIONS

PART IV comprises Sections 26 to 35, which deal with sensitive issues of national security, law enforcement in the spheres of crime, taxation, health and social work, and judicial appointments and legal professional privilege.

Section 26 Preliminary

26.–(1) References in any provision of Part II or III of this Act to personal data do not include references to data which by virtue of this Part of this Act are exempt from that provision.
(2) In this Part of this Act "the subject access provisions" means–
   (a) section 21 above; and
   (b) any provision of Part II of this Act conferring a power on the Registrar to the extent to which it is exercisable by reference to paragraph *(a)* of the seventh data protection principle.
(3) In this Part of this Act "the non-disclosure provisions" means–
   (a) sections 5(2)*(d)* and 15 above; and
   (b) any provision of Part II of this Act conferring a power on the Registrar to the extent to which it is exercisable by reference to any data protection principle inconsistent with the disclosure in question.
(4) Except as provided by this Part of this Act the subject access provisions shall apply notwithstanding any enactment or rule of law prohibiting or restricting the disclosure, or authorising the withholding, of information.

Section 26 provides definitions of "the subject access provisions" and "the non-disclosure provisions". "Subject access provisions" (Section 21 is relevant) give a data subject the statutory right to receive in writing a copy of the information based on his personal data. Also, under PART II, giving a power to the Registrar, the provisions define the extent to which that power is exercisable under data protection principle 7(a) (an individual shall be entitled, at reasonable intervals and without undue delay or expense, first to be informed by any data user whether he holds personal data of which the individual is the subject, and secondly the access to any such data held by the data user). It is clear, therefore, that exemption from subject access provisions will mean, in effect, that the data subject will not be able to obtain information based on personal data held in respect of him by the data user; and that any written request for such information would be unenforceable in the courts. Furthermore, the Registrar would not be in a position to proceed against the data user for contravention of the data protection principle 7(a).

Subsection 3 deals with the meaning of the "non-disclosure provisions" (Sections 5 (2)(d) and 15). Section 5 (2)(d) prevents personal data disclosure by any data user to a person not described in the entry on the register under Section 4, subsection 3(d). Section 15 prohibits the disclosure of personal data by a computer bureau without the authority of the person in respect of whom, or in respect of which, the computer bureau's services are made available. The practicalities in this case are that, in the event of exemption from the non-disclosure provisions, the prohibitions in respect of disclosure provided for in Section 5(2) (d) and Section 15(1) will be inapplicable and hence unenforceable. Further disclosure in such cases would not be the subject matter of an offence. In addition, subsection 3 provides that the term "the non-disclosure provisions" means any provision of PART II conferring a power on the Registrar to the extent to which it is exercisable by reference to any data protection principle inconsistent with the disclosure in question.

Subsection 4 provides that otherwise than as provided by PART IV the subject access provisions will be dominant and apply notwithstanding any enactment or rule of law prohibiting or restricting the disclosure, or authorising the withholding, of information.

Section 27   National security

27.–(1) Personal data are exempt from the provisions of Part II of this Act and of sections 21 to 24 above if the exemption is required for the purpose of safeguarding national security.
(2) Any question whether the exemption mentioned in subsection (1) above is or at any time was required for the purpose there mentioned in respect of any personal data shall be determined by a Minister of the Crown; and a certificate signed by a Minister of the Crown certifying that the exemption is or at any time was so required shall be conclusive evidence of that fact.
(3) Personal data which are not exempt under subsection (1) above are exempt from the non-disclosure provisions in any case in which the disclosure of the data is for the purpose of safeguarding national security.
(4) For the purposes of subsection (3) above a certificate signed by a Minister of the Crown certifying that personal data

are or have been disclosed for the purpose mentioned in that subsection shall be conclusive evidence of that fact.
(5) A document purporting to be such a certificate as is mentioned in this section shall be received in evidence and deemed to be such a certificate unless the contrary is proved.
(6) The powers conferred by this section on a Minister of the Crown shall not be exercisable except by a Minister who is a member of the Cabinet or by the Attorney General or the Lord Advocate.

Subsection 1 requires no comment.

Subsection 2 provides that any question as to whether the exemption is required for the purpose of safeguarding national security is a matter to be determined by a minister of the Crown, and that a certificate signed by a minister of the Crown certifying that the exemption is, or at any time was, so required, shall be *conclusive evidence* of that fact. Thus it will be impossible to question such a certificate signed by a minister on the basis that the exemption was not justified. Clearly the draftsmen of the Act have considered this to be a politically sensitive question, which it obviously is, and have given the ultimate discretion to ministers of the Crown to decide what is and what is not within the bounds of national security.

It is, of course, possible that exemption may be claimed on the basis of safeguarding national security without a certificate signed by a minister of the Crown which would provide conclusive evidence, but even in such a case it would not be a matter for the court to determine whether exemption was required for the purpose of safeguarding national security. Issues would have to be referred (Section 27, subsection 2) to a minister of the Crown for his determination.

Subsection 3 applies to personal data not held for the purpose of safeguarding national security, but which are disclosed in respect of that purpose. In that circumstance the data are exempt from the non-disclosure provisions.

Subsections 4, 5 and 6 require no comment.

Section 28 Crime and taxation

28.—(1) Personal data held for any of the following purposes—
   (a) the prevention or detection of crime;
   (b) the apprehension or prosecution of offenders; or
   (c) the assessment or collection of any tax or duty,
are exempt from the subject access provisions in any case in which the application of those provisions to the data would be likely to prejudice any of the matters mentioned in this subsection.

(2) Personal data which—
   (a) are held for the purpose of discharging statutory functions; and
   (b) consist of information obtained for such a purpose from a person who had it in his possession for any of the purposes mentioned in subsection (1) above
are exempt from the subject access provisions to the same extent as personal data held for any of the purposes mentioned in that subsection.

(3) Personal data are exempt from the non-disclosure provisions in any case in which—
   (a) the disclosure is for any of the purposes mentioned in subsection (1) above; and
   (b) the application of those provisions in relation to the disclosure would be likely to prejudice any of the matters mentioned in that subsection;
and in proceedings against any person for contravening a provision mentioned in section 26(3)(a) above it shall be a defence to prove that he had reasonable grounds for believing that failure to make the disclosure in question would have been likely to prejudice any of those matters.

(4) Personal data are exempt from the provisions of Part II of this Act conferring powers on the Registrar, to the extent to which they are exercisable by reference to the first data protection principle, in any case in which the application of those provisions to the data would be likely to prejudice any of the matters mentioned in subsection (1) above.

Subsection 1 requires no comment.

Subsection 2 provides exemption from the subject access provisions in respect of data held for the purpose of discharging statutory functions *and* which consists of information obtained for such a statutory purpose from a person who had it in his possession for
(a) the prevention and detection of crime; or
(b) the apprehension or prosecution of offenders; or

(c) the assessment or collection of any tax or duty.

Thus the Inspector of Taxes might receive personal data from an Officer of the Fraud Squad and it is provided by subsection 2 that such data would thereby be exempt in the hands of the Fraud Squad and the Inspector of Taxes if and insofar as the specific requirements of subsection 1 and/or 2 were complied with.

Subsection 3 provides an exemption from the non-disclosure provisions in respect of data disclosed for any of the purposes set out at subsection 1 *and* where non-disclosure would be likely to prejudice any of those purposes. Futher, a defence to proceedings is provided for on the basis of the person making the disclosure having had reasonable grounds for believing that the failure to disclose would have been likely to prejudice any of the purposes set out in subsection 1.

Subsection 4 provides that personal data are exempt from the provisions of PART II, which confer powers on the Registrar, if the information represented by the data has been obtained and processed fairly and lawfully, in any case of the application of the provisions of PART II where those provisions would be likely to prejudice any of the purposes set out in subsection 1. The reference in subsection 4 to data protection principle 1 clearly means that, in the event of personal data being obtained unfairly or unlawfully or having been processed unfairly or unlawfully, such data would not be exempt from the provisions of PART II conferring powers on the Registrar even if the application of the Registrar's powers would be likely to prejudice any of the purposes set out in subsection 1, i.e. the prevention or detection of crime, the apprehension or prosecution of offenders, the assessment or collection of any tax or duty. Thus, in the event of, for instance, the police unlawfully entering premises and thereafter obtaining evidence in connection with the preventing or detection of crime, or the apprehension or prosecution of offenders, the unlawful entry would take any personal data obtained or processed outside the provisions of data protection principle 1. Therefore such data would *not* be exempt as far as the

Registrar exercising his powers under PART II is concerned.

Data relating specifically to corporate bodies is not dealt with, save insofar as that data itself relates to a human being within such a corporate body. It is not the case, therefore, that the Act is in any way aimed at controlling or reducing the loss or seizure of industrial or corporate data as such.

It is clear that the Act in its definition of "data user" does not intend the inclusion of computer operatives generally, but rather those who commence the automatic processing of data with control over the contents and use of such data. Section 1, subsection 6, defines a person who carries on a computer bureau as being one who provides other persons with services in respect of data. A person is defined as providing such services as (a) agent for other persons when he causes data held by them to be processed automatically, or (b) he allows other persons the use of equipment in his possession for processing data automatically. By reason of the provision whereby a person will carry on a computer bureau if he allows other persons the use of equipment in his possession for processing data, those who sell, or lease, computers or other automatic processing equipment will not be liable as data users. Section 1, subsection 7, defines processing in relation to data as follows: "amending, augmenting, deleting or rearranging the data or extracting the information constituting the data and, in the case of personal data means . . . performing any of those operations by reference to the data subject."

It is clear that, in the event of a complaint being received from a data subject by the Registrar, the Registrar might conclude that exemption was not appropriate under Section 28 on the basis that the application of, for instance, the subject access provisions would not be likely to prejudice any of the purposes mentioned in subsection 1. In that event, the Registrar could serve an enforcement notice on the data user specifying the data protection principle breached, and requiring subject access to be provided within a specified period of time. We have already dealt with the method of appeal to the data protection tribunal by a data user in respect of an enforcement notice, and thereafter appeal on a point of law to the High Court.

It is the case that the data subject has two means of obtaining subject access from the data user. First, the data subject can make a complaint to the Registrar and the Registrar may, in his discretion, serve an enforcement notice upon the data user. However, secondly, the data subject is able to apply to the High Court or to a County Court to obtain an order that the data user comply with the request for subject access pursuant to Section 21, subsection 8. It is likely, in our view, that the data subject would first complain to the Registrar and, in general, would only resort to litigation by making an application to the court in the event of the Registrar refusing to issue an enforcement notice.

Section 29   Health and social work

> 29.–(1) The Secretary of State may by order exempt from the subject access provisions, or modify those provisions in relation to, personal data consisting of information as to the physical or mental health of the data subject.
> (2) The Secretary of State may by order exempt from the subject access provisions, or modify those provisions in relation to, personal data of such other descriptions as may be specified in the order, being information–
>   *(a)* held by government departments or local authorities or by voluntary organisations or other bodies designated by or under the order; and
>   *(b)* appearing to him to be held for, or acquired in the course of, carrying out social work in relation to the data subject or other individuals;
> but the Secretary of State shall not under this subsection confer any exemption or make any modification except so far as he considers that the application to the data of those provisions (or of those provisions without modification) would be likely to prejudice the carrying out of social work.
> (3) An order under this section may make different provision in relation to data consisting of information of different descriptions.

In subsection 1 it is clearly envisaged that personal data in respect of physical or mental health might be damaging to the data subject who is a patient of, for instance, a general practitioner or consultant, and might injuriously affect the doctor/patient relationship which should otherwise exist.

Subsections 2 and 3 require no comment.

Section 30   Regulation of financial services etc.

30.—(1) Personal data held for the purpose of discharging statutory functions to which this section applies are exempt from the subject access provisions in any case in which the application of those provisions to the data would be likely to prejudice the proper discharge of those functions.
(2) This section applies to any functions designated for the purposes of this section by an order made by the Secretary of State, being functions conferred by or under any enactment appearing to him to be designed for protecting members of the public against financial loss due to dishonesty, incompetence or malpractice by persons concerned in the provision of banking, insurance, investment or other financial services or in the management of companies or to the conduct of discharged or undischarged bankrupts.

This section is best explained by an example. Take the case of insurance companies being required to be registered with the Department of Trade and Industry (DTI) under the Insurance Companies Act 1982 to take a certain line of insurance. It may be that the Department would be concerned as to the ethics and past behaviour of directors of an insurance company wishing to be registered. In the event of the DTI holding personal data on such directors, the same would be exempt from the subject access provisions if the application of those provisions would be likely to prejudice the function of registration. We note that the determination of what would be "likely to prejudice the proper discharge of" functions designated by the Secretary of State is not dealt with by means of a conclusive certificate (as in the case of National Security; see Section 27 subsection 4). Hence we consider that the matter is open to determination by the Courts.

Section 31   Judicial appointments and legal professional privilege

31.—(1) Personal data held by a government department are exempt from the subject access provisions if the data consist of information which has been received from a third party and is held as information relevant to the making of judicial appointments.
(2) Personal data are exempt from the subject access provisions if the data consist of information in respect of which a

claim to legal professional privilege (or, in Scotland, to confidentiality as between client and professional legal adviser) could be maintained in legal proceedings.

Subsection 1 provides that personal data held by a government department are exempt from the subject access provisions if the data are represented by information which has been received from a third party and is held as data relevant to making judicial appointments. Thus, in the event of a judge sending a letter to the Lord Chancellor's department as to the competence and suitability of a barrister in respect of a proposed judicial appointment, and that information being then recorded as information such that it can be processed by equipment operating automatically in response to instructions given for that purpose, the data thereby held by a government department would be exempt from subject access provisions by reason of subsection 1.

Subsection 2 provides that personal data are exempt from subject access provisions if the data are representative of information in respect of which a claim to legal professional privilege could be maintained in legal proceedings. Thus, in the event of a complaint being made by a data subject to the Registrar, the Registrar would have to consider, no doubt by communicating with the data user, whether a claim for legal professional privilege existed; and if the Registrar considered that such a claim did exist, he would not issue and serve an enforcement notice upon the data user. Similarly, if the data subject brought legal proceedings under Section 21, subsection 8, the High Court or the County Court would have to consider whether there was a valid claim of legal professional privilege whereby the personal data in question were exempt from the subject access provisions, in which event the court would make no order in respect of subject access.

We consider that subsection 2 is curiously worded, in that personal data are exempt if representative of information in respect of which a claim to legal professional privilege "could be maintained" in legal proceedings. We take the view that this means that the Registrar, in considering whether or not to issue an enforcement notice or other notice under the Act, and the High Court or the County

Court in deciding whether to make an order under Section 21, subsection 8, must be satisfied that a valid claim of legal professional privilege exists in respect of the relevant personal data.

Section 32 Payrolls and accounts

32.–(1) Subject to subsection (2) below, personal data held by a data user only for one or more of the following purposes–
- (a) calculating amounts payable by way of remuneration or pensions in respect of service in any employment or office or making payments of, or of sums deducted from, such remuneration or pensions; or
- (b) keeping accounts relating to any business or other activity carried on by the data user or keeping records of purchases, sales or other transactions for the purpose of ensuring that the requisite payments are made by or to him in respect of those transactions or for the purpose of making financial or management forecasts to assist him in the conduct of any such business or activity.

are exempt from the provisions of Part II of this Act and of sections 21 to 24 above.

(2) It shall be a condition of the exemption of any data under this section that the data are not used for any purpose other than the purpose or purposes for which they are held and are not disclosed except as permitted by subsections (3) and (4) below; but the exemption shall not be lost by any use or disclosure in breach of that condition if the data user shows that he had taken such care to prevent it as in all the circumstances was reasonably required.

(3) Data held only for one or more of the purposes mentioned in subsection (1)(a) above may be disclosed–
- (a) to any person, other than the data user, by whom the remuneration or pensions in question are payable;
- (b) for the purpose of obtaining actuarial advice;
- (c) for the purpose of giving information as to the persons in any employment or office for use in medical research into the health of, or injuries suffered by, persons engaged in particular occupations or working in particular places or areas;
- (d) if the data subject (or a person acting on his behalf) has requested or consented to the disclosure of the data either generally or in the circumstances in which the disclosure in question is made; or
- (e) if the person making the disclosure has reasonable

grounds for believing that the disclosure falls within paragraph *(d)* above.
(4) Data held for any of the purposes mentioned in subsection (1) above may be disclosed—
  (a) for the purpose of audit or where the disclosure is for the purpose only of giving information about the data user's financial affairs; or
  (b) in any case in which disclosure would be permitted by any other provision of this Part of this Act if subsection (2) above were included among the non-disclosure provisions.
(5) In this section "remuneration" includes remuneration in kind and "pensions" includes gratuities or similar benefits.

Section 32 relates to personal data held by a data user for the purpose of calculating amounts payable as remuneration or pension money in respect of employees or office-holders or for the purpose of keeping accounts of money paid or received by the data user, or of keeping for accounting purposes records of goods or services supplied by or to the data user. By "accounting purposes" we refer to the verbose description of the range of activities referred to at subsection 1(b). Subsection 1 provides that such personal data held by the data user are exempt from the provisions of PART II and from Sections 21 to 24, dealing with the rights of data subjects.

Subsection 2 provides that exemption from the rights of data subjects is conditional upon the data not being used for any purpose or purposes other than the purpose or purposes for which the data are held and that they are not disclosed other than as allowed by subsections 3 and 4. We consider that the use of the phrase "the purpose or purposes for which they are held" means a purpose or purposes referred to in subsection 1 (a) or (b).

Subsection 3 provides specific instances in which data held for one or more of the purposes specified in subsection 1 (a) may be disclosed. Subsection 3 (a), (b) and (c) require no comment. Subsection 3 (d) provides that disclosure may take place if the data subject or a person acting on his behalf has requested or consented to the disclosure either generally or specifically as to the circumstances of the particular disclosure. Subsection 3 (e) is linked to subsection 3 (d) in that the data user may state that he had "reasonable grounds for believing" that the disclosure fell within subsection 3 (d). This could be open to certain abuse in that information contained in the data could be disclosed to someone over the telephone who states that he or she is a person whom the data user knows is authorised by the data subject to receive such information. In the event such a person might be an imposter, or might not. The "defence" as such is necessary but open to abuse by certain data users.

We take the view that disclosure of data includes the disclosure of information contained in such data.

Subsection 4 provides for further instances of disclosure of data held under subsection 1. This subsection is badly drafted. At subsection 4 (a) it is provided that such data may be disclosed for auditing purposes *or* where the disclosure is for "the purpose only of giving information about the data user's financial affairs". Clearly a data user could deliberately disclose a large amount of financial information and contain within it some crucial information about a particular data subject's remuneration, especially if that data subject is an employee. The draftsman seems to have missed the point that a data subject's remuneration is a relevant aspect of a data user's financial affairs. It would be very difficult to prove in many cases that a data user had some ulterior motive in disclosing information about "its" financial affairs.

Subsection 4 (b) is basically referring to exceptions to the non-disclosure provisions, such as national security under Section 27 or the prevention or detection of crime or the assessment or collection of tax under Section 28 in appropriate cases, and to other exemptions in the Act.

Section 33   Domestic or other limited purposes

33.—(1) Personal data held by an individual and concerned only with the management of his personal, family or household affairs or held by him only for recreational purposes are exempt from the provisions of Part II of this Act and of sections 21 to 24 above.

(2) Subject to subsections (3) and (4) below—

(a) personal data held by an unincorporated members' club and relating only to the members of the club; and

(b) personal data held by a data user only for the purpose of distributing, or recording the distribution of, articles or information to the data subjects and consisting only of their names, addresses or other particulars necessary for effecting the distribution,

are exempt from the provisions of Part II of this Act and of sections 21 to 24 above.

(3) Neither paragraph *(a)* nor paragraph *(b)* of subsection (2) above applies to personal data relating to any data subject unless he has been asked by the club or data user whether he objects to the data relating to him being held as mentioned in that paragraph and has not objected.

(4) It shall be a condition of the exemption of any data under paragraph *(b)* of subsection (2) above that the data are not used for any purpose other than that for which they are held and of the exemption of any data under either paragraph of that subsection that the data are not disclosed except as permitted by subsection (5) below; but the first exemption shall not be lost by any use, and neither exemption shall be lost by any disclosure, in breach of that condition if the data user shows that he had taken such care to prevent it as in all the circumstances was reasonably required.

(5) Data to which subsection (4) above applies may be disclosed—
- *(a)* if the data subject (or a person acting on his behalf) has requested or consented to the disclosure of the data either generally or in the circumstances in which the disclosure in question is made;
- *(b)* if the person making the disclosure has reasonable grounds for believing that the disclosure falls within paragraph *(a)* above; or
- *(c)* in any case in which disclosure would be permitted by any other provision of this Part of this Act if subsection (4) above were included among the non-disclosure provisions.

(6) Personal data held only for—
- *(a)* preparing statistics; or
- *(b)* carrying out research,

are exempt from the subject access provisions; but it shall be a condition of that exemption that the data are not used or disclosed for any other purpose and that the resulting statistics or the results of the research are not made available in a form which identifies the data subjects or any of them.

It is clear that in subsection 1 there are two prerequisites of personal data being exempt from the provisions of PART II and Sections 21 to 24 of PART III. First, the personal data must be held by an individual and, secondly, the personal data so held must be concerned only with that individual's personal, family or household affairs.

If an individual took home his business, professional or trade data which was personal data relating to individuals then there would be no exemption. Take the example of a personnel manager who, to keep up with his work and the times, takes home a wallet of floppy discs rather than a bulging briefcase. The floppies contain personnel records which he proceeds to analyse on his home computer. In this situation there would be no exemption.

Subsection 2 states that, subject to subsection 3, personal data held by an unincorporated members' club and relating only to members of the club (e.g. membership lists of names, telephone numbers, etc.) and personal data held by the data user solely for the purpose of distributing or recording the distribution of articles to the data subjects and consisting only of their names and addresses, are exempt from PART II and Sections 21 to 24 of PART III.

Subsection 3 provides a safeguard to the data subject in that he or she must be asked whether there is any objection to the data being held. The subsection is badly drafted because, whilst it is provided that the data subject can be asked whether he has any objection to the data being held, no provision is made as to what should occur in the event of the data subject indeed having an objection.

Subsection 4 provides that, in order to be exempt as personal data held only to distribute or record the distribution of articles of data subjects and consisting only of their names and addresses, the data must not be used for any purpose other than that for which they are held. Subsection 4 further provides that as to paragraphs (a) and (b) of subsection 2 it shall be a condition of exemption that the data are not disclosed except or permitted by subsection 5. It is further provided that the exemptions provided by subsection 2 shall not be lost in the case of subsection 2 (a) by use and/or disclosure, and in the case of subsection 2 (b) by disclosure, even in the event of the previous provision of subsection 4 being breached *if* the data user shows that he had taken reasonable care in the circumstances to prevent the use and/or disclosure.

Subsection 5 states that data may be disclosed if that disclosure has been consented to or requested by the data subject or there has been a general comment or request; or if the person making the disclosure had reasonable grounds for believing the disclosure had been so requested or consented to; or in the instance in which disclosure would be allowed by any other provision of PART IV of the Act if subsection 4 was included among the non-disclosure provisions. Here, basically, the provision as to disclosure for national security under Section 27 or for the prevention of or detection of crime or the assessment or collection of tax under Section 28 in an appropriate case, are being referred to, together with the other exemptions dealt with in the Act.

Subsection 6 provides that personal data held only for, firstly, preparing statistics or, secondly, carrying out research is exempt from subject access provisions. However, the safeguard is that such data is not to be disclosed for a purpose other than for preparing statistics or carrying out the research. Further, the resulting statistics or research must not identify the data subject in question. However, there is an apparent loophole in that the Act does not provide any protection in the event of disclosure made by the data user for the sole purpose of the research which the person to whom the data was disclosed then chooses to make known elsewhere. Thus the third party is not dealt with, and in our view this is a serious omission.

Section 34   Other exemptions

34.–(1) Personal data held by any person are exempt from the provisions of Part II of this Act and of sections 21 to 24 above if the data consist of information which that person is required by or under any enactment to make available to the public, whether by publishing it, making it available for inspection or otherwise and whether gratuitously or on payment of a fee.

(2) The Secretary of State may by order exempt from the subject access provisions personal data consisting of information the disclosure of which is prohibited or restricted by or under any enactment if he considers that the prohibition or restriction ought to prevail over those provisions in the

interests of the data subject or of any other individual.

(3) Where all the personal data relating to a data subject held by a data user (or all such data in respect of which a data user has a separate entry in the register) consist of information in respect of which the data subject is entitled to make a request to the data user under section 158 of the Consumer Credit Act 1974 (files of credit reference agencies)—

    (a) the data are exempt from the subject access provisions; and

    (b) any request in respect of the data under section 21 above shall be treated for all purpose as if it were a request under the said section 158.

(4) Personal data are exempt from the subject access provisions if the data are kept only for the purpose of replacing other data in the event of the latter being lost, destroyed or impaired.

(5) Personal data are exempt from the non-disclosure provisions in any case in which the disclosure is—

    (a) required by or under any enactment, by any rule of law or by the order of a court; or

    (b) made for the purposes of obtaining legal advice or for the purposes of, or in the course of, legal proceedings in which the person making the disclosure is a party or witness.

(6) Personal data are exempt from the non-disclosure provisions in any case in which—

    (a) the disclosure is to the data subject or a person acting on his behalf; or

    (b) the data subject or any such person has requested or consented to the particular disclosure in question; or

    (c) the disclosure is by a data user or a person carrying on a computer bureau to his servant or agent for the purpose of enabling the servant or agent to perform his functions as such; or

    (d) the person making the disclosure has reasonable grounds for believing that the disclosure falls within any of the foregoing paragraphs of this subsection.

(7) Section 4(3)*(d)* above does not apply to any disclosure falling within paragraph *(a)*, *(b)* or *(c)* of subsection (6) above; and that subsection shall apply to the restriction on disclosure in section 33 (6) above as it applies to the non-disclosure provisions.

(8) Personal data are exempt from the non-disclosure provisions in any case in which the disclosure is urgently required for preventing injury or other damage to the health of any person or persons; and in proceedings against any person for contravening a provision mentioned in section 26(3)*(a)* above

it shall be a defence to prove that he had reasonable grounds for believing that the disclosure in question was urgently required for that purpose.

(9) A person need not comply with a notice, request or order under the subject access provisions if compliance would expose him to proceedings for any offence other than an offence under this Act; and information disclosed by any person in compliance with such a notice, request or order shall not be admissible against him in proceedings for an offence under this Act.

Subsection 1 requires no comment.

Subsection 2 states that the Secretary of State may exempt personal data from the subject access provisions in the event of their disclosure being prohibited or restricted by statute in the event that he considers that the prohibition or restriction ought to prevail over the subject access provisions. Clearly, the Secretary of State is given broad power under subsection 2 to override by Order the generality that the subject access provisions shall take precedence over any other contrary enactment prohibiting or restricting disclosure. The importance of this power is such that it is placed in the Secretary of State's hands rather than those of the Registrar. Furthermore, any Order of the Secretary of State must be approved in draft form by a resolution of both Houses of Parliament. (See Section 40 subsection 4.)

Subsection 3 recognises that it would be otiose to have two statutes requiring disclosure of the same class of information, and recognises that, under Section 158 of the Consumer Credit Act 1974, files of credit reference agencies may be called for. In that respect the 1974 Act should continue to operate without being supplemented by the Data Protection Act. It is interesting to note that at subsection 3(b), in the event of a member of the public making a request in respect of data under Section 21, such a request should be treated for all purposes as if it were a request under Section 158 of the Consumer Credit Act 1974. This is a useful provision in preventing a member of the public being defeated by a technical mistake in requesting data under the wrong enactment.

Subsection 4 provides that "back-up" data retained only to replace other existing data in the event of the same being lost or destroyed are exempt from the subject access provisions of the Act.

Subsection 5 states that personal data are exempt from the non-disclosure provisions in the event of disclosure being required by or under any enactment or by an order of a court or made for the purpose of obtaining legal advice or for the purposes of or in the course of legal proceedings where the person making the disclosure is a party or a witness. We note that the "court" is not defined, although earlier at Section 25, it is stated that the jurisdiction conferred by Sections 21 and 24 is exercisable by the High Court or a County Court. In our view, it is probable that the exemption from non-disclosure provisions in the event of disclosure being required by or under any enactment or by an order of a court would probably include any Order of the European Court of Justice, and possibly also the European Court of Human Rights.

The word "witness" at subsection 5 (b) is not defined. We take the view that this may mean "potential witness" since technically a person is not a witness in legal proceedings unless called to give evidence on oath or that person has sworn an affidavit or prepared a Statutory Declaration filed and served in the proceedings. We take the view that a lack of proper definition here is liable to cause confusion and litigation.

Subsection 6 provides four instances at paragraphs (a), (b), (c) and (d) of personal data being exempt from the non-disclosure provisions. Subsection 6 (a) deals with disclosure to the data subject or to a person acting on his behalf (e.g. his solicitor or accountant). Subsection 6 (b) deals with the situation of a data subject or any such person acting on his behalf requesting or consenting to the particular disclosure in question. We consider this would include a general authority for disclosure to take place. Thus it would seem that the non-disclosure provisions can be waived specifically in particular cases, or generally. It is possible that in certain cases an employer might seek contractually to bind an employee to "contract out" of the non-disclosure provisions. Subsection 6 (c) provides for disclosure to a servant or agent of the data user or of a person carrying on a computer bureau to enable that servant or agent to carry out his functions as such. Subsection 6 (d) provides exemption where the person making the disclosure has "reasonable grounds" for believing the disclosure falls within paragraphs (a), (b) or (c) as referred to above. It appears to us that the presence of "reasonable grounds" is an objective test to be determined by the Courts, the Registrar or the Tribunal as the case may be.

Subsection 7 provides that the requirement of an entry in the Register of a description of any person or persons to whom the data user intends or may wish to disclose data (see Section 4 subsection 3 (d)) shall not apply to subsection 6 (a), (b) or (c); and that subsection 6 shall apply not only to the non-disclosure provisions as a basis for exemption, but also to Section 33 subsection 6 dealing with the restrictions on disclosure of personal data held only for preparing statistics and carrying out research.

Subsection 8 requires no comment.

Subsection 9 gives statutory force to what may be called the privilege against self-incrimination. Further, subsection 9 states that information disclosed by any person in compliance with a notice, request or order under the subject access provisions shall be inadmissible against him in proceedings for an offence under the Act. The courts are given no discretion to allow such evidence to be tendered in proceedings for an offence, and neither is the Registrar, nor the Secretary of State.

Section 35   Examination marks

35.–(1) Section 21 above shall have effect subject to the provisions of this section in the case of personal data consisting of marks or other information held by a data user–
  (a) for the purpose of determining the results of an academic, professional or other examination or of enabling the results of any such examination to be determined; or
  (b) in consequence of the determination of any such results.
(2) Where the period mentioned in subsection (6) of section 21 begins before the results of the examination are announced that period shall be extended until–

(a) the end of five months from the beginning of that period;
or
(b) the end of forty days after the date of the announcement, whichever is the earlier.

(3) Where by virtue of subsection (2) above a request is complied with more than forty days after the beginning of the period mentioned in subsection (6) of section 21, the information to be supplied pursuant to the request shall be supplied both by reference to the data in question at the time when the request is received and (if different) by reference to the data as from time to time held in the period beginning when the request is received and ending when it is complied with.

(4) For the purposes of this section the results of an examination shall be treated as announced when they are first published or (if not published) when they are first made available or communicated to the candidate in question.

(5) In this section "examination" includes any process for determining the knowledge, intelligence, skill or ability of a candidate by reference to his performance in any test, work or other activity.

Section 35 concerns itself with examination marks whereby the rights of data subjects under Section 21 of the Act have effect subject to the provision of this section. The personal data in question are provided at subsection 1 to consist of marks or other information held by the data user either to determine results of academic, professional or other examinations or to enable such results to be determined or held by reason of the determination of such results.

Subsection 2 provides that the 40 day time limit for compliance with a request supported by proper information, as provided for in Section 21, shall be extended, in the event of the period in question commencing before the announcement of the examination results, until the end of five months from the beginning of that period or the end of 40 days after the announcement (whichever is the earlier).

Subsection 3 deals with the situation of information being supplied outside the normal 40 day time limit. In such a case the information must be given by reference to the date of the request being made *and* by reference to the data held throughout the period until compliance takes place. This takes into account the fact that data may significantly alter during the course of such a period.

Subsections 4 and 5 require no comment.

PART V GENERAL
Section 36 General duties of the Registrar

36.–(1) It shall be the duty of the Registrar so to perform his functions under this Act as to promote the observance of the data protection principles by data users and persons carrying on computer bureaux.
(2) The Registrar may consider any complaint that any of the data protection principles or any provision of this Act has been or is being contravened and shall do so if the complaint appears to him to raise a matter of substance and to have been made without undue delay by a person directly affected; and where the Registrar considers any such complaint he shall notify the complainant of the result of his consideration and of any action which he proposes to take.
(3) The Registrar shall arrange for the dissemination in such form and manner as he considers appropriate of such information as it may appear to him expedient to give to the public about the operation of this Act and other matters within the scope of his functions under this Act and may give advice to any person as to any of those matters.
(4) It shall be the duty of the Registrar, where he considers it appropriate to do so, to encourage trade associations or other bodies representing data users to prepare, and to disseminate to their members, codes of practice for guidance in complying with the data protection principles.
(5) The Registrar shall annually lay before each House of Parliament a general report on the performance of his functions under this Act and may from time to time lay before each House of Parliament such other reports wiith respect to those functions as he thinks fit.

Subsection 1 provides a general and overriding duty of the Registrar to perform his functions under the Act in such a way as to promote the observance of the data protection principles by data users and persons carrying on computer bureaux. Clearly, this is a difficult duty to analyse and probably hard to enforce. However, in a case where the evidence is exceedingly clear that the Registrar has failed so to perform his functions, we take the view that the duty, being a statutory duty, will be enforceable by the courts in England and Wales and in Scotland. The appropriate venue is likely to be the High Court, Queen's Bench Division, Divisional Court, where the appropriate order would be an order of judicial review, being an order of Mandamus obliging the Registrar to perform his functions in accordance with Section 36.

Subsection 2 provides that the Registrar *may* consider any complaint that any data protection principle or provision of the Act has been broken or is being breached and *shall* do so if it appears to him to raise a matter of substance and to have been made without undue delay by a person directly affected (normally the data subject). In the event that the Registrar considers a complaint he must notify the complainant of the result of his consideration and of any action he proposes to take. We note that there is no provision for the Registrar to give reasons for not considering a complaint or for the result of any consideration or for the action he proposes to take or indeed for deciding to take no action.

Subsection 3 provides that the Registrar shall arrange for the public to be kept informed of the operation of the Act as he considers appropriate. Included within subsection 3 is a discretion for the Registrar, enabling him to give advice to any person on any matters within the scope of his functions under the Act.

Subsection 4 provides for the Registrar to encourage trade associations or other bodies representing data users to prepare and disseminate to their members codes of practice for complying with the data protection principles. The Registrar shall encourage such trade associations or other bodies where he considers it appropriate to do so. We find it difficult to perceive what form this encouragement might take. There are no provisions for Codes of Practice to be approved, but it may be that the Registrar would choose to do so to provide a "guide only" for data users in particular industries or professions. In that event, there would be real encouragement to produce an effective code of practice since data users would be far less likely to receive an enforcement notice or other proceedings if compliance with a code of practice could be shown – especially if such a code of practice had been brought into being by reason of encouragement from the Registrar. Compliance with a proper code of practice might also provide the basis for a defence to notices or proceedings served under the Act in an appropriate case.

We consider that it would be worthwhile for the Registrar's office to be able to provide general advice to members of the public and for easy-to-read booklets to be produced and made available. We hope this is what is intended by subsection 3.

Subsection 5 requires no comment.

Section 37   Co-operation between parties to the Convention

37. The Registrar shall be the designated authority in the United Kingdom for the purposes of Article 13 of the European Convention; and the Secretary of State may by order make provision as to the functions to be discharged by the Registrar in that capacity.

Section 37 requires no comment.

Section 38   Application to government departments and police

38.–(1) Except as provided in subsection (2) below, a government department shall be subject to the same obligations and liabilities under this Act as a private person; and for the purposes of this Act each government department shall be treated as a person separate from any other government department and a person in the public service of the Crown shall be treated as a servant of the government department to which his responsibilities or duties relate.
(2) A government department shall not be liable to prosecution under this Act but–
   (a) sections 5(3) and 15(2) above (and, so far as relating to those provisions, sections 5(5) and 15(3) above) shall apply to any person who by virtue of this section falls to be treated as a servant of the government department in question; and
   (b) section 6(6) above and paragraph 12 of Schedule 4 to this Act shall apply to a person in the public service of the Crown as they apply to any other person.
(3) For the purposes of this Act–
   (a) the constables under the direction and control of a chief officer of police shall be treated as his servants; and
   (b) the members of any body of constables maintained otherwise than by a police authority shall be treated as the servants–
      (i) of the authority or person by whom that body is maintained, and

(ii) in the case of any members of such a body who are under the direction and control of a chief officer, of that officer.

(4) In the application of subsection (3) above to Scotland, for the reference to a chief officer of police there shall be substituted a reference to a chief constable.

(5) In the application of subsection (3) above to Northern Ireland, for the reference to a chief officer of police there shall be substituted a reference to the Chief Constable of the Royal Ulster Constabulary and for the reference to a police authority there shall be substituted a reference to the Police Authority for Northern Ireland.

Subsection 1 states that, except as provided by subsection 2, a government department will have the same obligations and liabilities as a private person. In addition, each government department is to be treated separately. The term "government department" is included under Section 39 (General Interpretation), which states that the term "includes a Northern Ireland department and any body or authority exercising statutory functions on behalf of the Crown". We note in particular the use of the word "includes", which in itself leads to the conclusion that what follows is not meant to be an exhaustive definition of the term "government department". We take the view that it is unlikely that "government department" includes departments within local authorities, save insofar as those local authorities exercise statutory functions on behalf of the Crown.

Subsection 2 provides that a government department will be immune from prosecution under the Act, but goes on to provide that certain provisions will nonetheless apply to those departments. In particular, Section 5(2)(c), (d) and (e) apply to any servant of a government department whereby that servant will not obtain personal data or extract information represented by such data from any source not described in the registered entry, will not disclose any personal data to any person who is not described in the registered entry, and will not directly or indirectly transfer personal data to any country or territory outside the UK other than one named or described in the registered entry. Clearly, then, registration under the Act is required in respect of government departments as in respect of any other data user or computer bureau, and the enforcement provisions will apply to government departments with equal vigour, except that a government department will not be liable to criminal prosecution.

However, in respect of any person in the public service of the Crown, Section 6(6) and paragraph 12 of Schedule 4 apply, as they do in respect of any other person. Thus, if a person in the public service of the Crown in connection with an application for registration or for the alteration of registered particulars knowingly or recklessly provides the Registrar with information which is false or misleading in a material respect, he will be guilty of an offence. Further, such a person who intentionally obstructs a person in the execution of a warrant issued under Schedule 4, or who fails without reasonable excuse to give a person executing such a warrant such assistance as he may reasonably require for the execution of the warrant, will be guilty of an offence, as in the case of any other person.

Subsection 3 requires no comment.

Section 39 Data held, and services provided, outside the United Kingdom

39.–(1) Subject to the following provisions of this section, this Act does not apply to a data user in respect of data held, or to a person carrying on a computer bureau in respect of services provided, outside the United Kingdom.
(2) For the purposes of subsection (1) above—
  (a) data shall be treated as held where the data user exercises the control referred to in subsection (5)*(b)* of section 1 above in relation to the data; and
  (b) services shall be treated as provided where the person carrying on the computer bureau does any of the things referred to in subsection (6)*(a)* or *(b)* of that section.
(3) Where a person who is not resident in the United Kingdom—
  (a) exercises the control mentioned in paragraph *(a)* of subsection (2) above; or
  (b) does any of the things mentioned in paragraph *(b)* of that subsection.
through a servant or agent in the United Kingdom, this Act shall apply as if that control were exercised or, as the case may be, those things were done in the United Kingdom by the

servant or agent acting on his own account and not on behalf of the person whose servant or agent he is.

(4) Where by virtue of subsection (3) above a servant or agent is treated as a data user or as a person carrying on a computer bureau he may be described for the purposes of registration by the position or office which he holds; and any such description in an entry in the register shall be treated as applying to the person for the time being holding the position or office in question.

(5) This Act does not apply to data processed wholly outside the United Kingdom unless the data are used or intended to be used in the United Kingdom.

(6) Sections 4(3)*(e)* and 5(2)*(e)* and subsection (1) of section 12 above do not apply to the transfer of data which are already outside the United Kingdom; but references in the said section 12 to a contravention of the data protection principles include references to anything that would constitute such contravention if it occurred in relation to the data when held in the United Kingdom.

Subsection 1 provides that, subject to the provisions of Section 39, the Act does not, in general, apply to a data user in respect of data held or to a person carrying on a computer bureau in respect of services provided outside the UK. Clearly, one may have the situation of a data user based in the UK holding data outside the UK, and it would appear from the wording of Section 39, subsection 1, that a computer bureau might be carried on in the UK to provide services solely outside the UK, although the latter example is probably extreme and not contemplated by the draftsmen of the statute.

Subsection 2 defines the term "held" for the purposes of subsection 1 by cross-reference to subsection 5(b) of Section 1, which states that data are held by a person either alone or jointly, or in common with others, where that person controls the contents and use of the data comprising the collection. Further, in subsection 2(b) the term "services" is defined as being "provided" where the person carrying on the computer bureau does anything referred to in Section 1, subsection 6(a) or (b).

Section 40 Regulations, rules and orders

40.–(1) Any power conferred by this Act to make regulations, rules or orders shall be exercisable by statutory instrument.
(2) Without prejudice to sections 2(6) and 29(3) above, regulations, rules or orders under this Act may make different provision for different cases or circumstances.
(3) Before making an order under any of the foregoing provisions of this Act the Secretary of State shall consult the Registrar.
(4) No order shall be made under section 2(3), 4(8), 29, 30 or 34(2) above unless a draft of the order has been laid before and approved by a resolution of each House of Parliament.
(5) A statutory instrument containing an order under section 21(9) or 37 above or rules under paragraph 4 of Schedule 3 to this Act shall be subject to annulment in pursuance of a resolution of either House of Parliament.
(6) Regulations prescribing fees for the purposes of any provision of this Act or the period mentioned in section 8(2) above shall be laid before Parliament after being made.
(7) Regulations prescribing fees payable to the Registrar under this Act or the period mentioned in section 8(2) above shall be made after consultation with the Registrar and with the approval of the Treasury; and in making any such regulations the Secretary of State shall have regard to the desirability of securing that those fees are sufficient to offset the expenses incurred by the Registrar and the Tribunal in discharging their functions under this Act and any expenses of the Secretary of State in respect of the Tribunal.

Section 40 requires no comment.

Section 41 General interpretation

41. In addition to the provisions of sections 1 and 2 above, the following provisions shall have effect for the interpretation of this Act—
    "business" includes any trade or profession;
    "data equipment" means equipment for the automatic processing of data or for recording information so that it can be automatically processed;
    "data material" means any document or other material used in connection with data equipment;
    "a de-registration notice" means a notice under section 11 above;
    "enactment" includes an enactment passed after this Act;

"an enforcement notice" means a notice under section 10 above;

"the European Convention" means the Convention for the Protection of Individuals with regard to Automatic Processing of Personal Data which was opened for signature on 28th January 1981;

"government department" includes a Northern Ireland department and any body or authority exercising statutory functions on behalf of the Crown;

"prescribed" means prescribed by regulations made by the Secretary of State;

"the Registrar" means the Data Protection Registrar;

"the register", except where the reference is to the register of companies, means the register maintained under section 4 above and (except where the reference is to a registered company, to the registered office of a company or to registered post) references to registration shall be construed accordingly;

"registered company" means a company registered under the enactments relating to companies for the time being in force in any part of the United Kingdom;

"a transfer prohibition notice" means a notice under section 12 above;

"the Tribunal" means the Data Protection Tribunal.

Section 41 requires no comment.

Section 42   Commencement and transitional provisions

42.–(1) No application for registration shall be made until such day as the Secretary of State may by order appoint, and sections 5 and 15 above shall not apply until the end of the period of six months beginning with that day.

(2) Until the end of the period of two years beginning with the day appointed under subsection (1) above the Registrar shall not have power–

(a) to refuse an application made in accordance with section 6 above except on the ground mentioned in section 7(2)(a) above; or

(b) to serve an enforcement notice imposing requirements to be complied with, a de-registration notice expiring, or a transfer prohibition notice imposing a prohibition taking effect, before the end of that period.

(3) Where the Registrar proposes to serve any person with an enforcement notice before the end of the period mentioned in subsection (2) above he shall, in determining the time by which the requirements of the notice are to be complied with,

have regard to the probable cost to that person of complying with those requirements.

(4) Section 21 above and paragraph 1*(b)* of Schedule 4 to this Act shall not apply until the end of the period mentioned in subsection (2) above.

(5) Section 22 above shall not apply to damage suffered before the end of the period mentioned in subsection (1) above, and in deciding whether to refuse an application or serve a notice under Part II of this Act the Registrar shall treat the provision about accuracy in the fifth data protection principle as inapplicable until the end of that period and as inapplicable thereafter to data shown to have been held by the data user in question since before the end of that period.

(6) Sections 23 and 24(3) above shall not apply to damage suffered before the end of the period of two months beginning with the date on which this Act is passed.

(7) Sections 24(1) and (2) above shall not apply before the end of the period mentioned in subsection (1) above.

Subsection 1 provides a six-month period before Sections 5 and 15 have application, being six months after the appointed day.

Subsection 2 provides that the Registrar cannot over a period of two years, commencing with the appointed day, either refuse an application for registration or for amendment of registered particulars made under Section 6, except by reason of Section 7, subsection 2(a) (i.e., insufficient information), or serve an enforcement notice or de-registration notice or transfer prohibition notice, in the event of any of these notices having effect before the end of the two-year period. It is clear that such notices may be served before the end of the two-year period but with effect from and after the end of the two-year period on the basis of any of the data protection principles having been breached or being breached by a registered person. A warrant will be issued. However, notices may be served from the end of the two-year period on the basis of such past or present breach of the data protection principles (if the judge dealing with the matter is satisfied that these are reasonable grounds to suspect such a breach).

Subsection 3 makes provision for the Registrar in proposing to serve an enforcement notice before the end of the two-year period, to have regard to the cost of compliance in determining the time for compliance with the requirements. Here the Act takes notice of the large sums of money which may often be required to cope with the Act's provisions and that such money may only be available over an extended period of time. It is plainly not the intention of the Act to ruin businesses financially; nonetheless the Act must be complied with and a balance must be struck.

Subsection 4 is important in that the rights of access provisions under Section 21 will not apply until the end of the two-year period and that a warrant may not be issued.

Subsection 5 provides that the provisions in Section 22 as to compensation for inaccuracy will not apply to damage sustained before the end of the six-month period or to damage sustained thereafter insofar as that is caused by data held prior to the end of the six-month period. Further, it is provided that the inaccuracy of data held until the end of the six-month period is irrelevant to the Registrar's decisions as to whether to refuse an application for registration or alteration of registered particulars or to serve a notice (enforcement etc.). However, we would point out that the other data protection principles remain relevant in respect of such previously held data (such as the first data protection principle as to such data being obtained and processed fairly and lawfully).

Subsection 6 states that Sections 23 and 24, subsection 3 (relating to compensation for loss or disclosure and/or erasure), will not apply in respect of damage sustained before the end of a two-month period commencing with the date of the Act being passed.

Subsection 7 provides that Section 24, subsections 1 and 2, will not apply until the end of the six-month period and will not relate to data held prior to the end of that period.

Section 43 Short title and extent

43.—(1) This Act may be cited as the Data Protection Act 1984.
(2) This Act extends to Northern Ireland.
(3) Her Majesty may by Order in Council direct that this Act shall extend to any of the Channel Islands with such exceptions and modifications as may be specified in the Order.

Section 43 requires no comment.

PART III
AFTER THE ACT

Chapter 4
The Implications of the Act for Managers and Professionals

In this chapter we discuss from different viewpoints what we believe could be the effects of the Act. To start, we explain "access" and "access control" and the role of audits, then we help the lawyer to understand data protection in terms of computing and managerial issues; help senior staff, managers and specialists to appreciate the significance of the Act so far as fields of interest and managerial purviews are concerned; and help the computer professional to understand the relevant legal and managerial issues, and show him the need to adhere to high professional standards and how he might achieve them. We also try to help a discerning hobbyist or domestic computer user involved with personal data.

Lawyers practising in data protection will need a thorough understanding of each section; Chapter 3 is intended to assist in this understanding. Additionally, the lawyer should, ideally, understand certain facts about computers; some we give in this chapter and Appendix 2. Senior executives and professionals in general are likely to be affected by the consequential liability expressed in Section 20. They will thus need to understand the principles upon which the Act is based, and appreciate the importance of the security procedures described in the next chapter and how they need to relate to a corporate information policy. In addition, all non-legal professionals will benefit from an understanding of the relation between law and the computer, which we describe in this chapter and in Appendix 1. The domestic user (or hobbyist) needs to appreciate the full dimension of the problem he might encounter if he indulges in the practice of processing and storing personal data.

Access

A key issue in the Act is the right of a data subject to have access to data held on him by a data user. Access is mentioned in Section 21 and in other sections of the Act. We need to examine "access" in some depth because, in the context of data protection, it relates directly to the computer system on which the data are held and the environment in which the data user performs.

The term "rights of access" is easy enough to understand in the context of the Act. Difficulties lie in the technical achievement, bearing in mind the present state of development of much computer hardware and software.

In plain English, a data subject believing that there are certain facts about him held by a data user is legally entitled, after verification that such facts are held, to ascertain their accuracy and whether they are up to date. A data subject who has ascertained that such data are held on him is legally entitled to see them and, if necessary, to have them corrected and brought up to date.

A reverse situation is that the data subject is entitled to legal redress if the facts about him are accessed by someone other than the appropriate data user. Both situations have conditions and caveats attached, but in essence the above serves to define two properties – the right of access of a data subject and the denial of access to all other than the appropriate data user.

In everyday life it is a common enough act on the part of most individuals to wish to leave on display objects they do not mind others having access to. Conversely, most individuals have some objects which they keep under lock and key, thereby denying access to others. A commonplace happening, however, is burglary, where a third party obtains unauthorised access to objects.

The object may be a document such as a letter which would need to be read by eye by the individual with access. If the access is authorised, the document could be replaced or the owner might give permission for it to be copied or taken away. With unauthorised access the burglar has to make a decision – to take the original thereby leaving evidence in that the original will have vanished, or (most likely, in the case of a spy) to make a copy, leaving the original intact and no discernible evidence of the copying process.

Three more aspects of access are relevant to our purpose. One is the case where there is a hierarchy with some individuals allowed access to objects by others in the hierarchy who own the objects. The former are given discretionary access by the latter. A second concerns an object such as a letter when the owner may exercise discretion and allow another individual to read it. After, say, a minute the owner may exercise discretion, change his mind, and take back the letter, thereby denying further access. The third concerns the case where a member of a hierarchy, say individual A, imposes on others in the hierarchy non-discretionary modes which, in effect, remove from individual B the right to exercise discretion in granting to individual C access to an object owned by B. Thus A tells B that whilst he, B, can read his own letter, he cannot give C permission to read it.

There is a variant: A tells B that he, B, cannot allow C to read a letter which is deposited with B for safe-keeping, about Jones' sexual life, but he can allow C to read a letter, similarly deposited with B, about a sack of potatoes – a policy defining access. It follows, of course, that B will keep Jones' letter in a separate file from the one on potatoes.

Summarising the above, we have described the following:

(*a*) authorised access to objects,
(*b*) unauthorised access to objects,
(*c*) copying of an object,
(*d*) a hierarchy of individuals with a common interest in access,

(e) discretionary access,
(f) non-discretionary access,
(g) an individual with both discretionary and non-discretionary forms of access, and
(h) an access policy.

Hierarchies

The access rights of data subjects and data users are, we believe, fundamental to successful implementation of the Act, and in what follows we first place the data protection principles and sections of the Act in the context of a theoretical hierarchy. Matters are then discussed, by implication, in terms appropriate to executive, legal, managerial and professional roles.

Hierarchies will necesssarily differ between organisations. The one shown in Figure 4.1 is purely an example. It is not to be taken as a format for all organisations, neither do we imply that all the levels shown either do or should exist in all organisations. Clearly, larger organisations will have more corresponding levels than smaller ones. The order, too, may differ: for example, in certain cases the financial level (level 4) may be higher than that of legal executive (level 3); operations management (level 10) may be higher than systems development (level 9); the role of information executive (level 5) may not exist or the function may be known by another term, such as management support. A domestic or small business user may well attempt to combine roles.

The extent to which an organisation has had a sense of responsibility so far as data processing in general is concerned, and the adequacy of its existing control procedures, are likely to determine the immediate effect of the Act. Where in the past such matters have been taken seriously, high professional standards are applied, and the progress of the Bill through Parliament followed assiduously, then problems are likely to be confined to the technical aspects of access control discussed in Chapter 5. Where an organisation has not acted as described, difficulties may well be

Level	Function	Abbreviation
1	Board	B
2	Senior management	SM
3	Solicitor and legal executive	LE
4	Financial	FM
	Auditing	AD
5	Information policy	IP
	Personnel	PM
	Marketing and sales	MS
	Public relations	PR
6	Risk assessment	RA
7	Data control	DC
8	Security	SE
9	Systems development	SD
10	Operations management	OM

Note: Hierarchies will necessarily differ. Finance in certain cases will be at a level above legal executive; operations management above systems development. Figure 4.1 is not meant to be taken as a format for all organisations but rather to show that some attention needs to be paid to relative levels as part of information, access and security policies.

Figure 4.1
An example of an organisational hierarchy appropriate for data protection in a large organisation

encountered. This chapter is intended to be of help in those cases.

Although we believe that many organisations should restructure to protect the interests of data subjects and their own positions as data users, we recognise that such change may be unacceptable or thought to be too expensive. Value judgement will be necessary; in essence the issue becomes one of asset value, but assets of a different nature from conventional assets and with special problems arising from the fact that the assets are computer-based data.

Whilst such assets have many of the properties of conventional assets, one different feature is that inaccurate data (see Chapter 2) may well render a data user liable to prosecution. For example, an organisation may have personal data, perhaps of unknown source, of dubious accuracy. Further, there may be no remaining knowledge as to how many "copies" of the data are held and their specific locations. The cost of compliance with Section 21 subsection 1 may well be prohibitive. A situation could apply where a data subject, now with rights of access, obtains such access to the dubious data. The data user would have great difficulty in complying with Section 22 and principle 5 because, for example, of locating all versions of data in the computer file system (see Appendix 2).

We have already shown that data are representative of information. All organisations depend on information to conduct their business (which will include personal data) and cannot survive for long if information becomes corrupted, distorted, stolen, lost, loses its timeliness and so on. Computers have already had and are still having a profound effect on information; the combination of computer and information is, of course, "information technology", of which data protection is a part. We believe that the corporate information executive, level 5 in Figure 4.1, could assume responsibility for what used to be termed data-processing activities as part of "corporate information", which will include all an organisation's data. Information executives should be close to, if not part of, the corporate strategic centre because a fine balance will need to be struck between corporate assessments of all categories of data, their sensitivities, who should have authorised access to data and, more importantly and more difficult to enforce, who within an organisation, should be prevented from having access or given conditional access. The structure of Figure 4.1 is a basis of an access control policy developed further in Chapter 5 in the context of a security policy. Depending on an organisation's business, personal data will appear to a greater or lesser extent. For example, it will be prominent where life insurance mass marketing and debt collection are major purposes. At the other extreme, an organisation may hold only personal data on its own employees.

We do not believe there is a set of general solutions to problems; each organisation, large and small, will need to study each issue and their interrelations in terms of relevant sections of the Act. Here we draw attention to the need and suggest ways in which the right questions can be formulated;

policies will need to be defined and people found to assume specific responsibilities of the kind shown in Figure 4.1. Section 20 of the Act lists specific corporate positions; managerial responsibilities will need to be correspondingly defined. It could be appropriate to have, for example, a data controller, responsible for each clearly definable category of data, reporting to an information executive who should in turn be in a position to contribute to corporate information policy. The beginnings of a hierarchy for data protection emerge. The checklists (pp.172-8) develop this approach.

The Need for Inspection or Audits

The need for change is illustrated by an argument we make for the use of independent inspections or "data protection audits", although it must be made clear that there is no UK statutory requirement for such audits. They are not, for example, a part of the Act. We believe, however, that such audits would be wholly beneficial to both data subject and data user, and will reasonably ensure compliance with the Act. It is for this reason we continue as though they are an evidential requirement.

The situation we have in mind is one where an organisation could have a "data protection" audit carried out on, say, an annual basis, enabling such an organisation (assuming it passes an audit) to demonstrate publicly that it has survived an "effective and visible inspection activity" (to quote part of a CEC inspection clause[1]). We make the assumption that the Act's requirements can only be met in letter and spirit and attract public confidence (and the confidence of the business community outside the UK) if the effectiveness of the principles on which the legislation is based is manifest on a regular basis. The only point at issue, then, is that of determining who, in a professional sense, should carry out the "audit". The functional term "auditing" in Figure 4.1 (level 4 in the hierarchy) is loosely connected with this activity, although it can be taken to combine conventional auditing and accounting.

Data Protection Audits – Who Might Do Them?

In 1982 a joint report[2] by Deloitte, Haskins and Sells (DHS – an organisation with an established reputation over many years for carrying out financial audits of clients with computer-based systems), and the National Computing Centre (NCC – an organisation representing a large cross-section of computer users) argued the case for financial auditors as described above also to carry out data protection audits along with their statutory financial duties. It is worth considering the report and proposals in some detail.

The report first describes thirteen data protection principles which are an amalgam of the OECD Guidelines (see Chapter 1), the CoE Convention[3] and Younger[4] inspection procedures. These are discussed and a definition given of certain minimum skills required by an "inspector".

The DHS–NCC report goes on to discuss the possible conflicts which might arise between an auditor and his client when there is a difference of opinion leading to a "qualified" audit. The report, however, stops short of discussing the by no means improbable situation where a client might pass a conventional financial audit but fail a data protection audit. With different professional criteria applying but with one man acting as auditor, there could be an acute professional dilemma for client and auditor. Kelman and Sizer[5] show that in any case computer systems can present financial auditors with problems.

One broad objective of a financial audit is an examination of controls which have been incorporated in a system to ensure the reliability, accuracy and authenticity of computer processes as they relate to financial programs and data. The effectiveness of computer audit lies in the detection of control weaknesses. Hook[6] regarded the financial audit as a preventative rather than a detective mechanism. Some people, however, have already argued that data protection audits require a fundamentally different approach. Wilder[7], for example, points out that the strength of the case for data protection audits being carried out by financial auditors is not self-evident. Whilst the current UK interest is in the UK legislation, the protection of personal data in computer systems is an international problem; systems containing personal data, some crossing national boundaries, can reach a level of technical complexity which may well be beyond the range of the current professional interests and experiences of many financial auditors. Wilder cites as an example Project Universe – the linking together into one huge electronic system of 150 computers in various local area networks by means of a geostationary satellite.

He also poses a dilemma for the financial auditor thus. The DHS–NCC report states that inspection procedures "may involve the use of independent programs to access and review the data held on the computer files". In Wilder's hypothetical situation, the financial auditor's client could be guilty of the offence of "unauthorised disclosure" (see Section 2 subsection 2 and data protection principles 3 and 8 and see also Sections 17 and 23), for the auditors are unlikely to be named as authorised recipients and an audit may not always be a declared use (see Sections 10 and 11).

Summarising the foregoing, a data protection audit demands not only a specialised technical approach but also a need for an understanding of the legal requirements of, first, the other European countries concerned, then countries such as the USA and Australia. Coupling these with the need to understand the issues inherent in transborder data flow, distributed systems, the proliferation of cheap and powerful micro-systems, and the need for access controls by data users, underlines the importance of deciding who carries out a data protection audit. Wilder concludes that in the UK it should be a function of people with professional grade membership of the British Computer Society (BCS). The BCS has codes of conduct and practice which would apply to, say, certified "data inspectors"; disciplinary procedures support the codes. Such people would, in all probability, have another professional qualification as well.

We draw no conclusion as to which professional qualification and membership of professional body or bodies are best suited to carrying out data protection audits. We are, however, convinced that visible audit (inspection) procedures, carried out by independent professionally qualified people holding relevant professional qualifications in computing, are the best way of allaying public fears. Apart from protecting the interests of data subjects, proof of working to relevant standards and practices would serve a valuable commercial purpose world-wide in showing that the UK is dealing with data protection in a commendably professional manner. The checklists on pp.172-8 make clear that the processes in data protection audits will demand a knowledge of the underlying principles in the Act, for only in this way will those responsible as data users understand the subjective nature and context-related sensitivities of the data.

The Form a Data Protection Audit Could Take

A data protection audit would have a first level concerned wiith the data user's organisation, in line with our introductory remarks concerning business objectives, relationship within the organisation, with other companies and so on. There would be a need to determine the degree of awareness at senior management level of the aims and purposes of the Act itself and the Council of Europe Convention. If an organisation does business in the USA, then a knowledge of American legislation, case law and practice will be expected. The degree of managerial control will need to be established; professing knowledge of requirements is one thing, but ensuring that there is corporate conformity to standards and requirements is another thing altogether. Such conformity can best function effectively with information feedback.

The second stage in a data protection audit would concern the need for different data to be at different levels in line with a security policy. A number of categories may exist at each level. For example, data on employees may be at a higher level than data on competitors, customers and so on. Recalling that Section 2(3) of the Act deals with sensitive data, the audit should be aimed at revealing the corporate categories at a given level which allows certain people access to, say, religious beliefs of data subjects but not to, say, data subjects' racial or sexual lives. All such access "rights" must, of course, meet the Act's requirements. The audit cannot confirm that it is right to place certain data in a particular category as regards another, but it should be able to confirm that the possibly higher-rated level has, in fact, attracted a higher degree of awareness for security by the data user which is reflected in the security policy.

Risk analysis and risk management will play a part, so the different data categories and/or sensitivities need to be valued in an asset sense. A high data asset value will need to be ascribed to those data which are likely to attract attacks. All these aspects are covered in the next chapter.

An audit at the third stage would be concerned with the responsibilities of a specific data controller (level 7 in Figure 4.1) who would be responsible for managing activity concerned with data preparation, input, validation and amendment, and magnetic media. Other responsibilities might also include data communications, documentation, operating systems, operational procedures and contingency measures.

Data Protection and Information Technology (IT)

So far as data protection is concerned, information technology has four attributes which we regard as relevant to the "information" part of the term. These are (i) the transition from privacy to data protection; (ii) the proliferation of computer systems and the consequential high volume/low profit margin marketing scene; (iii) the evolution of "data processing systems" into "information systems"; and (iv) the disappearance of many of the large centralised data processing centres in favour of distributed processing either controlled (i.e. planned) or by a *laissez faire* process.

The influence of these four has often occurred simultaneously and has already had a considerable effect on some organisations. Of particular relevance to data protection matters has been the emergence of the information executive (level 5 in Figure 4.1). He was first identified by Rockart[8], who describes the new executive as seeing himself reporting at a "fairly high level" in an organisation, such as to the president or chief executive. Such an executive sees his role more as a general manager and less as a data-processing person, and he is well aware of his importance in controlling the information sources of the organisation, which would encompass, inevitably, those concerned with personal data. According to Rockart, such an executive appears to regard himself as a candidate for a top management position. He is highly motivated and has something of the evangelical spirit in bringing others to an awareness of the importance of the handling of information in organisations. It is likely that the new structure under such executives could consist of functions such as "data control level 7", "risk assessment level 6", "security level 8" and so on. These functions are concerned with the information aspect of IT.

The other part of IT is typified by the hardware now sold in such vast quantities. The visual display unit and keyboard should, it is maintained, be on everyone's desk. This means that the work patterns and modes of corporate behaviour of foremen, clerks, managers and chief executives are governed by the limits of keyboard interaction in such activities as process control, automated office environments, electronic mail and tele-conferencing respectively. Together these define the information systems environment.

In such environments the effects of the necessary extensive restructuring to adapt has, according to Nolan[9], had a significant effect on patterns of capital expenditure – a typical example given by Nolan is a capital spend on computing of $25,000,000 in 1970 and $90,000,000 in 1980. Whereas a "data processing manager" would have controlled the whole of the 1970 spend, he controlled only 60 per cent of the 1980 figure. In spite of this trend, which is repeated almost everywhere, with only the scale differing, Nolan's management survey reveals that many people and managements still operate as though the data-processing activity is centralised, whereas the reality is often quite different. An answer proposed by Nolan is that within an organisation the managing of the global information system should be by means of an executive steering committee. However, these do not exist yet in many cases, nor is even the need for them appreciated, so the handling of personal data takes place and will take place for some time in many instances where organisational procedures do not exist to satisfy even the first stage of a data protection audit.

A realistic scenario summing up the hazards in a data protection context is one concerning an office block shared by a number of independent, smallish companies such as a building society, an insurance broker, a travel agent and a mail order business. One floor of the block may be occupied by a computer bureau – a separate company – which provides a service to all the companies in the office block. The building will be wired for full communication facilities, providing terminal-based access points to the computer in all the offices of the separate companies. It is primarily the security features incorporated in the operating system of the computer and the security procedures enforced elsewhere which prevent staff of the building society, say, from deliberately or inadvertently accessing the insurance broker's files and *vice versa*. The level of risk to data subjects and data users alike is clearly very high.

Some Relevant Facts about Computers

In Appendix 2 we describe technical matters of peripheral concern to data protection. Here we present a few technical facts of which lawyers and managers should be aware, as they relate to computer systems which will be involved in data protection.

An organisation can meet its information-processing requirements in a number of different ways. These are, more or less in the order in which they appeared in time: (i) a central computing facility to which many remote terminals will be attached; (ii) a number of smallish computers connected by means of a "local area network" (LAN), where the LAN is usually confined within the physical boundary of an organisation; (iii) a combination of (i) and (ii); (iv) a geographically widespread network with virtually no physical constraints – e.g. satellite links providing world-wide network facilities.

Distributed processing is a term widely used in the context

of mini-computers, and it is nearly always assumed that "distributed" is synonymous with "geographically spread". It can be, but need not be. With the right software and a compatible range of equipment, a requirement for centralised facilities can be met by a collection of minis, sited within a few metres of each other, with a LAN – (ii) above. The point in making the distinction between a main-frame and a LAN is that there will be differences that could be important in terms of data protection. For example, the maintenance of a single set of master files can be more difficult in the case of a LAN and distributed computers, each with its own operating system. The control of, and responsibility for, data integrity and timeliness becomes difficult if not impossible.

A wider geographical spread (of computers) may also be more expensive, because the economies of scale accruing from centralised support may not be realisable. Further, standardisation of operating systems, software generally and documentation may well be more difficult to achieve, having an adverse effect on security and auditability (as explained in the next chapter). There are other hazards in decentralisation: local control is liable to result in the fragmentation of objectives, the dispersal of an organisation's reserves of expertise and the uncoordinated growth in applications software.

On the other hand, where there is no desire, or need, to have centralised control, then freely dispersed systems have many attractions. In our view, however, it is most unlikely that any organisation so organised would survive a data-protection audit. Of particular relevance in data protection is the reduction in security, with the increased risk of unauthorised access to files. In order to guard against some of these hazards, and so protect the interests of data subjects, there should always be a reasonable measure of central control.

The debate concerning decentralisation versus centralisation is not, however, the same as the one of mini-computers versus main-frames, although "centralised system" implies use of a main-frame, whilst decentralisation implies dispersed mini-computers or micro-computers. The real arguments, in fact, concern environment and purpose, and involve technological, organisational and economic issues.

The economic argument should take into account communications and manpower costs, both of which have risen significantly over the last few years. Of particular importance is the cost of maintenance, which, because of the shift to high volume/low profit margin, is rising and can become extremely expensive. Yet a lowering of maintenance cover by the data user can result in a lowering of operational standards, which should, in fact, be maintained at a high standard. The organisational aspects are difficult to review in cost terms because of their highly subjective nature. If they relate to manpower, internal reviews may allow the true costs to remain obscure, so any assessment of the changes in cost-effectiveness should be carried out by an independent investigation.

Steps to be Taken by Computer Professionals

We now see that data protection is part of general information handling, yet those parts of information which pertain to data protection are likely to be spread randomly over corporate information systems, perhaps crossing managerial boundaries. We have shown earlier that the effect of the change to information processing has had a marked effect on the way managers perform. The emergence of a dual reporting structure – line management and information source management – has been detected.

It is in such environments that the computer professionals practise. Whilst they may be untouched directly by many of the broader issues we have described above, they and managers will henceforth operate in a legal spotlight where data protection issues come into play, and they should therefore, in our view, need to know something about the law as it applies to computers. We describe some of those features of the law *per se* as they apply to data protection, in Appendix 1. We show here how the computer professional might need to prepare himself for his position as an expert in a situation where an infringement of the Act has resulted in his having to present evidence of procedures in force at the due time.

The situation will be similar to that where any evidence has to be presented in court. Computers have had an effect in this area and some studies have been carried out.[10] The Home Office is currently considering the admissibility of computer evidence in the Police and Criminal Evidence Bill, specifically Clauses 58 and 59.

Kelman and Sizer[11] have proposed the use of an affidavit or deposition, to be prepared by computer professionals, which could in certain circumstances be used in both criminal and civil cases and could be adapted for use in data protection litigations. A deposition could consist of seven parts, as follows.

1. Statement One could deal with the qualifications and experience of the person in charge of the registered system in question (in other words, the data user). This is to establish that he is qualified to swear such a document.
2. Statement Two could consist of a description of the registered system with reference to each of the components in the system by, in the case of hardware, make and model number, and, in the case of software, any descriptive title, version number and so on.
3. Statement Three could deal with the quality of the individual components by reference to the development time taken in their creation. For example, reference could be made here to any technical literature or manuals which were used, giving the number of man-hours in their original development.
4. Statement Four could deal with the testing and documentation standards applied to the applications software which is part of the registered system. Where this has been bought-in, the software house should provide information on the testing and documentation standards employed.
5. Statement Five could deal with the procedures for keeping records on modifications made to the software, and the qualifications of the staff employed.

6. Statement Six could deal with the relevant security features.
7. Finally, Statement Seven could indicate how the particular event occurred and how it relates to the Act's requirements.

The last statement would, of course, only be produced if the need arose. The others could be maintained all the time as part of good practice and retained for a sensible period of time. In a data protection case a deposition of the kind described would greatly assist in demonstrating that a data user had taken every reasonable precaution to meet the Act's requirements. It would also help in clarifying the extent to which his direct responsibilities could be affected. The Kelman/Sizer "Seven Stage Affidavit" will also be relevant in registrations to provide proof of adherence to standards and procedures.

A computer professional might well argue that most of the technical requirements reflect practices already adhered to by any well run, efficient and honest computing business. However, there is a world of difference between the man who, out of professional pride, produces a good system or runs a secure, efficient computing service, and the one who pays lip service to the technical requirements of data protection. The latter will have to aspire to and implement such standards, because to do otherwise may render him accountable legally, and will certainly result in his not surviving a data-protection audit.

Conclusion

A great deal of corporate analysis, heart-searching, technical appraisal and career shuffling is a likely outcome for those organisations and people working in areas covered by the Act. So far as the people are concerned, some already combine relatively high corporate or personal status with the requisite technical skills and knowledge that make them acceptable data users, and hence able to answer in law with impunity. In other cases, the person with the skills and knowledge to formulate information and security policies to ensure conformity may well be of too low a status to contribute meaningfully. Problems will exist in small to medium sized businesses where there is no one combining the relevant hierarchical status with the legal and technical knowledge of the issues involved in the processing and storage of personal data. Indeed the domestic user indulging in hobby activities concerning personal data is likely to be vulnerable to claims brought against him by a distraught or enraged data subject.

Working through the checklists below provides a valuable first step in assessing the current degree of protection afforded to data subjects and the degree of risk in processing personal data for all existing and intending data users. Also the checklists should provide some initial guidance as to whether the law is being complied with by the data user.

Checklists for Senior Management

Board level (B)

1. Is there knowledge in all cases of the purpose or purposes for which the personal data are held (Principle 2)?
2. Has information represented by the personal data been obtained fairly and lawfully (Principle 1)?
3. Has any application for registration or for alteration of the register been refused (Principles 1 and 2)?

Senior management level (SM)

1. Has information represented by the personal data been obtained fairly and lawfully (Principle 1)?
2. Have the personal data been processed fairly and lawfully (Principle 1)?
3. Is there knowledge in all cases of the purpose or purposes for which the personal data are held (Principle 2)?

4. Has any application for registration or for alteration of the register been refused (Principles 1 and 2)?
5. Are there adequate safeguards to ensure that all uses or disclosure of personal data are not incompatible, inconsistent or likely to mislead in respect of each and every specified purpose (Principles 3 and 8)?
6. Is there a means of independent monitoring of the security measures and a "feedback" to senior management (Principles 1 and 8) from lower levels?

Solicitor and legal executive level (LE)

1. Has the information represented by the personal data been obtained fairly and lawfully (Principle 1)?
2. Have the personal data been processed fairly and lawfully (Principle 1)?
3. Is there knowledge that any purpose for which the data are held is not lawful (Principle 2)?
4. Has each and every purpose for which the personal data are held been specified by
   (*a*) registration, or
   (*b*) an application for registration, or
   (*c*) alteration of the register, or
   (*d*) an application for alteration of the register (Principle 2)?
5. Has any application for registration or for alteration of the register been refused (Principles 1 and 2)?
6. Are any personal data being used or disclosed in any manner incompatible, inconsistent or likely to mislead in respect of each and every specified purpose (Principle 3)?
7. Have any personal data been used as in 6 above (Principle 3)?
8. Are there adequate safeguards to ensure that all uses or disclosures of personal data are not incompatible, inconsistent or likely to mislead in respect of each and every specified purpose (Principles 3 and 8)?

Financial level (FM)
Auditing level (AD)

1. Is there knowledge that any purpose for which the data are held is not lawful (Principle 2)?
2. Are there adequate safeguards to ensure that all uses or disclosure are not incompatible, inconsistent or likely to mislead in respect of each and every specified purpose for which data are held (Principles 3 and 8)?
3. Is knowledge of the provisions made available so that independent checks can be made that corrections or erasures specified in Principle 7b have been carried out (Principles 5 and 7)?
4. Is there a means of independent monitoring of the security measures and a "feedback" to senior management (Principles 1 and 8)?

Personnel level (PM)
Information policy level (IP)
Marketing and Sales level (MS)
Public Relations level (PR)

1. Is there knowledge in all cases of the purpose or purposes for which the personal data are held (Principle 2)?
2. Is there knowledge that any purpose for which the data are held is not lawful (Principle 2)?
3. Has each and every purpose for which the personal data are held been specified by
   (*a*) registration, or
   (*b*) an application for registration, or
   (*c*) alteration of the register, or
   (*d*) an application for alteration of the register (Principle 2)?
4. Has any application for registration or for alteration of the register been refused (Principles 1 and 2)?
5. Are any personal data being used or disclosed in any manner incompatible, inconsistent or likely to mislead in respect of each and every specified purpose (Principle 3)?

THE IMPLICATIONS

6. Have any personal data been used as in 5 above (Principle 3)?
7. Are the personal data adequate, relevant, and not excessive for the specified purpose in each and every case (Principle 4)?
8. Are the personal data accurate and up-to-date (Principle 5)?
9. Are the specified data in respect of any specified purpose kept longer than is necessary (Principle 6)?
10. Are individual data subjects allowed at reasonable intervals and without undue delay and expense
    (*a*) to be informed that personal data are held of which that individual is the subject,
    (*b*) access to all personal data of which they are subjects (Principle 7a)?
11. Have adequate security measures been taken to guard against personal data being the target of non-accidental unauthorised access (resulting in unauthorised alteration, deletion, destruction, disclosure, distribution) (Principles 1 and 8)?

Risk assessment level (RA)

1. Is there knowledge in all cases of the purposes for which the personal data are held (Principle 2)?
2. Is there knowledge that any purpose for which the data are held is not lawful (Principle 2)?
3. Are any personal data being used or disclosed in any manner incompatible, inconsistent or likely to mislead in respect of each and every specified purpose (Principle 3)?
4. Have any personal data been used as in 3 above (Principle 3)?
5. Have adequate security measures been taken to guard against personal data being the target of accidental unauthorised access (resulting in unauthorised alteration, deletion, destruction, disclosure, distribution) (Principles 1 and 8)?
6. Have adequate contingency measures been adopted to guard against accidental destruction of personal

data other than through unauthorised access (e.g. fire, flood, storm etc.) (Principles 1 and 8)?

Data control level (DC)

1. Are any personal data being used or disclosed in any manner incompatible, inconsistent or likely to mislead in respect of each and every specified purpose for which data are held (Principle 3)?
2. Are there adequate safeguards to ensure that all uses or disclosure of personal data are not incompatible, inconsistent or likely to mislead in respect of each and every specified purpose (Principles 3 and 8)?
3. Are the personal data adequate, relevant, and not excessive for the specified purpose in each and every case (Principle 4)?
4. Are the personal data accurate and up-to-date (Principle 6)?
5. Are individual data subjects allowed at reasonable intervals and without undue delay and expense
    (*a*) to be informed that personal data are held of which that individual is the subject,
    (*b*) access to all personal data of which they are subjects (Principle 7a)?
6. Are provisions made to have personal data held in respect of the data subject corrected or erased (Principle 7b)?
7. Is knowledge of the provisions made available so that independent checks can be made that such corrections or erasures have been carried out (Principles 5 and 7)?
8. Have adequate security measures been taken to guard against personal data being the target of non-accidental unauthorised access (resulting in unauthorised alteration, deletion, destruction, disclosure, distribution) (Principles 1 and 8)?
9. Have adequate contingency measures been adopted to guard against accidental destruction of personal data other than through unauthorised access (e.g. fire, flood, storm etc.) (Principles 1 and 8)?

Security level (SE)

1. Have any personal data been used or disclosed in any manner incompatible, inconsistent or likely to mislead in respect of each and every specified purpose (Principle 3)?
2. Are there adequate safeguards to ensure that all uses or disclosure of personal data are not incompatible, inconsistent or likely to mislead in respect of each and every specified purpose (Principles 3 and 8)?
3. Are individual data subjects allowed at reasonable intervals and without undue delay and expense
   (a) to be informed that personal data are held of which that individual is the subject,
   (b) access to all personal data of which they are subjects (Principle 7a)?
4. Are provisions made to have personal data held in respect of the data subject corrected or erased (Principle 7b)?
5. Is knowledge of the provisions made available so that independent checks can be made that such corrections or erasures have been carried out (Principles 5 and 7)?
6. Have adequate security measures been taken to guard against personal data being the target of non-accidental unauthorised access (resulting in unauthorised alteration, deletion, destruction, disclosure, distribution (Principles 1 and 8)?
7. Have adequate contingency measures been adopted to guard against accidental destruction of personal data other than through unauthorised access (e.g. fire, flood, storm etc.) (Principles 1 and 8)?

Systems development level (SD)

1. Are there adequate safeguards to ensure that all uses or disclosure of personal data are not incompatible, inconsistent or likely to mislead in respect of each and every specified purpose (Principles 3 and 8)?

2. Are personal data accurate and up-to-date (Principle 5)?
3. Are provisions made to have personal data held in respect of the data subject corrected or erased (Principle 7b)?
4. Have adequate security measures been taken to guard against personal data being the target of non-accidental unauthorised access (resulting in unauthorised alteration, deletion, destruction, disclosure, distribution (Principles 1 and 8)?

Operations management level (OM)

1. Are there adequate safeguards to ensure that all uses or disclosure of personal data are not incompatible, inconsistent or likely to mislead in respect of each and every specified purpose (Principles 3 and 8)?
2. Are the personal data accurate and up-to-date (Principle 5)?
3. Are the personal data in respect of any specified purpose kept longer than is necessary (Principle 6)?
4. Are individual data subjects allowed at reasonable intervals and without undue delay and expense
   (*a*) to be informed that personal data are held of which that individual is the subject,
   (*b*) access to all personal data of which they are subjects (Principle 7a)?
5. Are provisions made to have personal data held in respect of the data subject corrected or erased (Principle 7b)?
6. Have adequate security measures been taken to guard against personal data being the target of non-accidental unauthorised access (resulting in unauthorised alteration, deletion, destruction, disclosure, distribution) (Principles 1 and 8)?
7. Have adequate contingency measures been adopted to guard against accidental destruction of personal data other than through unauthorised access (e.g. fire, flood, storm etc.) (Principles 1 and 8)?

References

1. Commission of the European Communities – a report of the Council of Ministers
2. Deloitte, Haskins and Sells and the National Computing Centre, "The External Auditor as Privacy Inspector", *Information Age,* Vol. 5, no. 3, July 1983
3. Council Of Europe, "The Convention for the Protection of Individuals with Regard to Automatic Processing of Personal Data", Opened for signature January 1981
4. Younger, K. (Chairman), "Report of the Committee on Privacy", Cmnd 5012, HMSO, July 1972
5. Kelman, A. and Sizer, R., *The Computer in Court,* Gower, 1982, pp. 11-22, 52
6. Hook, P., Contribution to "Computer Generated Output as Admissible Evidence in Civil and Criminal Cases", BCS Monograph, March 1982
7. Wilder, K., "The DP Professional as Privacy Inspector", *Information Age,* Vol. 5, No. 3, July 1983
8. Rockart, J.F., "The Changing Role of the Information Systems Executive: A Critical Success Factors Perspective", *Sloan Management Review,* Fall 1982
9. Nolan, R.L., "Managing Information Systems by Committee", *Harvard Business Review*, July/August 1982
10. Hook, *op. cit.*
11. Kelman and Sizer, *op. cit.*

Chapter 5
The Security Aspects

There is a tendency to dismiss computer security as not being relevant to data protection. We have already expressed a contrary opinion, and in this chapter we show that much of the Act implies the use of practices and procedures which will be largely ineffective without the implementation of security in its totality. Various groups – the doctors, for example, through the BMA – laudably deliberate on who should have access to what information under what conditions at given times. It is argued, for example, that it is the doctor who should make decisions where accesses to patients' medical records are concerned. The facts of the matter are that, with the present state of many computers and much software, such deliberations are largely academic. The lack of those security features in many computer systems which can prevent non-authorised accesses means, in effect, that it is the criminal, the careless and the mischievous who will decide matters of access. With proper attention to detail, however, some computers can be made secure; security policies must exist and be implemented. In this chapter (amplified in Appendix 2) we discuss relevant aspects of computer security with the purpose of convincing the reader that its totality must be taken seriously in the context of legislated data protection, and that a security policy must be formulated for the computer, its

THE SECURITY ASPECTS 181

software, business environment and so on.

There is a wealth of literature on computer security, a minute fraction of which we refer to in this chapter. In what follows we have limited the depth to which certain matters are taken. We do not, for example, list known examples of computer insecurity but give references to two comprehensive analyses. Our purpose is to show what issues need to be considered in the formulation of a security policy. We emphasise the totality of security, likening it to a 'chain'. The links in the chain are represented by the state of corporate awareness, people, buildings, computer systems and operating systems software, modes of operation, communications, and so on. Somewhere there will be a weak link.

In most data processing activities all sorts of people will have access to computers handling a mix of data of differing sensitivities because, largely, that has been the way in which computers can be operated cost-effectively. In such "multi-user, multi-access" modes the Act can be contravened deliberately, unwittingly or carelessly. We label all three as "attacks"; largely the same measures are employed to minimise the effectiveness of any type of attack. Attacks will be successful at the weakest link in the chain.

Corporate Awareness

This chapter is written with a corporate data user in mind, but some or all of the techniques will apply to the "domestic" user (into which category we place the small or one-man business). Hereafter we do not distinguish between corporate and domestic data users, as we believe the distinctions are obvious and the reader can be selective as befits his personal interests.

PART II, Section 20, lays a clear responsibility for data protection matters on "any director, manager, secretary or similar officer of the body corporate". PART IV, Section 33, lays a similar responsibility on the individual or "domestic" data user in that exemption applies only where the data are not used or disclosed for any other purpose. In essence the only means that any of the above people will have of ensuring that unauthorised use, disclosure, destruction or amendment of personal data do not take place is to have adequate security procedures. Figure 5.1 depicts a security structure of universal application, but it should be noted that computers are not inherently secure; time, money and effort need to be spent to achieve a given standard of security. Even then the degree of security can only be expressed in terms of the probability of withstanding an attack. Norman[1] refers throughout his book to computer *insecurity* to make the point. Because of the need for standards, risk factor, data categories and procedures (all of which imply the need for a corporate policy, funds and personnel), senior management will need to appreciate that the successful implementation of data protection procedures depends on the physical and technical aspects of security – once again the total picture.

Data Protection and Security

Before dealing further with security it is necessary to draw a distinction between it and the "privacy" part of data protection. Although we have indicated already that security is the core of data protection, it cannot be assumed that the standard of the latter is always adequate just because "security" is high. Regrettably, certain breaches of the Act can occur in a "secure" environment. So, for the prudent, there should be the benefit of a specialised insurance policy. It is as well to recall that "invasion of privacy" is the act to guard against; paradoxically invasion of privacy can be accomplished effectively in a secure environment as the following hypothetical but realistic scenario shows.

A vendor has a business which is the selling of information. As raw material he acquires, legitimately, data from a variety of sources: for example, address lists, results of surveys, and the business client/customer records of various companies.* In a non-computer context, the data are prob-

---

*It is relevant to note here that receivers and liquidators recognise the asset value of data and sell them as such. Our vendor acquires sets of data by this process as well. However, our comment in the section on data as an asset (page 188) is of interest where liquidation of assets may be at issue.

THE SECURITY ASPECTS 183

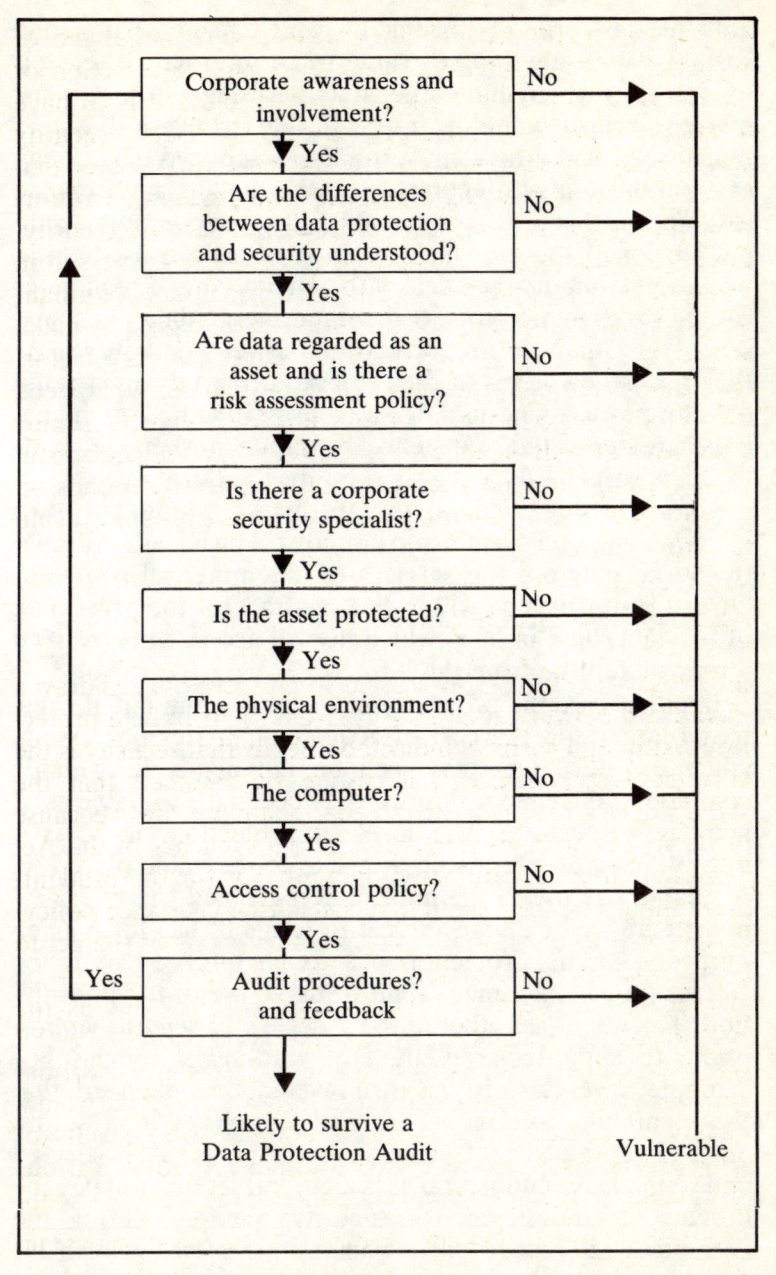

```
        ┌─────────────────────────┐ No
   ┌───▶│ Corporate awareness and │────▶
   │    │      involvement?       │
   │    └───────────┬─────────────┘
   │              ▼ Yes
   │    ┌─────────────────────────┐ No
   │    │   Are the differences   │────▶
   │    │ between data protection │
   │    │ and security understood?│
   │    └───────────┬─────────────┘
   │              ▼ Yes
   │    ┌─────────────────────────┐ No
   │    │ Are data regarded as an │────▶
   │    │   asset and is there a  │
   │    │  risk assessment policy?│
   │    └───────────┬─────────────┘
   │              ▼ Yes
   │    ┌─────────────────────────┐ No
   │    │   Is there a corporate  │────▶
   │    │   security specialist?  │
   │    └───────────┬─────────────┘
   │              ▼ Yes
   │    ┌─────────────────────────┐ No
   │    │   Is the asset protected?│───▶
   │    └───────────┬─────────────┘
   │              ▼ Yes
   │    ┌─────────────────────────┐ No
   │    │ The physical environment?│───▶
   │    └───────────┬─────────────┘
   │              ▼ Yes
   │    ┌─────────────────────────┐ No
   │    │      The computer?      │────▶
   │    └───────────┬─────────────┘
   │              ▼ Yes
   │    ┌─────────────────────────┐ No
   │    │   Access control policy?│────▶
   │    └───────────┬─────────────┘
   │              ▼ Yes
   │Yes ┌─────────────────────────┐ No
   └────│   Audit procedures?     │────▶
        │     and feedback        │
        └───────────┬─────────────┘
                    ▼
           Likely to survive a          Vulnerable
           Data Protection Audit
```

Figure 5.1

ably in the form of documents which need perusal and sorting before anything of value in an informative sense is obvious. Thus, anything other than perusing and sorting for a given purpose would be impracticable, owing to the sheer magnitude of the task and probable associated cost. However, in the context of computing (and making a reasonable assumption that the various data will be in computer compatible form) the amount of data is of little consequence, because a computer can deal with vast amounts. A computer can be programmed to sort the data, merge data items and search speculatively for correlation between data items. By this means new items of data can be produced which could be informative on perusal in a way never intended originally, have greater value and hence be more marketable items than the original data acquired by the vendor.

For processing the data, our information vendor may own his own computer system and employ his own staff. Alternatively, he may use the services of a commercial computer bureau with which he will have a contract for the processing of his data, held in files, which he will access from his own terminals remote from the bureau.

In either case the pre-processed data have an initial value based largely on the cost of acquisition. After processing, when the new data may well be the highly marketable commodity the vendor desires, they become a valuable asset needing protection. The level of protection, if he is a sensible vendor, will be appropriate to the value placed on the data. The use of the information gleaned from the new items may well be time–critical in terms of use for a given purpose, so the protection has to be afforded until the vendor judges the time is right to make use of the information. In either case, therefore, a degree of security appropriate to a particular method of working is sought. For example, a vendor with his own installation will ensure that the computer itself is secure and is housed in a secure environment, and that his staff are appropriately selected and trained. A vendor who uses a bureau service will pay the bureau for the degree of security required during the data-processing stage and when output is *en route* to his premises. He will also arrange to have the output of his processed data held under secure conditions once on his own premises.

These security requirements (and we show later in this chapter how they may be implemented) are typical of perfectly proper and professionally run data-processing activities. They are employed at many computer installations for entirely legal and laudable purposes, and are as socially acceptable as the security features used by banks. However, a different and sinister connotation results simply by implying that a vendor (now a data user under the term used in the Act) is processing personal data, and by the use of the correlation sorting and merging techniques already mentioned is identifying particular individuals and their likes, dislikes and details of their private lives. The data-processing activity would take place under the secure conditions described; security measures are, therefore, aiding the potential invasion of privacy of individuals. Would such a data user have registered his systems and if so as what?

Security

Security *per se* is not a new topic. In 1916 Henri Fayol, a French industrialist, analysed major functions of management and named security as one of them, describing it as, "all measures conferring security upon the undertaking and the requisite peace of mind upon the personnel". The word itself is derived from the Latin *securas*, meaning "to be free from care". For data-protection purposes, there are three general areas into which the totality of security can be split – the corporate security policy, the physical and personnel aspects (e.g. buildings and staff), and the computer system in question (hardware, software, communication etc.). Each of these is dealt with later in the chapter.

Most computer manufacturers have for years mentioned "security" features as being available with their products. In some cases security is claimed to be part of, or inherent in, a particular piece of software or hardware or both; in other cases security is offered as an "add on" facility. All of these claims are true to a greater or lesser extent, depending on what is understood by security. As defined in this chapter and Appendix 2 it is doubtful whether many of these claims would bear close analysis. However, taking them at face value for the present, security procedures must be easy to use. If complicated, a data user's staff may tend to ignore them, resulting in a lowering of the level of protection to the data subject and leaving the data user exposed to litigation. As an officer of such a data user may find himself in court as a result of the lower inadequate protection, the prudent officer will ensure that a watch is maintained and an independent assessment made of the effectiveness of security procedures.

Weissman[2] costed certain security features some years ago in the ADEPT 50 system. He claimed then that about 5 per cent of the total design time in man-hours and about 10 per cent of the coding time were spent in developing the security features, and estimated that 80 per cent of the code was concerned with five components of the total system; about 2 per cent of the computer's time (on a modified IBM 360/50) was spent in performing security checks during operation.

Certain security procedures even in kernelised systems (see Appendix 2) can be turned "on" or "off" by an operator. When turned on, the overhead in terms of a reduction in available computer power (the 2 per cent identified by Weissman) can be significant. Faced with a need to process as much work as possible in a given period of time, an operator may either voluntarily or as a result of pressure from management de-activate the more time-consuming checks. It should therefore be part of the security policy to determine the extent to which security procedures can be tolerated and, if adopted as part of data protection procedures, enforced. Enforcement should be monitored independently.

Where security is a corporate requirement, intermediate levels of management and specialists need to be constrained from placing their local interests above corporate policy. This need arises because in any multi-level multi-user environment there will be conflicts of priorities at all levels of management; pressure will sooner or later be brought to bear on a person responsible for a data-processing activity to make him resolve local conflicts of priorities by circumventing the security policy. Giving in to pressure of this kind will almost certainly introduce weak links in the security chain, resulting in turn in a potential danger to a data subject and the risk of litigation for the data user. We recall our comments on the "responsible person" in Chapter 1 – such a person should have his position protected if security is to be taken seriously, so that he can resist any pressures to degrade corporate security procedures without danger to his own job security.

Finally in this section it is worth pointing out that information on security procedures described in this chapter has been in the public domain for some years. This is not by default on the part of manufacturers and others but part of a deliberate policy originating with the Department of Defence of the USA.[3] Rein Turn summarised many of the basic principles in 1981 but in 1964 Baran[4] had argued that one could only use with confidence (in a security sense) a computer system whose security features had been placed in the public domain. The strength of Baran's argument still lies in the fact that computer security essentially consists of two parts – the security features, and the "keys" or "parameters" which cause the features to be implemented or activated. It is the keys and parameters which need to be guarded. The features, after Baran, can be discussed openly. It then becomes a commercially attractive issue to those concerned with security (like banks have been for some time) and so ensures that manufacturer A competes with manufacturer B in providing security features which can be independently validated. Potential customers can also assess the features meaningfully.

For the non-technical reader, the distinction between security features and keys is analogous to the distinction between advertised security features of a domestic alarm system and the manner in which they are used; the fact that some purchasers of these systems will elect not to use some features all the time (by not switching "keys" on) means that some premises are likely to be burgled more often and more easily than others – in effect as decided by the owners. A lax data user could parallel closely a lax owner of burgled premises.

Data as an Asset, and Risk Assessment

Data can be regarded as an asset requiring management and protection, as do other assets. Figures 5.2, 5.3, 5.4, illustrate recorded attacks on computer assets[5] which, although pertaining to events of some years ago, usefully relate the extent of losses, methods of attack, and the job positions of the attackers. The scale of the losses is impressive yet represents only a fraction of the total picture. Norman[6] gives many more later examples, as do Wong and Farquhar.[7]

Data assets are found usually in some form of central filing system in which data items are uniquely filed, located, retrieved, updated. Data are also commonly transferred, or distributed to other locations, over a network. Format, language, accuracy, relevancy, compatibility (with other data), ownership, rights of access, data identity, sensitivity, classification, associative relationships with other data, and who possesses the authority to read, write, copy, delete and amend data items, are all relevant issues for the data user. The list is not exhaustive. Risk analysis (see Figure 5.5) needs to be applied; where there is a high asset value, there is a risk-sensitive environment, a link under strain and a potential point of attack.

Comparisons can be made with general business assets. For example, it is often the case that companies or other organisations will choose to raise finance from their bankers by issuing debentures secured by a floating charge over all the assets of the company or organisation. This charge would generally be a legal charge under Section 95 of the Companies Act 1948. To be valid and enforceable such a charge must be registered within 21 days of creation (although an extension of time can be allowed under Section 101). In the event that the party with the benefit of the floating charge chose to enforce it because, for instance, a business loan was not repaid, then in our view it would apply to personal data as to all other assets. Therefore, to comply with data protection principle 8 the company or those controlling the organisation should in our view ensure that any floating charge or other charge or lien on assets does not include such personal data. Indeed we consider it prudent

		Brandt Allen	
		Average losses in computer frauds ($000's)	
	Type	Corporation	Banks
1	Payments to employees	139	3
	Payments to others	133	–
	Payments to creditors	324	252
2	Accounting/inventory	1300	195
	Collections/deposits	43	157
	Billings	6	–
	AV. loss totals	1945	607
			(Abridged)

Figure 5.2

		Brandt Allen
Schemes used		
Method	1	2
Transactions added or altered	40	44
Transactions deleted	2	3
File changes	6	3
Program changes	2	7
Improper operation	4	1
Miscellaneous	2	11
		(Abridged)

Figure 5.3

	Average loss related to job position				Loss ($000s)	
	Total	Alone	Inside	Outside	Total	Alone
Terminal op.	16	4	6	6	727	8
Clerk	19	11	5	3	58	37
Programmer	19	10	5	4	53	20
Manager	22	18	3	1	314	274
Operator	10	5	3	2	37	33
Others	5	4	1	–	92	48
Unknown	3	3	–	–	3096	–

Brandt Allen

(Abridged)

THE SECURITY ASPECTS

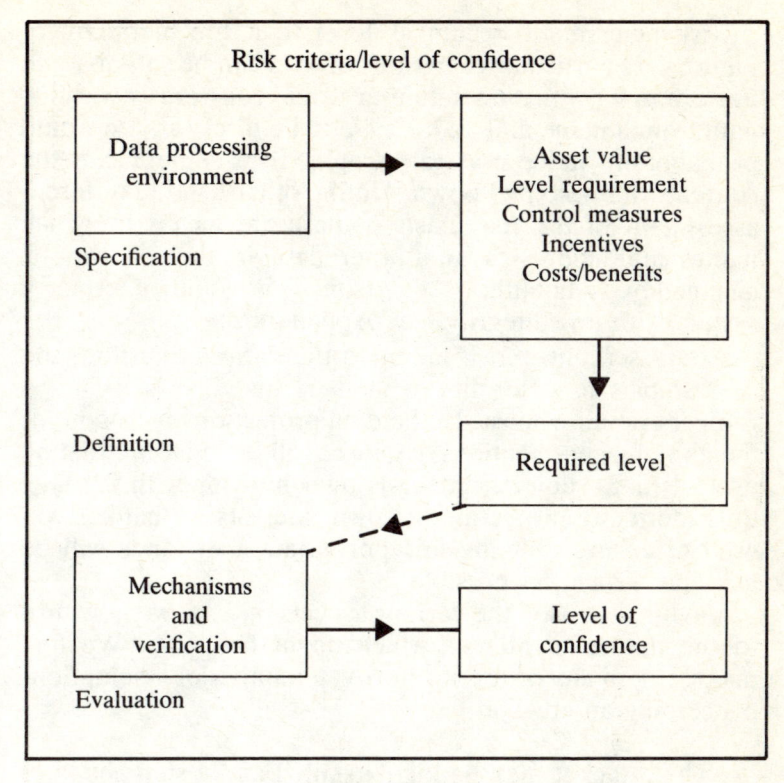

Figure 5.5

for such data to be expressly excluded.

Nevertheless, an asset value should be ascribed to data because the scope of a security policy needs to embrace fine judgement of what is a reasonable price to pay for security. As well as having such an asset value ascribed, data in a data protection environment need to be placed in categories with associated risk factors thus:

Category	*Risk factor*
Names and addresses	0 low
Club memberships	1
Career histories	2
Medical histories	3 high

Risk assessment occurs at level 6 in the hierarchy of Figure 4.1. Particular categories of data can be sub-divided. For example, whilst no data user would consciously wish for data from a name and address file to be disclosed, he would probably not judge it as catastrophic if by some means the contents did become known. On the other hand, a different assessment of the risk exists if there are means by which names and addresses and other data in the file can be changed by an unauthorised person. This would be termed a system with low integrity (see Appendix 2).

After ascribing a risk factor to the data in question, the next step is to determine what it is that one is trying to protect oneself against. In the data protection environment, the aim of a conscientious data user will be to ensure that he protects data subjects' interests by complying with the law, thus indirectly protecting his own interests. A banker will wish to ensure that the misappropriation of funds will be made as difficult as possible.

Having discussed the various aspects of data, we now turn to the nature of attacks which might be made. We first make, not in any order of priority, a number of assumptions concerning an attacker.

1. The attacker may be highly skilled and a step ahead of the data user in the technology involved.
2. The attacker may on the other hand be unskilled but have an innate ability to detect weak lines. Comer[8] has shown this to be a real and increasing threat as familiarity with the computer increases.
3. The attacker may be external to an organisation, business or family.
4. An attacker will sometimes be successful, so there must be a means of tracing the time, location and logical path of such attacks.
5. The attacker may be a member of the data users' staff or, a point to be noted by the hobbyist, a member of his family.

There are two consequential postulates:

1. No operating system or piece of software available commercially is absolutely secure.
2. Testing even by those independent of the designers and implementers of software will in general only minimise the risks; they will not be eliminated.

Parts of a typical computer system have varying degrees of vulnerability to attack. For example, where, in a given environment, there is a variety of terminals, communication protocols, communication lines and associated electronic equipments, the system is relatively more vulnerable. Systems are also more vulnerable where communication is via the public network and lines carrying data in the public domain are not encrypted. Certain items of computer equipment can radiate signals which, under certain conditions, represent the data being conveyed around the system. Thus anyone able to receive and decode the "transmitted" signals would, in effect, have access to the data. This is not in the realms of fantasy; a test was made some years ago with special equipment[9] in a van parked near a computer centre containing a printer. The electrical signals driving the printer were sufficiently powerful to be received and recorded on the equipment in the van. They were later used to produce the same eye-readable output as was printed at the centre. However, specialised knowledge and equipment are required to do such monitoring successfully, so attacks of this kind would only take place where the data attacked have an intrinsic value greater than the cost of mounting such an attack. Countermeasures can be taken but are relatively expensive. Clearly, in a data protection context where Section 15 of the Act makes unauthorised disclosure an offence in a bureaux environment, and Section 21 under certain circumstances gives a data subject a right of access to his personal data (which in most cases will be by means of eye-readable printed output), the safeguarding by a data user of the production of printed output on a line-printer or similar device at source will be of paramount importance, though whether it will ever warrant the application of measures to limit radiation is a consideration for the risk assessor.

Protecting the Asset

Some years ago the problems of protecting computer data from attack had easier solutions, because computers were simpler, and both computer and data were centralised. Protection (if it was implemented) could be achieved by containing both in a room with controlled physical access. This is no longer realistic; the use of remote terminals, distributed processing, micros on a wide geographic basis, and transborder dataflows, make such a *cordon sanitaire* an outmoded form of protection other than in very specialised circumstances.

We now consider asset protection in terms of physical environment, the computer, access control, audit procedures and encryption. For the reasons given above we do not consider the radiation problem any further.

Physical Environment

A computer "building" was once a highly visible target in that all the components were conveniently grouped and housed together, but was also inherently the least vulnerable link in the chain because it was relatively easy to devise and implement physical security procedures mainly concerned with controlled entry. Nowadays even the term "building" needs clarification. Until relatively recently one could point to the particular physical location where computing activity was carried out, usually "the computer centre". Such is now not always the case. The introduction of terminals, minis and micros already mentioned together with microcomputer-based office automation systems on a vast scale, means that there is probably no part of a business premises (and a great many homes) free from computing activity in some form or another.

To summarise, a building is no longer a key solution; terminals connected to a computer can breach physical security boundaries just as effectively as when the door of a bank vault is cut open by a thermal lance, though the illegal use of a terminal may, without pre-designed and implemented safeguards, leave no trace and hence is a more subtle and dangerous form of threat than the lance. Unauthorised use of a computer terminal is relatively easy with many present-day computer systems. The 1983 media-publicised penetration of a US military computer system by a schoolboy computer "whizz-kid" is just one example. Terminals can thus change a symbolic air-tight box into a symbolic colander unless precautions are taken.

Even with precautions, environment and system security can be compromised if staff are untrustworthy. Management thus has choices where physical environment is concerned. One choice (an extreme one) is to resort to a secure "building" formed by using, say, an underground concrete bunker with one entrance guarded continuously by at least two human beings and appropriate electronic devices. The computer system would have, say, three operators at all times to reduce the risk stemming from collusion. All personnel would be hand-picked. The computer would run one "job" at a time under (more than one) operator control; no terminals would be attached. With this choice the cost would be high, efficiency of operation low, security standard very high, risk factor low. Data protection would be achieved almost certainly at an unacceptably high cost.

Another choice (virtually the other extreme) is to have relatively easy access and only one operator at a time in attendance. Many remote terminals would be attached and the computer would run many jobs simultaneously – the multi-user mode. Here capital cost might still be high but so, now, would the efficiency of operation. Overhead costs would be low. However, standards of security would be low, with a high risk factor. Data protection could superficially be achieved relatively cheaply but at high risk of successful prosecution of the data user. This is more typical of the way most computer systems are now operated; fortunately, as we show later, a security policy can improve standards, giving a median between the two extremes.

The Computer

The heart of security in any computer lies in the operating system which should, ideally, be designed – for example, kernelised (see Appendix 2) – with security in mind. One example of embedded design philosophy is due to Elliott Organick[10] who described an operating system philosophy as follows: "Users compete for the computer's resources. They 'play' against each other in one way or another, fair or foul. Fair play . . . is to be encouraged. Foul play, as for instance one user inadvertently or deliberately destroying the data or procedures of another user or of the system itself, is to be more than merely minimised, discouraged or outlawed. It is to be prevented in toto. Multics is designed so that a large measure of fair play can be achieved by co-operating users, while at the same time every type of foul play that can be anticipated is prevented."

Sultzer describes access control lists, authentication and control of privileges. Karger and Lipner[12] describe similar features in VAX/VMS which in the experimental stage had authentication, auditing and integrity features. All of these features are being introduced into the commercial product. Both VMS and Multics have non-discretionary control on access (see page 157).

Discretionary control is relatively common and allows an owner of a file, say, to specify who can have access to his file. Non-discretionary control, however, is at a level above the file owner. Once non-discretionary control is implemented, the owner can only allow access as defined by the non-discretion rules. A powerful control results but, as Lipner points out, its application needs careful study. Once implemented, individuals in an organisation will be identified with a corporate information and access policy and constrained to a specific 'need to know' group corresponding not only to, say, public and confidential but also to categories at each level. Lipner points out that in researching for his paper he found that organisations were greatly concerned with the protection and integrity of financial data but less so with other data, regardless of its sensitivity. The Act will cause organisations to think out (or re-think) their scale of corporate concern for these matters.

We have already referred to data, as defined in the Act, as being contained in "files" (see Appendix 2). In essence a security policy is concerned with access; if to files, then what can be done with a file's contents once access has been obtained. The degree to which data are protected thus depends first on access controls, then on controlling where the data go (or flow) in the system after an access. Flow control describes this feature (see Appendix 2). Briefly, it can be illustrated here by an example. Suppose a file at a level higher than public is accessed, data from that file cannot flow to a file at public level. The restriction will apply whether the data user is the legal one permitted by the access policy, or an attacker who successfully reads the file. In data protection terms this means that an attacker reading an unauthorised file at level A (high) and obtaining illegal write privilege would be prevented from writing that file's contents to another file in the public domain. To obtain the information a second attack at a different point in the system would need to be successful.

Access Control

So far as the data user at a terminal is concerned the primary level of access control is likely to be the ubiquitous password by which he identifies himself to the computer when he requests service from his terminal. The password method of identification, though able to provide a measure of security, becomes increasingly vulnerable with use. Passwords can be stolen, deduced, monitored and overheard. Experience shows that a password is often poorly protected by a data user.

With a password system there is an essential requirement to store centrally the list of passwords in some highly protected part of the computer system and to control tightly authorised access to this list of passwords. There needs to be some form of access by, say, a password controller because, unfortunately, people forget passwords. Where this happens, a password should not be given out by the controller over, say, the telephone to a data user who claims to have forgotten his password, so a more positive method of proof of identity is necessary. The method by which this is done can be a weak link, as a clever potential masquerader would know precisely what to do to obtain a password, then to gain unauthorised access to the system. However, masquerading by means of a password previously obtained by impersonation is not the only form of weakness in the password system. It is possible to use a micro-computer at a terminal to try combinations of passwords until a successful one is found, though it is only fair to point out that a high level of skill would be needed by the potential intruder. Some computer systems, the ADEPT-50 in 1969, for example, detect and prevent this kind of attack. A prudent data user will be concerned to know about the availability of such safeguards.

The following list shows modes of access possible to computer-based data beyond the password level:

1. 'Read only', where the contents of a file can be 'read', say, on the screen of a visual display unit.
2. 'Write to and read', where a file can be opened and written to as well as previous contents being used as in 1.
3. 'Append', where the file can be added to but existing contents cannot be read or changed.
4. A file name can be changed.
5. A file can be deleted.

In addition there are more powerful modes known as system facilities, such as:

6. Allocation of access permissions.
7. Initiation of a computing process.
8. Allowing access through an intermediate computing process.

Weissman[13] formalised access control identifying users, terminals, jobs and files in a way now useful in data protection. He proposed three security properties – authority, franchise and category. Authority relates to the levels of security, franchise refers to a common need to know, and category permits "need to know" designation by identification. Lipner[14] took matters further and combined non-discretionary facilities with integrity in a commercial environment, showing how a security policy must distinguish between modification of system, development, production and application software. Clearly the first requires tighter control and higher integrity than the others.

An access control policy allows permissible links to be made between files and parts of a computer system such as memory, certain processes and output procedures. The effect of such links would be, say, to allow an accessed file to be linked to a real device such as a printer only under certain conditions consistent with the policy, which, in turn, would be based on a data protection principle. Saltzer[15] formalised such a technique (and in doing so formalised commonsense): use only the level of privilege (access) appropriate to the need; if no specific type of access is specified, allow no access of any kind; check every access for conformity with a previously defined profile of that access; make sure that an access request, to be successful, must meet with a number of criteria, not just one. Figure 5.6 is a loose interpretation of access links in terms of authorities and franchises, illustrating the basis of a security policy.

In a system with remote terminals, one of the criteria could, for example, be the privileges allocated to a given terminal and one or more of the read, write and execute modes of access. Figure 5.7 is an example of an access policy.

So far the discussion on access has been confined to files, but more is involved. There needs to be adequate control over the flow of data already referred to and between, say, an object on one level and an object at another (lower) level (see Appendix 2). Jordan[16] describes the additional facilities necessary to effect a more fundamental type of control where an object such as a segment (of memory) is at a given level (in a range from O, lowest level, to 7, highest level) and in one of 18 categories. With such a system, according to Jordan, when a person tries to obtain access to a segment, tests determine what, if any, access will be allowed before

Project	Health								Careers							
Authority	Public		Guarded		Sensitive		Confidential		Public		Guarded		Sensitive		Confidential	
Franchise	Read	Write	Read	Write	Read	Write	Read	Write	Read	Write	Read	Write	Read	Write	Read	Write
Data User	▨	▨	C	D	A C	D	B C	D	A C	C	C	C	B C D	C D	C	C
Terminal	▨	▨	3	4	1 3	4	2 3	4	5,6 3	3	3	3	2 3 4	3 4	3	3

Figure 5.6   An elementary access policy in terms of projects, authorities and franchises

Examples – In project "Health" no data user holds any franchise at level 'Public'.

In project "Careers" only data user C can read and write to a file at level 'Confidential' and only from terminal 3.

In project "Careers" data user A can read files at level 'Public' from terminals 5 or 6 but holds no other franchise.

THE SECURITY ASPECTS

Object	Subject	
	(User) A	(User) B
1	read, write	—
2	read, write, execute	read
3	—	read, write, execute

Figure 5.7   A simple access policy in matrix form

such access is obtained. A form of data flow control results as a data user must have the same or higher authority than that of the segment. Figure 5.8 represents the principle of flow control in simplified form.

Level	A 0	B 7
Categories	2, 3, 6	1, 2, 4, 5
In the above, flow would be permitted only from A to B in category 2. No flow could take place from B to A.		

Figure 5.8   Flow control in a hierarchy

Tight access control can itself result in problems. For example, in any well run computer-based activity there is a necessary and now legal requirement (Sections 22 and 24) to purge data from old and unwanted files. The tighter the access controls, the more the load falls on the owner of the files to do the purging, because he is the only one who has access. The safeguards in a properly designed and implemented system may well prevent a data controller, say, from knowing which data are in active use.

Audit Procedures

Most of what needed to be written in this book concerning audits was given in Chapter 4. We add here that the techniques for the audit of computing systems are still being developed, particularly in the case of networked and distributed computers. The objective, in broad terms, is to examine all aspects of the controls incorporated to ensure the integrity and accuracy of the data and the authenticity of accesses. A prudent data user should therefore examine closely the audit facilities incorporated in an operating system. ADEPT 50 (1969) provided extensive audit features.

Encryption

In deriving a security policy one searches for ways of bringing all potential weaknesses under control. We have shown the lengths to which a data user will have to go where security is taken seriously. Up to now we have concentrated on the areas directly associated with the computer system, though we have referred to instances where data on a communication line passes into the public domain on its way to or from a terminal or part of a network. The lines are usually owned by a public authority (PTT) in the UK and Europe, and by commercial organisations in the USA and elsewhere. Clearly, the lines themselves, their routes, installation and associated equipment are beyond the control of the organisation using them.

Technically, it is possible to "tap" such lines, and to monitor and record the data traffic without giving evidence of the tapping process. Encryption is a means of coding or scrambling the data so that anyone tapping a line perceives unintelligible data. Papek and Kline[17] discusses encryption and related matters in the context of secure computer networks.

There is more to encryption, however, than the protection of data whilst it is in transit on a communication line. One of the major problems in networks is to prevent the introduction of false, spurious and altered data. Sophisticated encryption techniques have been developed, as described by Davies, Price and Parkin,[18] which help to minimise these forms of attack. At present, use of encryption as described above is largely confined to the real-time on-line banking system, where the vast amounts of money represented by the electronic fund transfer processes demand the highest possible order of protection. In data protection the demand for encryption has still to be determined, but it would seem that where networks and distributed computing are the operational modes, then it will be necessary to use encryption techniques as digital signatures to prevent attacks on data arising from impersonation and insertion of false messages at parts of a network.

Contingency Planning

The previous sections have dealt with access control aspects of computer security as being particularly relevant to data protection. There are other aspects of computer security that have to be complied with to meet data protection principle 8 but which apply universally and are well covered in the literature. An important one is contingency planning which, briefly, is concerned with the standby arrangements which should be made for alternative means of processing work in the event of a disaster to the main computers. The arrangements entered into – such as agreements to use other facilities on a reciprocal basis – need to be a part of the overall risk assessment. Talbot[19] is one of the most recent authors to deal with the topic and a reader wishing to know more about contingency planning is referred to his book.

Summary

1. Management should be aware of the need for understanding of data protection principles, the implementation of security requirements and the need to integrate these with control and monitoring procedures relevant

to the corporate structure. Another look at the checklists on pp. 172-8 would be appropriate.
2. There should be an information policy based on data asset value and risk analysis.
3. There needs to be:
   (a) control of physical accesses to, and within, the data processing environment;
   (b) control of external access from, for example, remote terminals;
   (c) system software which provides different forms of authorised access to files and preserves barriers between the different forms of authorisation, such control applying at all parts of the system down to segment level;
   (d) a flow control policy;
   (e) physical records maintained of the usage of computer, magnetic tapes, removable discs and printing devices;
   (f) inspection procedures of such records by an independent authority;
4. There should be an awareness of the need to ensure that collusion is required before breaching of any of the foregoing can be attempted by a data users' staff.
5. The use of encryption techniques should be considered where networking and distributed processing are concerned.

We have shown that security is an important technical component of data protection – in effect, a core. Any organisation of any size dealing with personal data as defined in the Act will need the services of a specialist who understands not only the data protection issues but is technically competent. Figure 5.9 is a checklist, in matrix form, of protection measures such a person can take against threats. Figure 5.10 shows the areas of application of the above list.

The importance of having the correct mental attitudes to security is illustrated by the attitudes of people in the banking industry, where it is natural to assume that attempts will be made to misappropriate funds. To this end, banking

Threats \ Preventative measures	Encryption	Physical Access	Software Access	Activity man.	Authorisation	Labelling	Monitoring volume of I/O	Audit trails
Passive (electromag. sensing)	✓							
Active (Browsing)			✓	✓	✓	✓		✓
Impersonation (system level)			✓	✓	✓	✓		
Trapdoor				✓		✓	✓	✓
Personnel		✓		✓	✓	✓		
Theft of media	✓	✓						
Collusion				✓				✓

Figure 5.9

procedures for years have acknowledged the importance of separation of control; two or more officials are usually needed, each with a different key or part of a combination code necessary to open and close any place, such as a vault, where there is a concentration of valuable items. This same principle should form the basis of any activity concerned with a system on which personal data are stored and processed. Two people at least should be required each to perform the relevant parts of any transaction or process involved in the centralised transfer or handling of personal data.

Senior management should be concerned in security matters. It is their personal attitudes and their assessment of trade-offs in the measures that are applied to achieve a given degree of security which largely dictate compliance with the Act.

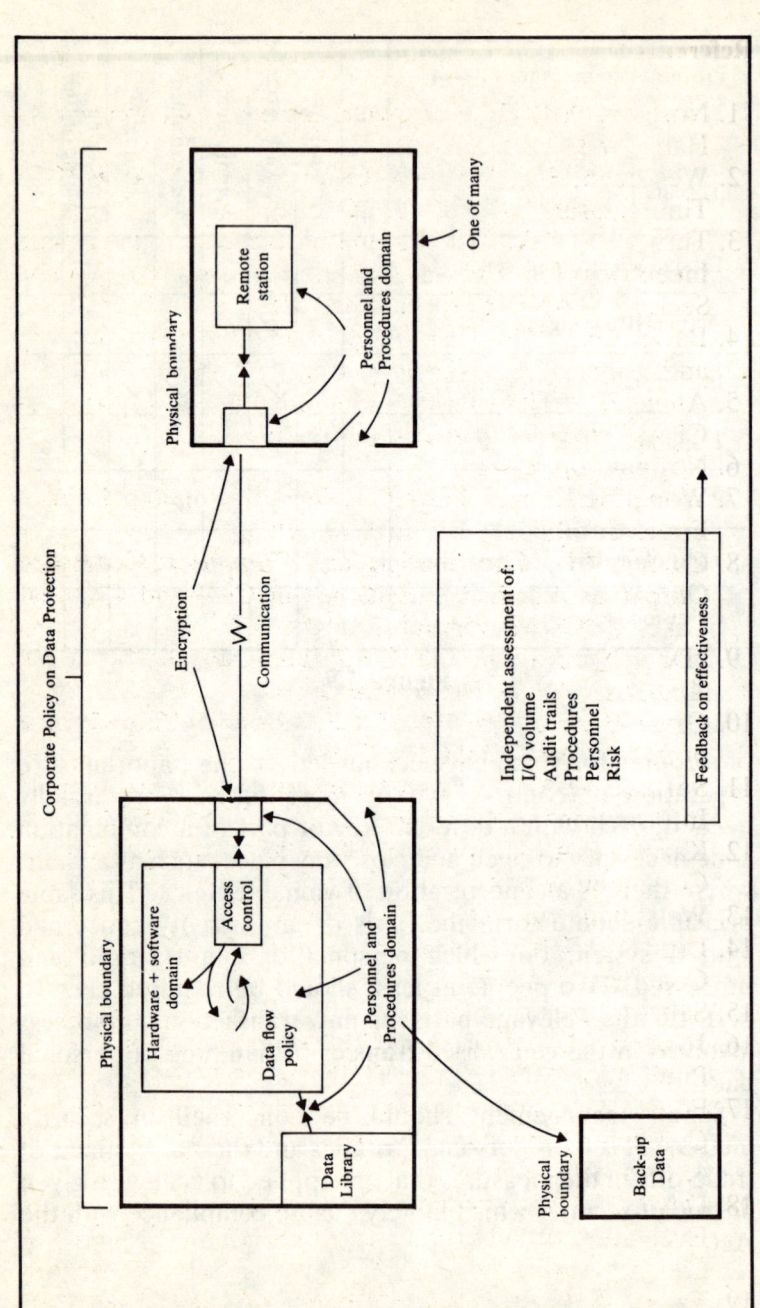

Figure 5.10 Possible application of techniques

References

1. Norman, A.R.D., *Computer Insecurity*, Chapman and Hall, 1983
2. Weissman, C., "Security Controls in the ADEPT-50 Time Sharing System", FJCC, 1964
3. Turn, R., "Trusted Computer Systems. Needs and Incentives for Use in Government and the Private Sector", RAND Corporation, 1981
4. Baran, P., "On Distributed Communication-Security and Secrecy", RAND Corporation, 1964
5. Allen, B., "The Biggest Computer Frauds: Lessons for CPAs", *Journal of Accountancy*, 1977
6. Norman, *op. cit.*
7. Wong, K.K. and Farquhar, W., "Computer Related Fraud Casebook", BIS Ltd, March 1983
8. Comer, M., Contribution to "Computer Generated Output as Admissible Evidence in Civil and Criminal Cases", BCS Monograph, March 1982
9. "Data Security in the Corporate Data Base", *EDP Analyser*, Vol. 8, No. 5, May 1970
10. Organick, E., *"The MULTICS System: An Examination of its Structure"*, MIT Press, 1972
11. Saltzer, J.M., "Protection and the Control of Information", *CACM*, Vol. 17, No. 7, July 1974
12. Karger, P.A. and Lipner, S.B., "Research Activities in Computer Security", IEEE, 1982
13. Weissman, *op. cit.*
14. Lipner, S.B., "Non-discretionary Controls for Commercial Applications", IEE, 1982
15. Saltzer, *op. cit.*
16. Jordan, D., "MULTICS Data Security", HIS Publication MN 12-2187: HUN 541-5505
17. Popek, G.J. and Kline, C.S., "Encryption and Secure Computer Networks", *Computer Surveys*, Vol. 11, No. 4, Dec 1979
18. Davies, D.W., Price, W.L. and Parkin, G.I., "An Evaluation of Public Key Cryptosystems", NPL Report CTU 1, April 1980
19. Talbot, J.R., *Management Guide to Computer Security*, Gower, 1981

Appendix 1
Some Legal Facts Associated with Computers

In this appendix we describe, for the non-legal reader, some of the fundamental legal problems presented to the law by computers.

With computers now performing a role in every walk of life, computer output forms evidence of one sort or another in many cases before the courts, and can present courts with problems of accuracy and admissibility. Reliance is often placed on the use of expert witnesses, and the course of justice may be made more difficult by the combination of jargon (in which computing abounds) and the lack of sufficient knowledge on the part of lawyers to mount an effective cross-examination. We examine each of these in more detail, but emphasise that we barely scratch the surface.

Whilst not so in every case, one of the general problems of computer output used as evidence is that it may be classified as 'hearsay' evidence. Until the widespread use of computers, courts in countries having the common law system (such as England and Wales) did not usually have a problem in deciding what was hearsay evidence and whether, in a given circumstance, a piece of evidence was admissible. Briefly, courts in such countries insist on the presence of a witness who can be cross-examined as to the truth of a given piece of evidence. We now explain the meaning of hearsay by means of a simple example.

A man grows cabbages on a piece of land. He finds that some of the cabbages have been eaten and suspects a goat belonging to a neighbour. To prove this, he needs evidence which will stand up in court. The most common form of evidence in such a case (which would be a civil case) would be the production of a witness who will have seen a goat eating the cabbages and, under oath, will testify that on a certain day at a certain time he saw the neighbour's goat eating the cabbages. He is then cross-examined, when it may be revealed that he cannot tell one goat from another and he is therefore discredited as a witness. On the other hand, the cross-examination may reveal that he is an expert in goat recognition; he will not be discredited and the case will be won.

So far we have not demonstrated 'hearsay' but have illustrated the role of cross-examination: we thought this a necessary first step as the English legal system is founded on such an adversarial base, in which each of the parties is represented by a lawyer who argues against the other, and cross-examines the opposing litigant and witnesses.

There is also a difference between civil and criminal cases which must be noted at this stage. In the latter, the majority of cases are decided in a magistrates' court with, normally, laymen on the bench. Sometimes a legally qualified stipendiary (being an experienced solicitor or barrister) may sit. Such courts decide questions of law and fact. The highest criminal court at first instance is the Crown Court, with both judge and jury; the former decides questions of law, the latter questions of fact.

In civil cases, the County Courts handle cases where claims for damages range up to £5,000; High Courts decide matters generally in excess of £5,000. A judge normally sits on his own and decides on law and fact, except where a case involves libel, slander, false imprisonment or malicious prosecution, where a jury may decide facts. It is here that much computer-generated evidence appears, and is likely also to be where data protection cases take place.

To return to hearsay, having illustrated cross-examination, we develop another scenario, still based on a goat and cabbages. The man whose cabbages have been eaten fails to find a witness who saw a goat eating his cabbages, so he consoles himself with a drink at a local inn. He learns from the barmaid that she had served a man the night before who had seen a goat eating cabbages. Under common law, the barmaid could not be called as a witness to make this statement because she could not be coss-examined as to the truth of what the man saw. In other words, such 'evidence' would be hearsay.

A real situation would normally be more complex and, generally, differ in civil and criminal cases. Also, over the years, exceptions to the hearsay rule have been developed. For example, the barmaid could be called to give evidence that the owner of the goat had told her that his goat had eaten the cabbages.

Goats, cabbages and barmaids are well removed from data protection, computers and output, but they have served to establish two issues – cross-examination and hearsay evidence – which are germane to our purpose.

Under statutory exceptions to the hearsay rule, written (printed) evidence is admissible, but restrictions are placed upon such evidence. The statute taken to be relevant to computer generated evidence was drafted many years ago, when such evidence would commonly have been a product of the technology of the time – for example, handwritten, typed or printed; whichever it was, a human being somewhere would have been directly involved in its production and could have been called to testify as to its validity. However, no new common law exceptions have been created since 1876, and in 1964, in Myers v. the Director of Public Prosecutions, the House of Lords confirmed that any further matters concerned with hearsay must be decided by Parliament.

There is no discretion in a court to admit legally inadmissible evidence. However, in respect of hearsay evidence in the form of out-of-court statements as evidence of the facts stated, a witness's previous statement which if proved would be evidence of the facts stated, and statements produced by computers, it is provided by Order 20 rule 15 of the County Court Rules 1981 and Order 38 rule 21 of the

Rules of the Supreme Court that a party to proceedings who wishes to tender in evidence any statement (by virtue of sections 2, 4 or 5 of the Civil Evidence Act, 1968) shall not less than 14 days before the trial or hearing give notice of his desire to do so. However, by Order 20 rule 20 of the County Court Rules, 1981 and Order 38 rule 29 of the Rules of the Supreme Court, the Court has a discretion to allow such evidence to be tendered without a notice having been served. The basic rule requiring a notice to be served is to prevent a party being taken by surprise by the production of hearsay evidence.

Unless a given piece of evidence falls within an established class as admissible, it is inadmissible. The law, therefore, may not be appropriate for the kind of documentary record produced by the computing process where it is not always possible to find a human being in the process, as the following case of R. v. Pettigrew (a criminal case), shows.

Briefly, a house was burgled and £650 in new £5-notes was stolen. The notes had earlier been supplied to the victim by a branch of the Trustee Savings Bank. Later, Stewart Pettigrew was arrested by the police and found to have in his possession three new £5 notes. At his trial, the prosecution submitted as evidence a computer-generated and printed listing of bank note numbers. The listing, provided by the Bank of England, identified the serial numbers of a bundle of £5,000 worth of notes traceable through the TSB to the victim. Pettigrew was convicted and that might have been the end of the matter. Pettigrew, however, appealed against the conviction on the point that the information recorded on the listing had not been supplied by a person who had or could reasonably have had personal knowledge of the matters dealt with in the information.

In exploring the matter, the Court of Appeal learned that whilst an operator noted, in a given bundle of printed notes, the serial number of the first note, automatic equipment read that number and subsequent numbers as notes were counted and checked. The notes were then stacked automatically in numerical sequence save for any which had been rejected.

After due deliberation, it was held that the listed numbers

and the process by which they were produced could not be said to be in the personal knowledge of the operator or in the mind of anybody. Pettigrew was acquitted. It was held subsequently that a gap had been exposed in the Criminal Evidence Act 1965.

The relevance of Pettigrew to data protection is seen if one imagines that the data concerns not bank note numbers but a person's lifestyle, habits, financial standing, career prospects and so on. Some of the data may have been derived by correlation, a computational process 'not in the personal knowledge of the operator'. Worse still, the author of the software which performed the correlation may not be known, and his program so poorly annotated that the logical design can neither be followed nor comprehended in principle. This is by no means an infrequent occurrence in computing. With this in mind, if a data subject were to succeed in bringing a data user to court for a breach of the Act, where would proof and redress lie? We find a possible answer by examining R. v. Pettigrew in terms of what might have happened.

The prosecution could have acted differently and called an expert witness (a computer professional, say), to testify that in that particular case the Bank of England computer had been functioning correctly during the relevant period. Such an expert witness would need to have based his opinion on some tangible form of evidence, such as a record of operations often called a log, and source-form* documentation of any problems involved. These could have been introduced in evidence to support his testimony. It may not be easy, however, because of the cross-examination process – but we show in Chapter 4 how steps may be taken by a data user to ensure that there is factual evidence of a responsible and professional approach to computing activity in his organisation.

Section 5 of the Civil Evidence Act 1968 is said to be incomplete where computers are concerned. One can only speculate as to the reasons for the alleged incompleteness, as it is impossible to know what was in the draftsmens' minds at

---

*For the non-technical reader 'source form' can roughly be interpreted as the human comprehensible version of a program or set of data.

the time. It is a fact that the Civil Evidence Act makes no distinction between hardware and software, the implication being that only the hardware need be functioning correctly. However, Tapper's[1] interpretation of the Act is worth reading, as is Cross on Evidence[2] which quotes the South Australia Evidence Act 1972. This Act is couched in terms often used by computer professionals and is well worth reading by such people.

In the case of UK legislation, recalling that fifteen years ago virtually all the software was sold by the manufacturer along with the hardware ("bundled" is the term used to describe the practice) the assumption was probably made by the draftsmen that software was error-free. We explain in Chapter 1 that the assumption was always unsound and today the situation is worse, as many computers can now have software which may have been written by the manufacturer but is more likely to be produced by third parties. Some manufacturers of micro-processors do not provide software, other than the most elementary, so a customer is bound to go to a third party; software errors are commonplace.

We now describe further facts concerning computers, hardware and software upon which a knowledgeable lawyer could build a cross-examination. Reference should be made to Appendix 2 for clarification of term.

Bearing in mind that under cross-examination an honest man can be made to look a liar if he does not consider his words carefully, the computer professional as an expert witness is going to have to be very sure of his ground and be aware of the difference between a fact and an opinion. In a given situation, for example, where he may be required to testify that a computer was functioning correctly, he will need to prove that the hardware and software were working properly at the relevant time. No reader should need to be reminded that output (in whatever form) can contain errors or that a computer can malfunction. It is, however, a salutary and valuable experience to see the facts as a knowledgeable lawyer might see them.

An improperly briefed and unskilled (in court procedures) computer professional might simply state, in answer to a question from Counsel: "The computer was working properly". This, however, is an opinion, not a fact. With complex systems (see Appendix 2), it is doubtful whether any single person could have sufficient knowledge about such systems to be capable of producing facts. A series of independent experts on the hardware, software and communications sub-systems may be required with, say, the data controller testifying that no faults came to his notice at a particular time. Each of the specialists would need to support his own particular testimony with documentary evidence. If this had not been regularly maintained due to lax or non-existent operational standards, then a lawyer could show the whole group to be incompetent.

Such a lawyer would know, for example, that errors could be numerous and arise from a number of sources. The hardware or software may be inherently faulty or may develop faults when interacting with other components in, say, a particular system; the hardware may develop faults because it is working in an unsuitable environment (e.g. too warm an office): the software may be inadequately tested and contain hidden errors; faults may be produced by telecommunication lines used for transmission of data between computers in a network; application programmers may be inadequately trained. The lawyer would also know that most computer systems have built-in safeguards, but that it is possible for these to be bypassed.

In the case of a larger computer, the operating system (see Appendix 2) will usually be produced by the computer manufacturer. The purpose of the operating system is to control jobs submitted to the computer; to handle files and messages passing between the computer and its peripherals; to maintain a record of the resources used by individuals; to keep a record (log) of errors and to carry out other operational processes.

Operating system software for computers is rarely in a finalised state and is constantly being updated and improved by the manufacturer. There is usually strict control over the distribution of amendments by the manufacturers, who also provide managers of installations with advice and instructions on how amendments are to be implemented.

A computer installation run in a professional manner will have documentary control over amendments and a data controller should know exactly which version of an operating system is running at a given time.

A knowledgeable lawyer will know that a claim that a given operating system is free from errors should never be taken seriously. Errors can always be present which have not been detected by any of the tests carried out by the manufacturer. The likelihood of such errors being present decreases with time as the particular version of operating system is used on various computer installations, and errors are notified and rectified. Nevertheless, it is always possible that an unusual set of circumstances may produce an error that was not discovered in the original testing procedures or spotted in use. The 'latest release' of an operating system must always be treated as suspect until time (and progressively fewer errors) build up a level of confidence. More confidence can be placed in the accuracy of output emanating from a computer whose operating system has undergone several years of development than one with a relatively new operating system where the manufacturer may still be relying on usage to reveal errors.

Errors can remain undetected in application software if one or more programs have been inadequately tested. Testing can only prove that errors exist. It is impossible to prove that a complete program is completely free from error. With only a few decision points in a program, an enormous number of logical paths exists.

When a computer is replaced with one from another manufacturer, existing programs and data will, in all probability, need to be converted so as to run under a new operating system on a computer with a different logic design. During this period of conversion, errors will almost certainly be produced. In a professionally run installation, a close watch will be maintained over the system for some time until all the obvious errors have been corrected and the new system is running satisfactorily.

All computers should be run in a professional manner. Management should ensure that the computing processes are supervised and that testing continues to reveal latent errors. However, it is possible for unauthorised and not easily detectable modifications to be made to the hardware, software or data in the computer, and management should ensure that the measures mentioned are implemented as a minimum standard.

The experienced computing professional will have found nothing unusual in any of the above because in his mind he knows that there is usually a reasonable explanation to account for faults. Among his peers, these would scarcely merit comment. In a court of law, however, where the computer professional will not stand among his peers, a different situation exists. Facts (and no doubt vast experience) retained in his head or conveyed in jargon will count for little.

There is no-one more vulnerable than the pedantic specialist who lapses into jargon when justifying an opinion. His competence is soon brought into question, as is shown by the court room scene in *The Computer in Court*[3], where the expert witness is subjected to informed cross-examination and shown to be incompetent. Yet lawyers and computing professionals must work together in the development of computer evidence law. To this end, the computer professional should remember that computer-generated evidence can only be admissible if it is reliable. It is worth repeating that a court needs facts, not unsupported opinions. This applies as much in data protection as in any area of computing activity.

To summarise, the ephemeral nature of the computational process needs to be taken into account and evidence of, for example, function and malfunction should be collected and recorded continuously.

References

1. Tapper, C., *Computer Law*, Longman, Essex, 1982.
2. Cross, R., *Cross on Evidence*, Butterworths, Kent, 1980.
3. Kelman, A. and Sizer, R., *The Computer in Court*, Gower, 1982.

Appendix 2
Some Relevant Technical Facts about Computers

Nothing is more obvious at the present time than that computers are widespread, their uses covering almost every aspect of private and business life. For this reason and because of the constantly evolving nature of the technology it would be pointless to describe particular computers so we confine the contents of this appendix to issues which are relevant to data protection. We make no attempt to explain how computers work.

Computers can be used in a variety of ways (or applications). For present purposes we classify these as business applications, scientific applications and process control applications. In data protection the last plays no part; scientific applications are of partial concern because they include statistical analysis and research which are carrying exemption from subject access provisions (see Section 33 subsection 6); business applications are of major concern and are found in each of the three categories of computer.

Computers fall broadly into three categories – main frames, mini-computers and micro-computers but 'computer' is a loose term; what most people are familiar with is actually a 'computer system' typically, in a minimal form, comprised of a central processor, printing device, keyboard and visual display unit, and additional memory units. A computer system can be huge, occupying a large amount of floor space, or small enough to fit into a briefcase. Hereafter we take the word 'computer' to mean 'computer system'.

The title 'main frame' owes its origin to the first large computers and their direct descendants. These are still manufactured in large numbers and sold world-wide. A main frame, originally physically very large and expensive, can now be relatively small because advances in the technology of large scale integration (LSI) make it possible physically to reduce the size as well as increasing processing power. Hardware prices have fallen; thus the only worthwhile distinction to be drawn between the main frame and the more powerful of the mini-computers is one of overall system costs, and the scale of the service a given computer provides to its users.

In general a main frame needs special buildings, large-scale air conditioning, special power supplies, and directly identifiable support and operations staff. Operating the main frame will be regarded as a business, with management, accounting and cost control procedures. Main frames can be expanded as need dictates and, broadly, with expansion, still appear as one computer system to the users, and one cost centre to management. A main frame can perform usefully as the centre, or major resource, in a 'network of computers'. Such a network, combining main frames with mini-computers, experiences no geographical boundaries as communications can be by means of satellites.

The mini-computer particularly in its largest form can have the power of, and perform easily the functions of, the large main frame of a few years ago. There is, however, sometimes a difference in that whilst some makes of mini computers can be expanded by the coupling together of two or more of the same make to get more 'power', such coupling does not always result in a system which looks or behaves as a single system (as can be achieved with most main frame expansions). In the context of data protection, security and auditing this is an important difference between the main frame and some makes of mini-computer.

Computers can be connected together to form a network. Often the term 'distributed processing' is applied to such arrangements. Many earlier centralised main frames have been replaced with (geographically) distributed mini-computers.

For present purposes it is sufficient to confine the details of any further difference between the main frame and the mini to the manner in which files (described later) are handled by the computer and whether there is a single file (or system) control process or more than one. For the non-technical reader we should explain that having more than one system controller (a piece of software), as can sometimes happen when two or more computers are coupled together, is analogous to having two captains of a ship simultaneously trying to be captain.

The micro-computer is now familiar to most people. We need do little more than state that whilst the actual computers are extremely small and compact, many of the associated system components such as mass storage devices (discs), printers and eye-readable displays, are still relatively large so a complete system can occupy far more space than the actual computer. The same possibility of expansion problem can apply with a micro as with some minis.

Micro-computers can present problems not encountered with main frames and mini-computers. By and large the two older categories are manufactured by long established companies with years of experience of hardware, software, maintenance, documentation, education and support of customers. Essentially, they can be termed as a low volume high profit margin activity, the latter providing funds for the essential and expensive support, maintenance and documentation services. The bulk of the micro-computer industry is the reverse – a high volume low profit-margin activity mainly (though not exclusively) hardware oriented with a vast independent software industry providing the packages now available in the High Street. In these circumstances it is not always possible to achieve the same high standards of support, maintenance and documentation which have been achieved and still apply with main frames and minis. The effects of low standards could be serious where data protection and security issues are concerned. Several of the larger old-established computer companies are now manufacturing micro-based system – the well-known pcs (personal computers) which are compatible with the relevant company's existing main frame and mini hardware and software. They enjoy all the benefits of established maintenance procedures, documentation and customer support services which are vital to successful use of any computer system.

Analysts forecast some time ago that a vicious market place would develop, not entirely of benefit to computer users. This has happened remarkably quickly; the market place for software (and hardware) is now viciously competitive. Product selling price is directly related to scope, the number of incorporated facilities and other features of a given "package". The price will also reflect development overheads. There are, therefore, several commercial pressures to keep all these to a minimum, consistent with the mass-market environment. The effect of data protection legislation is likely to be wholly beneficial in forcing up standards appertaining to software in applications covered by the Act.

We now consider the computer 'file' which can be regarded as the principal repository of the data to be protected regardless of whether the hardware is a main frame, mini or micro. For the non-technical reader it is useful to compare the computer file with the old established manila file. Both contain information in the form of characters (data) forming records (e.g. a personnel record). A computer file is a set of related records, treated as a unit and bears relevant functional resemblances to the manila file. These are worth describing though (again for the non-technical reader) the physical properties are totally different.

The manila file (consisting of paper pages in a stiff card cover) is stored in a filing cabinet in a file registry, each file will have a title and nearly always a reference number, and be stored in a certain sequence. A particular file will be located by the number, and the contents checked by reference to the title. Such a file can be opened, the contents read, worked on, added to, deleted, then the file can be closed. For security purposes the cabinets will be locked (as will the door of the registry when the registry is unmanned). A clerk will control access to and distribution of files.

Most computers nowadays have a file registry (or store) organised in a way similar to that described above, by the system controller. Each file will have some form of coded reference number enabling the computer, after a user has requested access, to locate it and send the contents, provided certain criteria are met (see Chapter 5), to be displayed in eye-readable form at, say, a visual display unit. A data user can open a new file, read the contents of an existing one, work on, amend, append, delete, and then close the file and return it to the file store all by key-board instructions. Conversion to and from eye-readable form takes place somewhere in the computer system between the file store and the visual display unit.

For security purposes access to the file store will be controlled by means which we describe in Chapter 5 but it is relevant here to note that, just as a file registry has to be organised if it is to be run in an efficient and secure manner, so have the files in any computer system. We referred earlier to the analogy with having two captains in charge of a ship. The dangers of running two separate filing systems can be just as great. The difficulties of complying with Sections 22 and 24 of the Act are self-evident.

Organisation in a computer file system usually starts with a directory which is a structured list of all the files in a hierarchy of files. The directories and files will be protected, and there are many ways of doing this, but a typical one is the password system. For convenience, the non-technical reader can imagine a safe with a combination lock. The person who knows the combination (pass-word) can open it to find, inside, a box itself bearing another combination lock. Only if the person knows that combination as well can he open the box and get at its contents. Computer directories and files can be protected in this manner to a considerable depth; that is, boxes within boxes within boxes, each requiring the use of a unique pass-word to access the next level down though in practice neater security procedures would apply.

It is essential to control authorisation, identification and authentication procedures so far as access to files is concerned. For example, access in general is usually permitted only to authorised users, whilst only those with a 'need to know' should have the right of access to a given file so that access is then possible only from identifiable specific computer terminals. In such a case, something more elaborate than pass-word controls would be necessary before a person could get access from a given terminal to a particular file directory and then to any subordinate file.

Before dealing in more detail with computer security a few general comments are appropriate on software and networks as applied to data protection as errors may arise from a number of sources and we now describe a few of these.

The hardware or software may be faulty or may develop faults when interacting with other components in a particular computer: the hardware may develop faults because it is working in an unsuitable environment such as a poor electrical power supply: the software may be inadequately tested and contain hidden errors: faults may be produced by a network or communication system by which data is transmitted between points in the network. Most computer systems have safeguards which prevent undetectable corruption of output but it is possible for errors of a particular kind to bypass these safeguards.

We give now some basic security considerations which we believe will apply when attempting to comply with the Act. First a security policy will need to be devised which corresponds with a given data protection policy. The scale of this will be a function of the scale of the relevant organisation's data processing activity. Such a policy will need to take into account the type of system (main frame, distributed minis, networked etc) on which systems and users are registered. We assume that all systems will employ remote terminals and be multi-user in concept.

To satisfy the Act's requirements yet being sensibly cost effective, the security policy should:

1. be describable in simple terms so that verification of enforcement (and adherence) can be carried out.

2. have a measurable and acceptable effect on the efficiency of operations in their totality.
3. combine a number of levels of authority (eg highly sensitive, less sensitive) with a number of projects (eg markets, insurance, health) and defining who needs to know what from which terminal etc.
4. allow the "owner" of a file to grant certain types of access to certain files under certain conditions (discretionary) and prevent an owner granting certain accesses to certain files regardless of attempts by the owner to grant such access (non-discretionary).
5. enforce a rule which stipulates that presence of a right (of access) is always more powerful than its absence.
6. ensure so far as is practicable compatibility with existing applications.

The basic aim of any security policy is to control accesses to data such that only permitted accesses under defined conditions are possible; illegal accesses are made as difficult as possible and evidence is accumulated on such accesses. Additionally, and this is what makes computer security different from other types of security, restrictions must be placed on data flows.

We assume that all the systems will be used for a variety of purposes by a number of users for, as we have described in Chapter 1, only in this way can computer systems be operated cost-effectively. The terms "multi-level" and "multi-user" describe such systems. In most data protection applications not all the users of the system will need to function at the same authorities; concomitantly a given user will not need to operate with the same authority and on the same project all the time. A system needs, therefore, to be able to adapt dynamically where authorities and projects attach to all relevant features of the system – subjects and objects, for example, as described in Table A2.1. The system must constrain any relationships between authorities to those which are valid according to the policy.

For a system to perform in such a manner, bearing in mind the policy requirement for verification, a computer system

Table A2.1

Three useful terms

Subject Users and processes are 'active elements' for which data accesses must be controlled. 'Subject' is used as a generic title for such elements.

Object Data need to be contained (in a repository sense). Access to containers needs to be controlled – by a kernel for example. Object is used as a generic title for such containers.

Kernel Certain requirements define a security policy (see main text). These requirements are met by features of the operating system contained in the kernel. It is axiomatic that the kernel contains nothing other than those features.

needs to be designed from first principles. Writers from the mid 1960s have been unanimous in declaring that security in a multi-level system cannot be achieved by add-on system software features. Where security has been a design requirement the operating system assumes the form of a 'kernel' (see Table A 2.1) which contains nothing other than those system processes necessary to satisfy the requirements of the policy.

Such kernels tend to be smaller than the whole system and have a better chance of being correct and verifiably so. It is axiomatic that such kernels must be protected from attacks and that all accesses to real system components are via the kernel.

Before leaving this over-view we describe three terms: security, integrity and "Trojan horse". Security (with which integrity is often confused) is taken to mean the implementation processes and procedures which control access to data and place constraints on data flow. Integrity we take to mean the state achieved when data cannot be modified or new data generated illegally. We use these descriptions in the main text. "Trojan horse" is a technique whereby an apparently innocuous program once accepted by a computer as an authorised "job" generates code designed to create attack points in computing processes. These attack points would be concealed from the data user but locatable by the attacker at some appropriate time.

Index

Acceptance/refusal of registration application 76-81
Access controls 155, 158, 182 *see also* Data access, Data flow control, Security
  access policy 158, 199-201
  and security 192-201, 203-6
  data controller 161, 165, 176
  discretionary 157, 196-7
  modes of access 198
  non-discretionary 157, 196-7
  password identification 197-8, 223
Access to premises
  warrant for inspection 98-105
Affidavit, 7-stage 170
Amendment of registered data 74-6, 118-21 *see also* Data user
Appeal tribunal 41-2 *see* Data protection tribunal
Application for registration 74-6 *see* Register of data users
Assessment of protection checklists
  board level 172
  data control level 176
  finance/auditing levels 174
  marketing, sales and PR 174-5
  operations management level 178
  personnel/information policy 174-5
  risk assessment level 175-6
  security level 177
  senior management level 172-3
  solicitor/legal executives 173
  systems development level 177-8
Assets *see also* Data subject, Data user, Security
  computer-based data 159-60
  data and security 188-94
  market value 183-5
  recorded attacks on 188-91
  risk analysis 191-3
Auditing *see also* Data protection audits
  disclosure for 132-4
Authority, franchise and category 198-201

British Computer Society (BCS) 19, 23, 163

INDEX

British Medical Association 180

Capital expenditure on computing 166
Civil proceedings 40-1 *see also* County Court
Codes of Conduct 163
Code of practice 144, 163
Company secretaries *see* Officers of corporate bodies
Compensation
  inaccuracy of personal data 43-4, 114-16
  loss or unauthorised disclosure 117-118
Computer bureaux *see also* Data user, Principles of data protection, Register of data users, Security
  access control 197-201
  appeals 92-7
  audit procedures 164-5, 182, 202
  compensation
    for inaccuracy 114-16
    for loss or unauthorised disclosure 117-18
  corporate security 180-95, 203-6
  crime and taxation exemptions 126-9
  data held outside UK 147-8
  definitions 49, 54, 58
  encryption 202-3
  entry and inspection 98-105
  national security exemptions 123-5
  obligations of govt depts 145-7
  prosecutions and penalties 106-9
  protection assessment checklists 172-8
  rectification and erasure 118-21
  registration 68-9, 71

  regulations and interpretation 149-50
  right of access and complaints 109-14
  service of notices 106
  transitional provisions 150-2
  unauthorised disclosures 40, 97-8
  unregistered holding 72-4
Computer file 222-4
Computer outputs in Court 17, 170-1, 209-17
Computer professional 155 *see also* Computers, Computer bureaux, Data user
  affidavit for Court 170-1
  and data protection 169-71
  as expert witness 214-17
Computers *see also* Access control
  and legal facts 209-17
  discretionary/non-discretionary controls 163, 196-7
  domestic 5, 21, 155
  modes of access 198-9
  password identification 197-8
  relevant facts about 167-9
  security *see* Security
  system security 196-7
  technical facts about 219
  with audit features 196, 202
Computing Services Association (CSA) 19
Consequential liability 155
Consumer Credit Act 1974 139
Corporate bodies *see* Officers of corporate bodies
Corporate information policy 155, 160-1 *see also* Security
  and access policy 196-7
  control and conformity 164, 169-71
  corporate planning 181-7
  data and basic security 183-7

230 INDEX

operation and access 188-201
protection awareness 181-3
total security 180-1, 188-94, 203-6
Council of Europe Convention 31, 35, 69, 145, 164
transfer prohibition notices 89-92
County Court 210
computer output as evidence 209-17
damages *see* County Courts Act 1959
inaccurate data 43-4
jurisdiction 121-2
legal privilege 130-2
County Courts Act 1959 43-4, 122
Court of Session (Scotland) jurisdiction 121-2
Criminal convictions 36-8, 57
Criminal Evidence Act 1968 16
Criminal Justice Act 1982 73
Criminal proceedings
R. *v* Pettigrew 212-3
unregistered holding of data 73
Crown Court 210

Data access 40, 42-3 *see also* Access control, Data subject, Exemptions, Personal data
and hierarchies 157-61
and the computer system 155, 158
enabling order 111
exemptions 44-5, 124-42
inspection of register 82
purpose 111-12
security and control 192-201, 203-6
subjects' rights 27, 42-5, 109-14, 156-8
Data controller 161, 201
responsibilities 165

protection assessment checklist 176
Data flow control 198-201, 225
Data inaccuracy 43-4, 159-60
Data inspectors 55, 163
Data integrity 168
and audit 202
definitions 226-7

Data processing *see* Processing data
equipment seizure 101, 107, 108-9

Data protection audits 21, 55 *see also* Computers, Security
computers with facilities 197, 199-201
form of 164-5
need for 161-4
procedures 182, 202

Data Protection Registrar 35, 62-4
acceptance/refusal for registration 76-81
and the European Convention 145
appeal proceedings 94-5
application for registration 74-6
compensation 114-18
de-registration notices 87-8
determination of appeals 95-7
duration and renewal of registration 81-2
enforcement notices 77, 82-7
entry and inspection 98-105
exemptions
crime and taxation 126-9
domestic purposes 135-7
examination results 141-2
financial services 130
judicial appointments 130-2
legal privilege 130-2
national security 124-5
other various 137-41

INDEX

general and overriding duties 143
inspection of registered particulars 82
non-disclosure definitions 123-4
policing 55, 107
powers in registration 41-2
prosecutions and penalties 106-9
provision of information immunity 105
rectification and erasure 118-21
regulations and interpretation 149-50
rights of access and complaints 109-14
rights of appeal 92-4
status and appointment 62-6
subject access definitions 123
transfer prohibition notices 89-92
transitional provisions 150-2
Data protection tribunal 41-2, 62-4, 66-8
appeals proceedings 94-5
determination of appeals 95-7
entry and inspection exemptions 99-100, 103-5
provision of information immunity 105, 128-9
rights of appeal to 92-4
Data purpose 40, 55, 58-60, 68-9, 69-70
and criminal disclosure 73-4
assessment by Registrar 70
payroll and accounts exemptions 132-4
protection assessment checklists 172-8
Data subject *see also* Data Protection Registrar, Data user, Exemptions, Personal data, Secretary of State
access exemptions 123, 126-9

additional safeguards 36-7, 60
and criminal prosecution 213-17
compensation
for inaccuracy 42, 114-16
for loss or unauthorised disclosure 117-18
consent to data use 22
definition 3, 49
de-registration notices 77, 87-8, 91, 92
destruction of material 107, 108-9
enforcement notices 82-7, 128-9
inaccuracy of personal data 42-4, 159-60
inspection of register 82
integrity of 162, 226-7
limits to definition 51-2
national security exemptions 44-5, 123-5
non-disclosure provisions 123-4, 126-9, 130-42
obligations of government depts 145-7
protection assessment checklists 172-8
protection principles 35-6
register content 68-9
representation on tribunal 64
rights of access 20, 40, 42-3, 109-14, 156-8, 193
stipulations for data use 22
transfer prohibition notices 89-92
transitional provisions 150-2
Data user *see also* Computer bureaux, Data Protection Registrar, Personal data, Security
access rights 155-61
access rights exemptions 123-5, 126-9, 130-4, 134-7

INDEX

and data purpose 55, 58-60, 69-70, 172-8
appeals proceedings 94-7
audit procedures and encryption 202-3
compensation
 for inaccuracy 114-16
 for loss or unauthorised disclosure 117-18
contingency planning 203
controlling access 196-201
corporate security 180-95, 203-6
data held outside UK 147-8
data subjects' rights 22, 42-5, 109-14, 156-8
definition 3-4, 49
deposition by professional 170-1
de-registration notices 87-8
domestic user 5, 21, 134, 155-6 181
enforcement notices 82-7
erasure 43, 118
incorrect data 42-4
limits to definition 52-4
motive and risk assessment 14
obligations of government depts 145-7
powers of entry and inspection 98-105
problems of evidence in court 213-17
prosecutions and penalties 106-9
protection assessment checklists 172-8
rectification 43, 118
register 35, 68-9, 82
registration 41-2, 74-6, 76-81, 81-2
regulations and interpretations 149-50
representation on tribunal 64
responsibilities 22-4, 35-6, 57-8, 109-11
rights of appeal 92-4
sensitivity of data 164
transfer prohibition notices 89-92
transitional provisions 150-2
transnational transmission 25, 88, 89-92, 163
unregistered holding 72-4
De-registration notices 77, 87-8, 91, 92
DHS/NCC report 162-5
Director of Public Prosecutions 107
Directors *see* Officers of corporate bodies
Disclosure of data *see also* Data subject, Personal data, Principles of data protection
 definitions 49
 exemptions 44-5, 123-42
 in register 68-9, 73-4
 interpretation 58-60
 limits 56
 non-disclosure definition 123

Electronic passport 24-5
Encryption 202-3
European Data Protection Convention *see* Council of Europe Convention
Exemptions *see also* Personal data
 crime and taxation 126-9
 domestic and other purposes 135-7
 examination results 141-2
 financial services 130
 health and social work 129
 legal privilege 130-2
 national security 123-5
 other various 137-41

INDEX

payrolls and accounts 132-4
personal data 44-5

General regulations of the Act
interpretations 149-50
rules and orders 149
transitional provisions and title 150-2

Government depts and police
obligations and liabilities 145-7

Health *see also* Law enforcement
mental 36-8, 57, 60-2
physical 36-8, 57, 60-2
sexual 36-8, 57, 60-2

Hierarchies 158, 159

High Court 210
computer output as evidence 170, 209-17
damages 122
inaccurate data 43-4
jurisdiction 121-2
legal privilege 130-2

Hobbyist and personal data 21, 155-6

Identity documentation 9-10
Information 15
Information executive 165
levels of risk and security 166-7
Information technology (IT)
data protection and 165
deposition for control 169-71
evolution 165-7
LAN and control 167-9

Injunction *see* Mareva injunction

Inspection *see also* Powers of entry, Rights
CEC 161
matters exempt 99-100, 103-5
need for 161-5
register particulars 82
Younger 162

Issue of warrants 98-9, 101-2

Judicial appointments *see* Legal privilege and judicial appointments

Law enforcement
crime 126-9
health and social work 129
taxation 126-9

Lawyers 155
protection assessment checklist 173

Legal privilege and judicial appointments
exemptions from access 130-2

Liability *see also* Consequential liability, Data user
officers of corporate bodies 40-1, 109

Local area network (LAN) 167-9

Managers *see* Officers of corporate bodies

Mareva injunction 38-9

Micro-computers, main frames and mini-computers 21, 219-22

Myers *v* DPP, House of Lords ruling 211

National Computing Centre (NCC) 19, 162-5

National security *see also* Security
exemptions 44-5
safeguards and certificate 124-5
subject access and non-disclosure 123-4

Officers of corporate bodies *see also* Computer bureaux, Data user, Principles of data protection
appeals 92-7
compensation for inaccuracy 114-16

corporate awareness of data
    protection 161, 181-3
data as asset 188-94
liability for breaches 40-1, 109,
    155
operational security 183-7
powers of entry and inspection
    98-105
protection assessment checklist
    172-8
provision of information
    immunity 105
risk and environmental security
    194-203
service of notices 106
suggested hierarchy 159
total security 180-1, 202-6
unauthorised disclosure 97-8
Official Secrets Act (1911) 105
Organisation for Economic Co-
    operation and Develop-
    ment (OECD) 24
  endorsement of Guidelines 29-
    30
  Guidelines 26-30
  International Chamber of
    Commerce 29

Personal data *see also* Data
    subject, Data user,
    Principles of data
    protection, Register of data
    users, Secretary of State,
    Security
additional safeguards 36-7, 60
appeals 92-7
compensation
  for inaccuracy 114-16
  for loss or unauthorised
    disclosure 117-18
corporate security 180-7, 197-
    201, 203-6
definition 49, 57-8
de-registration notices 87-8

enforcement notices 77, 82-7
exemptions 44-5
  consumer credit and others
    137-41
  crime and taxation 123-4,
    126-9
  domestic and others 134-7
  examination results 141-2
  financial services 130
  health and social work 129
  legal privilege 130-2
  national security 123-5
  payrolls and accounts 132-4
false description of data 74-6
held outside UK 25, 88-92, 147-
    8, 163
hobbyist 155-6
inaccuracy 42-4, 159-60
inspection of registered
    particulars 82
inspection or audit 161-5
interpretation 58-60
limits of definition 50-1
obligations of government
    depts 145-7
powers of entry and inspection
    98-105
registration 68-9
rights of access 40-3, 109-14,
    156-8
seizure of equipment 101, 107,
    108-9
transfer prohibition notices 89-
    92
transitional provisions 150-2
unregistered holding 72-4
Police and Criminal Evidence Bill
  admissibility of computer
    evidence 170
Political opinions 36-8, 57
Powers of entry 40 *see also* Data
    Protection Registrar,
    Inspection
  copies of seized material 102-3

INDEX

execution of warrants 99-102
exemptions from seizure 99-100, 103-5
issue of warrants 98-9
request for receipt 99, 102
Principles, Data Protection 35-6, 57-8 *see also* Data Protection Registrar, Personal data, Register of data users, Secretary of State
interpretation 38-9, 58-62
protection assessment checklists 172-8
Privacy 4-5 *see also* Security
data subject stipulations 22
data user responsibility 22-4
financial credit 8
invasion of and insurance 183-5
legal aspects 13, 14-17
motive for invasion 14
national problems 9-13
philosophical identification 7-14
technical arguments 17-21
Processing data *see also* Data user, Security
compensation
for inaccuracy 114-16
for loss or unauthorised disclosure 117-18
data value and risk 183-94
definition 49
exemptions and user definitions 128-9
limits of definition 50, 54-6
Prosecution and penalties 40, 106-9

Racial origin 36-8, 57, 60-2
Register of data users 35, 41-2 *see also* Computer bureaux, Data Protection Registrar

acceptance/refusal 41-2, 76-81
appeal proceedings 94-7
applications and amendments 74-6
assessment of purpose 70-1
compensation 114-18
content 68-9
de-registration notices 77, 87-8
duration and renewal 81-2
enforcement notices 82-7
inspection of particulars 82
powers of entry and inspection 98-105
rights of appeal 92-4
transfer prohibition notices 89-92
Registration 41-2 *see* Data Protection Registrar, Register of data users
Religious beliefs 36-8, 57, 60-2
Responsibility
data users 22-4
government depts 145-7
Registrar *see* Data Protection Registrar
Secretary of State *see* Secretary of State
Rights 155-61 *see also* Computer bureaux, Data subject, Data user
Risk management *see also* Security
checklist for protection assessment 175-6
contingency planning 204
data assets 188-94
risk analysis 191-3
sensitive data 165

Secretary of State *see also* Data Protection Registrar, Register of data users
and additional safeguards 36-7, 61-2

and the regulation of financial
services 130
enabling order for access 111
precedence of disclosure/access
137-41
variations for health and social
work 129
variations in register content
69, 71
variations to rights of appeal 94-6
Security 8-10 *see also* Data
Protection Registrar, Data
user, Personal data,
Privacy, Register of data
users
addresses and proof of identity
20-1
assessment checks 172-8
corporate policy 164-5, 180-1
access control 197-201
and basic security 185-7
audit procedures 202
checklist 224-5
computer environment 194-5
contingency planning 203-5
corporate awareness 181-3
data as asset and risk
assessment 188-94
data protection 183-5
encryption 202-3
operating system 196-7
summary 203-5
data protection principles 35-6,
56-60
data subject consent 22
data user responsibility 22-4
definition 226
early beliefs 10-14
executive checklist 177
kernel system 226

liability of corporate managers
40-1
national attitudes 9-13
obligations of government
depts 145-7
OECD Guidelines 26-30
powers of entry and inspection
40, 98-105
processed records 19-20
prosecution 40-1, 106-9
service of notices 40, 98-9
systems and software
standardisation 168
Trojan horse 226-7
unauthorised disclosure 40,
117-18
Sensitive data 8, 17, 19, 60-2 *see
also* Data user,
Exemptions, National
security, Security
and corporate information
policy 160-1
and corporate security policy
224-5
sensitivity rating 8, 19, 160-1,
166, 196-7, 224-5
Service of notices 40, 98-9, 106
see also Issue of warrants
Sheriff (Scotland) jurisdiction
121-2

Taxation 123-4, 126-9
Transfer prohibition notices 89-92

Unauthorised disclosure 97-8, 163
by computer bureaux 40
compensation for 117-18
United Nations Declaration of
Human Rights 8